THE
ARCHAEOLOGY
of SHAKESPEARE

THE MATERIAL LEGACY OF
SHAKESPEARE'S THEATRE

JEAN WILSON

SUTTON PUBLISHING

First published in the United Kingdom in 1995 by
Alan Sutton Publishing Ltd, an imprint of Sutton Publishing Limited
Phoenix Mill · Thrupp · Stroud · Gloucestershire · GL5 2BU

This edition first published in 1997

British Library Cataloguing in Publication Data

A catalogue record for this book is available from the British Library.

ISBN 0-7509-1727-X

Cover illustration: reconstruction of the first phase of the Rose theatre by C. Walter Hodges (Museum of London)

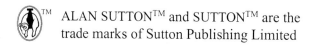 ALAN SUTTON™ and SUTTON™ are the
trade marks of Sutton Publishing Limited

Typeset in 11/13pt Bembo.
Typesetting and origination by
Sutton Publishing Limited
Printed in Great Britain by
WBC, Bridgend, Mid Glam.

CONTENTS

For B.W.
&
In Memoriam A.H.W.

ILLUSTRATIONS

PREFACE

I began this book, after the discovery of the remains of the Rose playhouse, in response to the general degree of ignorance and misunderstanding about what we knew of the playhouses of Shakespeare's London, and the paucity of real information from which that knowledge was derived. Because the direct evidence was so sparse, I also wanted to suggest that some expansion of the data from that on which scholars have hitherto based their theoretical reconstructions of the playhouses was in order. Too often, the everyday material remains of literate societies are overlooked by those who concentrate on their writings.

This explains my choice of title: *The Archaeology of Shakespeare*. Archaeology is the study of the human past, in all periods and everywhere, from the material remains that survive. Stone tools at Olduvai Gorge, the earthworks of Avebury, and the ruins of Tintern Abbey are all material evidence from our past; archaeology begins yesterday. I have used details from the secular architecture and funerary monuments of the Shakespearean period to suggest how the playhouses and the plays staged within them may have been presented.

Professor Colin Renfrew first suggested that I should write this book, as well as supplying its Foreword, and I am extremely grateful to him on both counts. Individual acknowledgements are made throughout the book, but I would like to thank all the owners of the materials illustrated, some of whom have chosen to remain anonymous, together with the staffs of the British Library, Cambridge University Library and Conway Library at the Courtauld Institute, who have been particularly helpful. My greatest debt is to my husband, Professor Norman Hammond, who has encouraged me to persevere with the book and provided many of its illustrations.

FOREWORD

by
Colin Renfrew

> Not marble, nor the gilded monuments
> Of princes shall outlive this powerful rhyme;
> But you shall shine more bright in these contents
> Than unswept stone besmirched with slutted time.
> When wasteful war shall statues overturn,
> And broils root out the work of masonry . . .

Shakespeare reaches out beyond the limits of space and time. Yet despite this immortality and the vast industry of subsequent scholarship, he remains for us a somewhat shadowy figure. A few signatures upon deeds, some disputed manuscript texts, a series of doubtful portraits, a will, a tomb – these are all the remaining substance of Shakespeare the man. *The Archaeology of Shakespeare* sets out to rectify, as far as possible, some of these deficiencies by investigating systematically the material evidence which remains and which bears upon the theatre and theatrical presentations in Elizabethan and Jacobean England.

The subject was transformed in 1989 by two unexpected and rather astonishing discoveries. The first was the discovery in Southwark, during building works, of the foundations of the Rose theatre. Already one of the best documented theatres of Elizabethan times through the account of Philip Henslowe, the case became a *cause célèbre* when the theatrical world of today united to prevent the destruction of the site. Although the documented links of the Rose with Shakespeare himself are rather tenuous, the forces of conservation won, and the site was saved for further investigation which is still continuing. Later that same year, in further building developments, the site of Shakespeare's own Globe theatre was found, and partial excavations undertaken. The results of these investigations are assessed here in relation to what is known of the other outdoor (and indoor) theatres of the London of the time. They serve to confirm and extend what some of the best theatre historians had been able to infer from the scanty records available, while correcting other theories.

Yet the material evidence can take us much further, as Jean Wilson shows us in this pioneering study. For she is able to set the conventions of theatrical presentation upon the Elizabethan stage within the much wider context of the visual representation of the human world. For the theatrical tableau finds its counterpart not only in the scenery and installation for the pageant and the masque of contemporary revels. Its conventions were employed also in the 'speaking pictures' which are found in tomb sculptures, in the monumental title pages of books such as John Speed's great conspectus of Jacobean England *The Theatre of the Empire of Great Britaine*, and in formal decorative installations such as screens, arches and even chimney pieces. (It is no coincidence, perhaps, that John Speed's book offers an early representation of an Ancient Briton, who is clearly modelled upon the dress and material culture of the American Indians: it was thus this same imaginative convention of the 'speaking picture' which first brought together, in what is today termed 'ethnographic analogy', the vision of prehistoric England and the living natives of the New World.)

To an archaeologist it seems ironic that we know less about the Shakespearean stage itself and the façade of scenery forming the backdrop to the action (the 'tiring-house') than we know of comparable installations in the Roman theatre. For in Greece and Turkey, Classical theatres are preserved where this monumental backdrop, the *scaenae frons*, still stands. Moreover the wall paintings of Roman Pompeii and Herculaneum seem to be in large measure inspired by the stage scenery of the Roman theatre. The visual analogy which Jean Wilson draws, linking together the conventions of stage presentation and monumental architecture – the 'speaking picture' – holds for the Classical theatre and Classical art also. Indeed the analogy goes even further, for many of the monumental tomb façades cut in the rock at the great city of Petra in Jordan, dating from Roman times, have strong resemblances with the Pompeian wall paintings, and the rhetoric of theatrical presentation seems to be one of the components of their decidedly ostentatious monumentality. The author is here rightly indicating a rich field of enquiry which merits further development: the interaction between the visual elements of literature, most clearly seen in the theatre, and the literary inspiration of the graphic arts. *The Archaeology of Shakespeare* indicates the way towards a more general 'archaeology of the theatre', and thus, as the author clearly shows, to the intersection of the visual and the literary arts.

There are moreover many details to catch the attention in this fascinating book beyond its principal general themes. I particularly enjoyed the hint that Dr Johnson's friend Mrs Thrale may have been already in the eighteenth century a pioneer in 'the archaeology of theatre' when she was apparently the first to observe the ruins of The Globe (she lived with her husband at the brewery then on the site) which archaeologists in our own day have so enthusiastically uncovered.

Shakespeare may indeed be one of those few great writers of whom it may be said that the work transcends the specific historical context of his time. But as Jean Wilson shows, our appreciation of his work is enriched by our understanding of that context.

CHAPTER ONE

THE LIFE OF SHAKESPEARE: HIS THEATRICAL AND SOCIAL MILIEU

The facts known about Shakespeare's physical life are scanty; about his emotional life non-existent. His childhood was spent in bourgeois security; his adolescence was marked by some loss of family prosperity; and his adult life was passed mostly in London, in the acquisition of wealth, which he invested in property in his home town. He died in middle age, after a short retirement among the fruits of his theatrical endeavours. Any attempt to recount the events of his life must involve a sketch of the middle-class country-town ambience of his childhood, and the history of the company of actors – first the Lord Chamberlain's Men, and subsequently the King's Men – with whom all but his earliest years in London were passed and with whose growing prosperity his own was intimately involved.

SHAKESPEARE'S FAMILY BACKGROUND

William Shakespeare was born in Stratford-upon-Avon a few days before 26 April 1564. He was the third of the eight children of John Shakespeare and his wife Mary, née Arden, preceded by two daughters one of whom certainly, and the other of whom probably, died in infancy. In the absence of a precise date, the choice of 23 April for celebrating his birthday seems as plausible as any other. Of his two younger sisters and three younger brothers, Anne, born in September 1571, died at the age of seven, but Joan (born 1569), Gilbert (born 1566), Richard (born 1574) and Edmund (born 1580) all attained adulthood. To raise five out of eight children to maturity was at this date a considerable feat, and says much for the family's inherited health and Mary Arden's prowess as a mother. Her administrative ability is suggested by the fact that her father named her as one of the executors to his will in 1556, before her marriage to John Shakespeare.

At the time of their marriage, which took place sometime between March 1556, when Robert Arden drew up his will, and September 1558, when Joan Shakespeare[1] was christened, John Shakespeare had been for at least eight years a resident of Henley Street in Stratford, and had owned property there since at least 1556. He must have been born by 1530, possibly several years earlier, and his wife by 1535, as it is unlikely that she would be named as executor to a will while still a minor. The history of her

The rear view of Shakespeare's birthplace in Stratford-upon-Avon – the town house of a prosperous sixteenth-century bourgeois. (Norman Hammond)

childbearing, as recorded in the Stratford registers, would seem to bear this out – the gap between her last two successful pregnancies (baptismal registers do not record stillbirths and miscarriages) suggest a decline in fertility appropriate to a woman in her forties, whereas the spacing of her previous pregnancies indicates that she probably breast-fed.

Mary Arden was born in the village of Wilmcote, the daughter of a prosperous farmer, from an ancient Warwickshire family. William Shakespeare spent his childhood in social and material comfort. His father, a glover, wool-dealer and occasional money-lender, was involved in local politics, holding progressively more important civic offices during Shakespeare's early childhood. Shakespeare would have grown up used to sitting in the pews reserved for local dignitaries at services in Holy Trinity Church, and to seeing his father and mother dressed as befitted an alderman and his wife. The family hovered on the borderline between the prosperous bourgeoisie and the minor gentry. Both John Shakespeare and his son set out to obtain proof that the family was to be placed on the gentry side of that line: John Shakespeare by making preliminary enquiries about a grant of arms in about 1568, William by finally obtaining it for his father in 1596.

With the exception of William, the Shakespeare family followed the marriage-pattern for gentry families at this period – a pattern designed to consolidate family property. Younger sons in such families tended to remain bachelors or to marry late, after they had become established in their professions, so that the family's wealth was not dissipated on supporting them and their offspring.[2] All three of William Shakespeare's younger brothers died unmarried.

During William Shakespeare's early childhood his circumstances were those of the son of one of the leading families in a small country town: the play which depicts the milieu closest to that in which he grew up is *The Merry Wives of Windsor*, with its affluent bourgeoisie. Stratford was small but it was not poor, being a prosperous market town sited on a major crossing of the Warwickshire Avon, which divided the sheep-raising Cotswolds and mixed farming Feldon to the south from the scattered woodlands of the Forest of Arden to the north. The wealth of the town may be gauged from the number of sixteenth-century monuments in Holy Trinity Church; that this prosperity was not a new thing is attested to by the magnificence of the church itself, and by the number of handsome sixteenth-century buildings which still survive. There was an excellent free grammar school, whose masters,

The monument in St Andrew Undershaft to Sir Thomas Offley, d. 1582, Lord Mayor of London, probably from the Cure workshop (personal communication by Dr G.F. Fisher). Although Offley was far more prosperous than John Shakespeare, this shows the dignity to which the mercantile classes active in public life might aspire. (Conway Library, Courtauld Institute of Art)

during the years when William Shakespeare almost certainly attended it, were better qualified (and more highly paid) than their contemporaries at Eton.

In his *A Description of England* of 1577–87, William Harrison describes the comfortable interiors of contemporary bourgeois households:

> in the houses of knights, gentlemen, merchantmen, and some other wealthy citizens, it is not geson to behold generally their great provision of tapestry, Turkey work, pewter, brass, fine linen, and thereto costly cupboards of plate, worth five or six hundred or a thousand pounds . . . even . . . the inferior artificers and many farmers . . . have, for the most part, learned also to garnish their cupboards with plate, their joined beds with tapestry and silk hangings, and their tables with carpets and fine napery . . . [3].

Harrison was given to patriotic aggrandizement, but when Robert Arden, William Shakespeare's grandfather, died in 1556, his goods included eleven painted cloths (used

High Street, Stratford-upon-Avon, showing the grammar school – a street-view virtually unchanged since Shakespeare's childhood. (Norman Hammond)

as a cheaper substitute for tapestries), copper pots and brass pans. The household would not, at this date, have comprised only the Shakespeare family: there would have been servants, and probably also lodgers. (When he became a rich man William Shakespeare himself had lodgers in his great house, New Place.)

For the first twelve years of Shakespeare's life his father progressed steadily in prosperity and local importance. He bought property around the town, and held the offices of alderman and high bailiff (the equivalent of mayor). He made business trips to London on behalf of the town. In 1576, however, he seems to have experienced a series of reverses, either in his commercial or (less probably) in his personal life. In a time of general national recession, John Shakespeare's business ventures began to fail. He and his wife were forced to mortgage the lands in Wilmcote that were her inheritance, and they never succeeded in regaining them, although they and their son went to law in an effort to do so. He stopped attending council meetings, although his fellow-councillors were reluctant to accept his departure and did not elect a new alderman to take his place until 1586, and he ceased to attend church, for fear, it was claimed, of being arrested for debt. However, John Shakespeare was not reduced to desperate poverty. He sold land, but he retained the Henley Street house where he carried on his business, and he was still held in enough respect in the town to be asked to perform various responsible tasks and civic duties. In 1579 he was able to afford to pay for a bell and pall for the funeral of his seven-year-old daughter, Anne.

The fact that one of the manifestations of John Shakespeare's difficulties was a refusal to attend church, combined with the discovery, in the eighteenth century, of a Catholic document inscribed with his name (which was accepted by the great scholar Edmund Malone, but has subsequently been lost) in the rafters of the Henley Street house, when taken with other indications that his son and granddaughter may have had Roman Catholic sympathies, has led some scholars to argue that John Shakespeare was a Catholic, and that his difficulties from 1576 onwards were due not to debt but to recusancy – refusal to attend the services of the Church of England. The balance of the evidence seems to be that his difficulties were probably financial; possibly religious. The last quarter of the sixteenth century was a time of national financial recession, and if John Shakespeare prospered less than he had formerly done, there were many others in a worse state. The document in which his non-attendance at church is noted differentiates between those who stay away for religious reasons, and those who are in fear of process for debt and names John Shakespeare among the latter. John Shakespeare's difficulties seem to have begun in 1576, but the government stringency towards recusants did not become truly oppressive until the early 1580s, with the arrival of the first missionary priests from the Continental seminaries. If the Shakespeare family were Catholic, they were to a great extent conformists, not the stuff of martyrs.

A sixteenth-century table setting, showing the type of houseware available in a middle-class household. (Museum of London)

LATE ADOLESCENCE AND MARRIAGE

At some time during the last years of the 1570s, William Shakespeare must have left Stratford grammar school and embarked upon some training which would lead to an eventual trade. The most likely course for him to have followed would have been to be apprenticed to his father, a likelihood which is strengthened by the fact that we know the occupations of two of his three younger brothers, and they were not glovers. Gilbert became a haberdasher, a trade linked to gloving, and Edmund, the youngest, became an actor in London. Since Edmund was born in 1580, his eldest brother was well-enough established in the London theatrical world to arrange Edmund's apprenticeship as a player when he was old enough to leave home. Apprenticeship usually began between the ages of ten and fourteen. The fact that the second son did not follow in his father's trade suggests that the eldest had already done so. There is an early tradition that Shakespeare spent some time as a schoolmaster in the country, and some scholars are inclined to give weight to this.[4]

He certainly spent his late adolescence in Stratford. After the record of his christening, William Shakespeare's first appearance in the documentary record is as a teenager about to be married. He was eighteen, his bride twenty-six. The remarkable aspect of the age of the partners in William Shakespeare's marriage is not, as many biographers have suggested, the age of the bride, but the youth of the groom. The average age of the partners in a first marriage at this date was twenty-six for men and twenty-four for women among the lower classes, possibly about a year earlier among the more prosperous middle-classes. The aristocracy married earlier, at about twenty for women and twenty-one for male heirs (their younger brothers married late or not at all). Anne Hathaway may therefore have been marrying a little late, but her husband was marrying exceptionally young. Such age-discrepant marriages were not uncommon at the period, but they tended to involve widows, and are unusual in first marriages.[5]

The emotional circumstances which led up to this wedding are matters for speculation; the physical ones certainties. At the time of her marriage, in November 1582, Anne Hathaway was three months pregnant. Banns could not be called between Advent Sunday and the Octave of Epiphany – 2 December to 13 January in 1582/3 – which probably explains the fact that the marriage was performed by special licence. If the marriage were to be postponed until the second half of January, it would be impossible to conceal the bride's pregnancy. It has been suggested that the marriage may have followed a betrothal, which, under Elizabethan law, if followed by sexual intercourse, represented a binding marriage, and that Shakespeare and his bride were not, therefore, guilty of immorality. If this were the case, then it is difficult to see the need for the special licence. To judge by the date of christening of Susanna Shakespeare, Anne Hathaway must have been aware of her condition by the beginning of November, which would have allowed ample time for the calling of banns, in order to regularize her position. The scramble for the licence so that the banns might be called at least once before 2 December suggests that a certain amount of persuasion had been entailed – whether of bride, bridegroom or bridegroom's father, who would have to give his consent to the marriage of a minor, it is impossible to say.

The circumstances of the marriage are made more confusing by what may be no more than a clerical error on the part of the Worcester Diocesan Court clerk. On 27 November 1582 the clerk entered the grant of a licence in the Bishop's Register to 'Willelmum Shaxpere et Annam Whateley de Temple Grafton'. On 28 November he entered a marriage licence bond, with the sureties being two Shottery farmers, friends of the Hathaway family, permitting 'William Shagspere . . . and Anne hathwey of Stratford' to marry after one calling of the banns. It is uncertain if we are dealing with two women, two men (unlikely) or only one of each. Whateley is a common Warwickshire name, and the clerk was careless, as other entries show; but while one might possibly mishear, or mistranscribe, 'Whateley' for 'Hathaway', it is inconceivable that the same process could translate 'Stratford' or 'Shottery' into 'Temple Grafton'. It has been suggested that Temple Grafton was perhaps the bride's residence at the time of the marriage, or the location for that marriage. Since it was to be performed at such short notice (the only date on which the banns could be called was 30 November, so the wedding must either have taken place then, directly after the calling of the banns, or shortly thereafter), it is conceivable that the minister of Temple Grafton, described four years later as 'old . . . Unsound in religion', unable to preach or read well, and notable only for his skill in curing diseased hawks, was the only local clergyman free to perform the ceremony. The mention of unsoundness in religion implies Catholicism, and is one of the pieces of evidence produced in support of Shakespeare's being a Catholic.

Shakespeare was a minor at the time of his marriage, and his father's consent was therefore necessary to the obtaining of a marriage licence. If two Annes were involved it seems odd that John Shakespeare should give his signed consent to two marriages within two days. For an eighteen-year-old male of Shakespeare's class at that date to be planning one marriage was unusual enough; to be proposing alternative domestic arrangements seems a near-impossibility.

Whether William Shakespeare was involved with two women or only one, it was Anne Hathaway he married at the end of 1582, and she was the mother of his children – Susanna, christened on 26 May 1583, and the twins Hamnet and Judith, christened on 2 February 1585. Apart from being linked with his parents in a lawsuit in 1588 (when his presence in Stratford was not necessary) William Shakespeare then disappears from the records until 1592, when he emerges in London as an actor and playwright. The sentimentality of some biographers has led them to date his departure from Stratford as subsequent to the birth of the twins; in fact he could have left any time from early May 1584 onwards.

THE MOVE TO LONDON

The usual age for the ending of an apprenticeship was twenty-one. If Shakespeare was apprenticed to his father and completed that apprenticeship, then he may not have left for London until 1585, or even as late as 1587, a date tentatively put forward by Schoenbaum and others. Other biographers have pointed to the extensive training known to have been necessary for the Elizabethan actor and have implied a rather earlier attachment to the London theatre. If the earliest suggested dates for the *Henry VI* trilogy – 1588–90 – are correct, Schoenbaum's proposed departure date would mean that Shakespeare wrote his first hits after very little experience of professional theatrical life. It is into these 'lost years' that Shakespeare's time as 'a schoolmaster in the country', if it existed, must also be fitted.

Many scholars believe that by 1592 Shakespeare had written at least eight plays: *The Comedy of Errors, The Taming of the Shrew, The Two Gentlemen of Verona, King John, Titus Andronicus* and all three parts of *Henry VI*. This volume of composition, while small compared with the output of some of his contemporaries, argues a considerable number of years of involvement with the London theatre. Later in his career he would produce between one and two plays a year:[6] if this rate of production was an echo of his previous practice, then he must have begun his career as an independent composer of plays by 1588.

We have, essentially, no knowledge of Shakespeare's prentice-work: no true juvenilia. Ben Jonson, who also started as an actor, is known to have begun his literary career as a part-author of plays, a participant in the then common process by which a play's plot was devised by one author and the various acts farmed out to others. Jonson was also the author of several early works which are now lost, as he did not think them worthy of inclusion in his collected works. The degree of accomplishment evident in

Shakespeare's earliest plays suggests that he too served some sort of literary apprenticeship, both as an actor, learning the arts of dramatic craftsmanship through performing in the works of other writers, and possibly through the same sort of early participation as Jonson's in the assembly side of the Elizabethan entertainment industry. In accounting for the seven or eight 'lost years', this process must be taken into account.

By 1592 Shakespeare was established as an actor and as the author of at least one hit – *Henry VI Part III*. It is this work which is misquoted in a pamphlet published under the name of, and probably by, the then recently deceased playwright Robert Greene. In it Greene addresses three fellow-playwrights, all, like him, university graduates, and warns them against the player who has dared to set himself up in rivalry to them:

> there is an upstart Crow, beautified with our feathers, that with his *Tygers hart wrapt in a Players hyde*, supposes he is as well able to bombast out a blanke verse as the best of you: and beeing an absolute *Johannes fac totum*, is in his owne conceit the onely Shake-scene in a countrey.[7]

Greene died in squalor. Of the three playwrights he is probably addressing, Christopher Marlowe was killed in 1593 in a pub in a squabble over the bill for drinks, Thomas Nashe died in obscurity sometime between 1599 and 1601, and George Peele died in 1596. The despised, comparatively under-educated actor outlived them by twenty years, and became one of the richest men in his home town, and a gentleman, a designation as prestigious as 'Master of Arts'.

THEATRICAL ASSOCIATES

Once he arrived in London, William Shakespeare's biography becomes inseparable from the history of the theatrical company with which he became associated as both leading actor and leading playwright, the Lord Chamberlain's Men. It is not known with which company or companies he spent the early part of his career. In 1592 a major outbreak of the plague forced the closure of the London theatres, and they stayed closed until the summer of 1594, except for one brief period early that year. This caused an upheaval in the English theatrical scene. Those companies which could, went on the road; others collapsed. When the theatres finally reopened, London was dominated by two adult companies: the Admiral's Men and the Lord Chamberlain's Men. They shared a playhouse at Newington Butts for a brief season in June 1594, alternating two- or three-day sessions, perhaps while their own playhouses, the Rose (which had been used for three performances in mid-May) and the Theatre, were prepared for their reopenings. After that they returned to their separate playhouses: the Admiral's Men to the Rose in Southwark, and the Lord Chamberlain's Men to the old Theatre in the Liberty of Holywell, now under or just north of Liverpool Street Station. At Christmas 1594 the Lord Chamberlain's Men presented two plays at court. On the following 15 March, three members of the company were paid for these performances: William Kempe, William Shakespeare and Richard Burbage. Shakespeare was now a leading member of the company.

The family at the heart of the Lord Chamberlain's Men – James Burbage and his sons Richard and Cuthbert – had Warwickshire connections. James Burbage, trained as a joiner,[8] had turned to acting, and had at one stage been the leader of Leicester's Men, the theatrical troupe under the patronage of the Earl of Leicester, the most powerful nobleman in the kingdom. Leicester was Queen Elizabeth's 'favourite favourite' (in Schoenbaum's phrase). His seat was at Kenilworth Castle, some twelve miles from Stratford, and his brother, the Earl of Warwick, was lord of Stratford and also patron of a company of players. Leicester's Men acted at Stratford in 1573, 1576–7 and 1586–7,[9] Warwick's Men in 1575. Leicester's Men may have been involved in one of the most spectacular of Elizabethan entertainments, mounted by the Earl of Leicester for the Queen at Kenilworth Castle in the summer of 1575.[10]

In 1576 James Burbage, together with his brother-in-law, John Brayne (who had previously put up the first purpose-built playhouse so far known to have been erected in London, the Red Lion), built the Theatre, which was to become the first home of the Lord Chamberlain's Men. Leicester's Men broke up after their patron's death in 1588, and it is difficult to trace the steps by which the Lord Chamberlain's Men were formed.[11] By this time the leading player was no longer James Burbage but his son Richard.

As with the brother Earls of Warwick and Leicester in the 1570s and 1580s, the patronage of the main theatrical companies in late-Elizabethan London was a family affair. The Lord Admiral, Charles, Lord Howard of Effingham, later created Earl of Nottingham, was the son-in-law of Henry Carey, Lord Hunsdon, the Lord Chamberlain. When Hunsdon died, in 1596, his heir took over his patronage of the theatrical company (and, shortly afterwards, his position of Lord Chamberlain), so at the time of Elizabeth's death in 1603, the companies were under the protection of brothers-in-law. Both men were also relatives of Elizabeth, and among her inner circle of friends. Lady Howard of Effingham (the former Catherine Carey) was among Elizabeth's favourite ladies-in-waiting, and her death was among the events which seem to have precipitated the depression which led to the Queen's last illness. Howard himself, commander of the fleet which had defeated the Spanish Armada, was a trusted adviser and confidant. He was a remote cousin of the Queen: both were descended from Thomas Howard, second Duke of Norfolk, by different wives. Henry Carey, Lord Hunsdon, was a much closer relative of Elizabeth. He was the son of Mary Boleyn, elder sister of Elizabeth's own mother, Anne, and her predecessor as Henry VIII's mistress. Since Mary Boleyn's liaison with Henry VIII continued for some time after her marriage to William Carey, it is possible that Hunsdon, as well as being Elizabeth's first cousin, was also her half-brother. Hunsdon was also the uncle of Leicester's widow, Lettice Knollys, who seems to have extended her patronage to Leicester's Men for a short time after her husband's death. James Burbage was fortunate – or shrewd – in his choice of patrons for his companies: the Queen's favourite favourite was succeeded by the Queen's favourite cousin.[12]

PATRONAGE AND PROSPERITY

The Burbages, Brayne and the owner of the land on which the Theatre stood were all joint proprietors of the real estate used by the Lord Chamberlain's Men. Apart from its playhouse, which might be used only intermittently, and be rented from an impresario, the capital investment of an Elizabethan theatre company consisted of its costumes, properties and playbooks. Apart from *Titus Andronicus*, and possibly *Henry VI Part I*, before 1595, all Shakespeare's plays were certainly associated only with the Lord Chamberlain's Men, suggesting that he retained their ownership. It was presumably his playbooks which comprised Shakespeare's entitlement to a major holding in his theatre company: he seems, after what must have been the lean years of 1592–4, to have speedily reached prosperity. In 1596 he carried through the application for a grant of arms which his father had been forced to abandon in the mid-1570s, and in 1597 he bought the second biggest house in Stratford, New Place. If the Shakespeare family had felt shamed by their financial reverses in the 1570s, William Shakespeare's house purchase twenty years later showed how far those reverses had been overcome.

Impresarios and their families made money in the Elizabethan theatre; actors and playwrights did not. Philip Henslowe, the impresario of the Admiral's Men, paid Thomas Dekker and Ben Jonson eight pounds in September 1599 for the script of the play *Page of Plymouth*. Ten days later he spent ten pounds on a gown for one of the female characters.[13] His account books consistently record a far greater expenditure on costumes than on playbooks, and a succession of debt-stricken playwrights and actors receiving loans to be paid back at interest appear in the records of his business. Edward Alleyn, principal actor in the same company, died extremely rich, the founder of the magnificent College of God's Gift at Dulwich, but he was Henslowe's stepson-in-law. Those actors who formed the nucleus of the Lord Chamberlain's Men were the exception to this rule. They lived lives of, as far as is known, quiet respectability, and they prospered. John Heminges and Henry Condell were churchwardens in the upper-middle-class parishes where they made their homes, and died wealthy men; Richard Burbage's estate was greater than Shakespeare's. If none of them achieved the plutocratic status of Edward Alleyn, they all succeeded in making themselves more than comfortably off. William Shakespeare's prosperity was unusual for an actor and playwright in the general context of the Elizabethan theatre; but he was typical of his company, in itself an anomaly among Elizabethan companies both for its cohesiveness and for its duration.

Nevertheless Shakespeare's sudden access of prosperity in the mid-1590s is remarkable, and has not been adequately explained. Two years after his purchase of New Place he was to be engaged in yet another enterprise requiring major capital, when he became one of the joint proprietors of the new Globe playhouse, which the Lord Chamberlain's Men built for themselves on the south bank of the Thames in Southwark.

The composition of *Love's Labour's Lost* is generally dated to the years of closure of the theatres, when Shakespeare also published his two narrative poems, *Venus and Adonis* and the *Rape of Lucrece*, dedicated to the young Earl of Southampton. Much scholarship has been expended on this unremarkable young man, who seems to have followed a pattern of life not unfamiliar among the aristocracy of any date: a somewhat wild and silly youth, followed by a respectable middle age spent divided between the pleasures of domesticity and public service, and a seat on the board of several business companies.[14] He was an astute choice on Shakespeare's part as the dedicatee of a fashionably erotic narrative: twenty-one years old, and a comparative newcomer to court, known, from his patronage of the translator John Florio, to be seriously interested in promoting the arts; and a member of the circle of extravagant young aristocrats who had attached themselves to the Earl of Essex. He was also spoilt and extravagant, and had a poorly controlled temper. As a leader – but not, unlike the royally-connected Essex,[15] *the* leader – of the younger faction at court, he was not so overwhelmed with dedications as not to feel the compliment of being the addressee of an avant-garde work produced by a high-quality printer.

Richard Field, who printed the poems, was an older schoolmate of William Shakespeare, being born in 1561, the son of a tanner of Bridge Street in Stratford. John Shakespeare and Henry Field, Richard's father, knew each other, and did business together, and when Field died, John Shakespeare carried out the duties of a friend and neighbour in helping to assess his goods. Richard Field had been apprenticed to the Huguenot printer Thomas Vautrollier, and had married his master's widow. Operating at the luxury end of the printing trade, Field had moved to the capital in 1576 and succeeded there. His presence there, and Shakespeare's use of him for the publication of his poems, is another indication of the comparative ease with which it was possible to transfer from Stratford to London, and the close connections which were maintained between them. Shakespeare did not go up to the capital, at whatever date he made that transition, as an unknown provincial youth with no connections.

The poems became fashionable best-sellers, and Shakespeare himself became something of a pin-up to poetically minded youth, if we are to trust the authority of the satirical *Parnassus* plays, staged by the students of St John's College, Cambridge.[16] An early tradition asserts that Southampton rewarded Shakespeare with a gift of £1000. The sum must inevitably have suffered the multiplications of gossip, but some substantial gift from his patron would explain Shakespeare's prosperity after the two-year closure of the theatres, when one would have expected those connected with the stage to be going through a period of financial stringency. The dedication to *The Rape of Lucrece* (1594) is considerably warmer and more intimate in tone than that of *Venus and Adonis* (1593), and suggests that the author has had concrete proof of his patron's generosity. But Shakespeare did not continue as a fashionable poet: once the theatres reopened he became involved in the setting-up of the Lord Chamberlain's Men, and remained attached to this group of colleagues for the rest of his theatrical career.

THE GLOBE

The Lord Chamberlain's Men did not stay for long at the old Theatre. In 1597 the lease expired, and the company was forced to look for a new playhouse. James Burbage had tried to negotiate a renewal of the lease with the ground landlord, Giles Allen, but these negotiations had come to nothing. He had then embarked on plans to establish the company in a new indoor playhouse, and to that end had taken over part of the old Dominican priory of Blackfriars, and devoted several hundred pounds to converting the *frater*, the friars' dining-hall, into an indoor playhouse. But the Blackfriars was a fashionable residential district, and its inhabitants (who included the company's patron, Lord Hunsdon) had no wish for their exclusivity to be invaded by a crowd of common theatre-goers. They petitioned the Privy Council on the matter, and Burbage's project was stopped.

In January 1597 James Burbage died, and by the end of the year negotiations with Allen were in such a bad way that the Lord Chamberlain's Men had moved from the Theatre to the neighbouring playhouse, the Curtain. Through 1598 the Burbage sons tried to renegotiate their lease, but Allen was intransigent. He disapproved of the theatre: he would pull down the playhouse and convert its materials to 'some better use'. The Chamberlain's Men determined that he might get the land, but he should never have the playhouse. On the night of 28 December 1598, Cuthbert and Richard Burbage, accompanied by their mother, their financial backer, their carpenter Peter Street and ten or a dozen workmen, pulled down the Theatre and transported its timbers across the Thames to London's other theatrical district, the Bankside. There the old Theatre became the basis for the new Globe. By 16 May 1599 the new playhouse was finished, and by September the Lord Chamberlain's Men were playing in it.

Allen assumed that with the lease expired, the land would come back into his possession with the buildings which had been erected on it. The players' move across the river with the Theatre was posited on the argument that although he owned the land, they owned the building, and were entitled to remove it. The subsequent lawsuits went on until 1602.[17]

The location the Lord Chamberlain's Men chose for their new playhouse was close to that of Henslowe's Rose, and was attractive for the same reasons: freedom from City jurisdiction and accessibility, either on foot across London Bridge or by water-taxi to the nearby river-steps. Henslowe did not welcome the rival establishment. The Rose had been built on swampy ground, and was already in bad condition; Henslowe commissioned Peter Street, who had built the Globe, to build his company a new playhouse about half a mile from the site of the old Theatre, north of the City, in the Liberty of Finsbury. The new playhouse was to be built in a similar manner to the Globe, but square; Henslowe called it the Fortune.

The building of the Globe involved Shakespeare in yet another major expense. At the Theatre, he had been a sharer in the company which acted in a building whose proprietors were the Burbages and their associates. At the Globe he, along with four other members of the Lord Chamberlain's Men, joined the Burbages in becoming a joint proprietor of the building. The Burbages held half the lease; the five other actors – Shakespeare, William Kempe, John Heminges, Augustine Phillips and Thomas Pope – held the other half. Shakespeare thus had a one-tenth share in the playhouse itself. Until 1608, when the Burbages finally managed to obtain the use of the Blackfriars playhouse, the Globe was the only home of the Lord Chamberlain's Men.

PROPERTY HOLDINGS

In London Shakespeare lived in a succession of lodgings in respectable bourgeois districts. An early tradition claims that he spent a period of each year at his home in Stratford; it is not known whether he was there in the summer of 1596 when his eleven-year-old son Hamnet died. His father died in 1601, having lived to see his son achieve a prosperity far greater than his own. Although New Place was only the second-biggest house in Stratford, it had more symbolic associations than the largest, having been built by an earlier local-boy-made-good, Sir Hugh Clopton, Lord Mayor of London and builder of Clopton Bridge, the starting point for any Stratfordian who wished to make the journey to London. Unlike his father, William Shakespeare did not become involved in local politics, but he did over the years increase his property holdings in the Stratford area. In May 1602 he bought about 107 acres of arable land in Old Stratford, with rights of common entitling him to pasture livestock in the outlying fields. In September of the same year he bought the title to a cottage which stood in a quarter of an acre of garden opposite the garden of New Place. In July 1605 he bought a half-interest in a lease of tithes in the area of Stratford and some surrounding parishes. On his father's death he had inherited the house on Henley Street in which he was born. On at least one occasion – the purchase of farmland – Gilbert Shakespeare acted as his brother's agent, and it may be that he took care of Shakespeare's business affairs in Stratford,[18] but the general administration of what was from 1597 onwards a considerable household, including family, servants and lodgers, would have fallen on Anne Shakespeare. The prosperity of William Shakespeare's affairs during his considerable absences suggests that, whatever the emotional state of his marriage, Anne was a good and trustworthy business partner.

Shakespeare made his last purchase of real-estate in March 1613: the gatehouse of the old Blackfriars priory, the *frater* of which James Burbage had converted into a theatre, and which had been the winter playhouse of Shakespeare's company since 1608. The gatehouse was in a desirable residential district, and close not only to the Blackfriars theatre but also to Puddle Wharf where one could take a water-taxi to Bankside and the Globe. The house cost £140, but Shakespeare seems never to have lived in it.

RETIREMENT AND DEATH

On 29 June 1613 the Globe theatre burned to the ground during a performance of *Henry VIII*. If we exclude the parts of *The Two Noble Kinsmen* possibly by him, William Shakespeare wrote no more plays. The Globe was rebuilt, at huge expense, within a year, but Shakespeare wrote nothing for it. John Fletcher succeeded him as the resident playwright for his company, and Shakespeare retired to Stratford.[19]

The theatrical company which he left was no longer the Lord Chamberlain's Men.

On 24 March 1603 Queen Elizabeth Tudor died, to be succeeded, as James I, by her third cousin, James VI of Scotland. James was a clever (although not intelligent) and cultivated man, determined to be seen as a patron of learning and the arts. His wife, Anne of Denmark, was an active patron of the arts with a passion for amateur theatricals. The patronage of the London dramatic companies now came directly under the Crown. The pre-eminence of the Lord Chamberlain's Men was recognized by their becoming the King's Men; the Admiral's Men enjoyed the patronage of the heir to the throne, Prince Henry, while the third-ranking company, Worcester's Men, became the Queen's Men. Shakespeare and his fellows were now Grooms of the Chamber to the King, entitled to livery, and in 1604, in their function as Grooms of the Chamber, they were required to wait upon the new Spanish ambassador and his train at Somerset House, on the occasion of the negotiations for a peace treaty which would bring to an end the long-running war between England and Spain. It is pleasing to note the lengths to which the English were prepared to go to impress the Spanish suite: the ranks of courtiers were swelled by actors playing courtiers. Twelve of the company were paid £21 12s between them for eighteen days attendance in August.[20]

The new status as the King's own company of players meant that they were called upon to perform at court far more often than in the previous reign. In the last decade of Elizabeth's reign they performed at court, on average, three times a year; in the first decade of James's the average was thirteen times a year. These figures relate, of course, only to known performances: there may have been other, unrecorded ones. A court performance would have meant adapting the play to a stage temporarily erected in a hall; and further adaptation was required after 1608, when the company to which the Blackfriars theatre had been leased was suppressed on the King's order. In August 1608 the King's Men assumed the lease of the Blackfriars theatre, and by autumn 1609 they were playing in it. From then on it seems that the King's Men used the Blackfriars as a winter home, and went to the much larger and less expensive Globe during the summers.

Shakespeare's connection as an actor with the Blackfriars theatre may have lasted for as little as two years; certainly for no more than four. Although he continued to make visits to London he spent the last years of his life in Stratford. His daughters married: Susanna well, to Dr John Hall in 1607; Judith much less satisfactorily, to Thomas Quiney in 1616. Ten weeks after her wedding Shakespeare himself was dead.

Of the circumstances of his death we have no reliable information. It has been argued that the signatures to his will, executed within a month of his death, are shaky, and may be those of a dying man, but judgements like this, however distinguished the paleographer who makes them, are ultimately subjective, and the knowledge that the signatory of a will died within a month of its execution is likely to create a prejudice in favour of his having been ill at the time.[21] The will was first drawn up in January 1616, possibly in anticipation of Judith Shakespeare's marriage; it was revised soon after that event, presumably in the light of a sexual scandal involving Shakespeare's new son-in-law. The overall intention of the document was to ensure that the property accumulated by John and then by William Shakespeare should pass intact to a male heir: one who would not (since Hamnet's death) bear the name Shakespeare, nor perhaps Hall (for Susanna was by this time thirty-three and had only one daughter, Elizabeth, born in 1608) but to Susanna's grandchildren. The property was entailed after Susanna's death to her male descendants: to her sons, were she to bear any, otherwise to the sons of her daughter. If the Hall line failed, then the property was to pass to the male heirs of Judith Quiney. Judith Quiney received £150, tied up so that her husband would not be able to get his hands on the principal, and a silver-gilt bowl. Shakespeare's only surviving sibling, his sister, Joan Hart, was left £20, Shakespeare's wearing apparel, and the right to stay on in the Henley Street house where she and her brother had been born, for the rest of her life. Her sons, Shakespeare's nephews, got five pounds each. Friends, colleagues and godchildren, both from Stratford and from the King's Men, were left small sums of money, some for memorial rings. And, in the most famous provision of any will ever made, Anne Shakespeare, née Hathaway, got the second-best bed.

Shakespeare's intentions were frustrated by genetics. Elizabeth Hall married twice, but remained childless. Judith Quiney's descendants died before Elizabeth Hall, by then Lady Bernard, and the estate was dispersed. Joan Hart's descendants remained in possession of the house in Henley Street until 1806, long enough to ensure its survival, but New Place was demolished in 1759. The Blackfriars gatehouse seems to have been demolished in the eighteenth century, and the various lodgings in which Shakespeare

All that now remains of New Place. (Norman Hammond)

had spent his London years vanished in the Great Fire of 1666. All the property he so carefully accumulated during his lifetime has vanished. Only the house acquired by his father to be the foundation of the Shakespeare fortunes, and in which the poet spent the first part of his life, survives. On the site of New Place some foundations survive, and the garden is in keeping with a house of its date. But nothing remains that we know with certainty to have been touched, or worn, or used by Shakespeare.

Seven years after William Shakespeare's death, two senior members of the King's Men collected his dramatic works in folio. The choice of format was important: folios were normally reserved for serious scholarly books, for the works of established classical poets. They were expensive: they made the statement that a work published in that format was itself a classic. When Ben Jonson had earlier collected his own works into a similar volume, the first living English poet to do so, he was subjected to a good deal of ridicule. Shakespeare's former colleagues John Heminges and Henry Condell, now the senior members of the King's Men (Richard Burbage had died in 1619) were affirming their belief in the stature of the dramatist who had made them the premier dramatic troupe in London – a stature which the passage of time has endorsed.

CHAPTER TWO

THE BACKGROUND OF THE ELIZABETHAN THEATRE

THE MEDIEVAL DRAMA

Although William Shakespeare was born three years before the first known purpose-built playhouse, John Brayne's Red Lion, was erected in London, at the time of his birth England had a long-established theatrical tradition, albeit a principally amateur one. The end of the medieval drama overlapped with the establishment of the Renaissance tradition: the last performances of the York Corpus Christi cycle of plays took place in 1572, when the Red Lion had already been built. In 1575 the Coventry Hock Tuesday play was performed for Elizabeth Tudor on her visit to the Earl of Leicester at Kenilworth Castle, a performance which it would have been possible for Shakespeare to have attended.[1] The following year James Burbage, the leader of Leicester's Men, perhaps a participant in the festivities at Kenilworth, built the Theatre in London.

The erection of purpose-built amphitheatres to provide permanent homes for companies of professional actors was revolutionary in Elizabethan London; but the idea of a visit to, or participation in, a dramatic performance as a means of recreation was not. For centuries, all over England, amateur actors had been putting on plays for the amusement of themselves and their neighbours.

There are almost no material remains of the great mass of English medieval drama. It may be traced mainly through local records – payments to performers, both professional and amateur, occurring in civic and household accounts; court cases, when entertainers had overstepped the mark of acceptability; descriptions in chronicles of particularly splendid dramatic events, usually celebrations connected with the court, and the occasional drawing, either of a specific event or of a generalized theatrical figure, such as a minstrel. Despite this general paucity of information, and perhaps because medievalists are more accustomed to think in terms of material culture than their Renaissance colleagues, scholars have been more diligent in their search of areas other than the literary for evidence of the manner of medieval stage presentation, and have produced in evidence carvings both in wood and stone, paintings and picture books.[2]

The survival of four manuscripts of mystery cycles is due to chance: the York manuscript because Archbishop Grindal called it in in 1572 to examine it for religious suitability, and never returned it (it is now in the British Library); the Wakefield manuscript in the private library of the Towneley family, whence it passed into the possession of the Huntington Library in San Marino, California; the Chester manuscript (this cycle was last performed in 1575) and the N-town manuscript (whose provenance is the subject of debate) in the British Library.[3] For the manner of their staging – the properties, costumes and settings used – we must rely on scholarly reconstruction from the manuscripts, from the visual arts and from the accounts concerning their performance.

Because of the accidental survival of their manuscripts, the medieval drama is thought of mainly in terms of the great mystery cycles, and of morality plays such as *Mankind*, but this is to limit its multifarious pervasion of life. The mystery cycles were essentially civic events, involving not only the celebration of the central narrative of the Christian religion in a form which would educate those involved, but also a celebration of the town which produced them – a manifestation of civic pride and piety, an ambiguous display of wealth and humility. Their production involved the whole town: those who represented the biblical characters, or saw to the staging; and those who came to watch, who found themselves in the position of the crowd at the foot of the cross, implicated in the events which had led to their salvation.

The mystery cycles are the products of the later Middle Ages, but sacred drama existed for centuries before their emergence, along with a flourishing entertainment industry. Acting was a principally amateur pastime, but professional entertainers – musicians, troubadours, jugglers, acrobats, attendants of performing animals, fools (both natural and professional) – were well established, both in the households of great men, and in peripatetic troupes, which may have claimed the patronage of a particular nobleman.[4] In an age in which literacy was limited, all literature had something of the nature of performance. The frontispiece to the manuscript of *Troilus and Criseyde* which shows Chaucer reading his poem to Richard II and his court[5] may be an imaginary scene, but most people would perforce absorb literature through the performance of the reader or storyteller, and the oral delivery of literature must be mimetic if it is to be successful. There is a case for seeing the seeds of professional theatre in the one-man show of the poet reading his own romances. Much of Chaucer's poetry depends for its effect (an effect lost to the modern reader) on a mimetic tension between the narrator of the poem and the writer/deliverer of it: the sophisticated public servant who wrote the poem, and his own creation/presentation of himself – the tubby, naive, inept narrator. Hearing Chaucer deliver one of his own poems must have been a dramatic experience much like hearing Garrison Keillor reading *The Prairie Home Companion*.

In the Middle Ages, theatre had an element of intimacy. It is worth stressing the small scale of life. At the time of Shakespeare's birth, Stratford-upon-Avon was a fairly large town, yet its population was between 1,200 and 1,400 people – the size of a large modern school, and less than the estimated capacity of the tiny Rose theatre. We are dealing with communities in which, if everyone did not know everyone else personally, they might know who everyone else was and something about them. Watching one of the mystery cycles was an experience closer to attending a local amateur dramatic society production in a small village than to attending a modern professional theatre. With the performers known to most of their audience, it would not have been possible to forget the player in the role. Medieval audiences of both civic religious celebrations and of court disguisings saw those whose lives were connected with their own enter for the course of the entertainment the role of another, but the experience must have been different from that of the audience at a professional performance, where a much smaller proportion of the audience (and one which decreased substantially over the years) would have been connected with the performers in this way. The considerations which this might entail may be seen in the modern productions of the Oberammergau Passion Play, where the casting of the Virgin Mary has been attended by considerable controversy.

Even the early small professional troupes, which developed from the late fourteenth century onwards, and were attached to various aristocratic households, spent time away from those households on tour, returning at set times of the year to set locations,[6] so they were known to the audiences before whom they played and, in the cases of the households that provided their bases, were entertaining their masters and fellows. The theatrical ancestry of Elizabethan drama had an intimacy which can now be recaptured only among amateurs.

RELIGIOUS AND CIVIC PAGEANTRY

The range of medieval theatrical experience was much greater than in most twentieth-century societies. It encompassed religious and political discourse as well as folk ritual and court entertainment. One part of the ancestry of religious drama is the liturgy of the Church, itself mimetic – at the consecration of the host, the heart of the Mass, the celebrant re-enacts the events of the Last Supper (and, by symbolic extension, the Crucifixion), while the congregation, attending his words and actions, are simultaneously themselves and represent and identify with the Apostles present at the Last Supper and the crowd witnessing the Crucifixion. Gradually the liturgy extended its mimetic scope to include dramatic representations of the crucial events of Easter – such as the coming of the four Marys to the empty tomb – and so paved the way for a fuller use of drama to celebrate and represent the Gospel. At the same time, clerical playwrights were looking for inspiration to classical drama, familiar from the school and university curriculum.[7] In England, the religious drama created from the fusion of these two traditions eventually came out of the churches and passed into the administration of the civic authorities, as represented by the guilds, although it was not until after the Reformation that the plays came under the control of those authorities. The great cycles were related to pageantry, attached to the feast of Corpus Christi, which was processional in intention, giving an opportunity for the public display of devotion in religious pageantry through the town.

Pageantry could be secular as well as religious. The public progress of the ruler through his kingdom, the display of his power and wealth this achieved, and the symbolic shows mounted to welcome him formed a major strand in the medieval dramatic world, and one which continued throughout the Elizabethan period. The appearance of the ruler, surrounded by courtiers, was an enactment of his or her position in the kingdom. Since the ruler embodied the kingdom, the splendour of the

Queen Elizabeth I Carried in Procession, *by Robert Peake the Elder. Such theatrical manifestations of court ceremonial were common in sixteenth-century London. (Private Collection)*

ruler's clothes and jewels displayed the kingdom's wealth. The appearance of the courtiers was equally important: a modest court argued a modest kingdom, while a display of splendour and extravagance argued prosperity and power. The theatrical nature of a royal public appearance may be gathered from the painting by Robert Peake of *Queen Elizabeth I Carried in Procession*. A crowd, the privileged at upper windows, the humbler citizens behind a row of halberdiers, watches as Elizabeth Tudor passes by in the company of her court. Preceded by six Knights of the Garter, one of whom bears her ceremonial sword, symbolizing her power, Elizabeth, in her triumphal chair, seems to float ethereally above the rest. She is shaded by a canopy or cloth of estate (another symbol of royalty) which is embroidered with emblematic flowers, symbolizing the cults of youth, beauty and virginity which were celebrated in honour of her at the late stage in her reign when the picture was painted. Her face is the portrait type known as the 'mask of youth', the face of a young goddess, not of a woman in her sixties. She wears a crown based on the design of a pyramid, symbolizing eternity, and her dress is white, with gauze puffs, again standing for her purity. The design of the piece is based on the concept of a triumph, both that of an imperial conqueror and the Petrarchan triumph of art in which the lady's eternal virtue is celebrated.[8]

What Peake has recorded in this picture is a moment of street theatre. On the occasions of formal royal processions, entries to towns, coronations and festivals, the town through which the royal person was to pass would respond with theatrical presentations of its own. These were as monitory as the procession of the ruler. If the rulers showed themselves as icons of wealth and power, the city would respond with images of what the regime should be. On the occasion of Elizabeth's coronation procession, a *tableau vivant* demanded that she make a commitment that her regime would be Protestant, and she responded and made that commitment both verbally and, for the sake of those who were too far away to hear the words addressed to her, visually, taking the English Bible which Truth the daughter of Time was proferring and kissing it with great fervour.[9] The sites chosen for these tableaux were often ones which themselves were important public works of the community involved, and stood for its own wealth and coherence. Market crosses were favourite sites for such displays, as were in London the various conduits or public water fountains, which usually ran with wine for the occasion. On a practical level, such structures, often elaborate and raised

Hobson's Conduit, Cambridge. This seventeenth-century conduit is typical of the structures which were used as the sites of and backgrounds to pageants in the Renaissance period. (Norman Hammond)

above the ground, provided convenient foundations for the erection of a raised acting area to enable the participants in the pageant to be easily visible. The *mise-en-scène* of a royal visit was triangular: the royal visitors were presented with a spectacle which demonstrated what the community visited required from them, the commercial power and coherence of the community which entitled them to make such a demand – this would be demonstrated both in the lavish cost of the tableau and in the site chosen for it, a piece of public work important either socially (a conduit which provided clean water) or defensively (a town gate) – and the advantages to be gained from submitting to the city's demands – demonstrated in the form of a gift, sometimes symbolic, sometimes crudely pecuniary. The city was presented with the embodied power – fiscal, temporal and spiritual – of the rulers and their court. The symbolic meeting of royal guest and civic host was viewed by a third group, the crowd of spectators, who were themselves arranged according to rank. Everyone both participated in the spectacle and, by observing everyone else, learned about their own place in the social hierarchy.[10] In this they resembled the audience at the mystery cycles, who both learned from the actions presented to them by the actors and themselves participated as the biblical crowd who were the witnesses to Jesus's life.

PERFORMANCE SITES

Both royal entries to towns and some mystery cycles seem to have depended on an ad hoc arrangement of temporary raised scaffolds and street area to accommodate the spectators of the events taking place on the raised structures. But there is evidence for the performance of some medieval drama in amphitheatres, and it has been suggested that temporary amphitheatres were also constructed for events such as tournaments and trials by combat. The origins of these amphitheatre structures is debatable. Roman theatres, such as the one at Silchester, were known and recognized, but whether they were the origins of the circular playing-places of Cornwall, or whether a circular shape is the logical one for the optimal accommodation of an audience, is debatable. By the time Ben Jonson (notorious for the detail of his learning) published his *Workes* (1616), a distinction was made between theatre and amphitheatre. Jonson and the title-page designer, William Hole, distinguish between the primitive origins of the theatre in Greece (Jonson saw himself in a line of descent from the classical theatre, rather than depending on a native tradition) and its development in the sophisticated Roman period. His amphitheatre is an excavated rural one, looking much as both Silchester and the Cornish playing places must have looked in his time, while the theatre is a fairly accurate representation of a Roman one with the superstructure of the Roman *frons scenae* read as a version of the Elizabethan stage-cover or heavens.

The title-page to Ben Jonson's Workes *(London, William Stansby, 1616). This title-page is designed to place Jonson in the context of the classical theatre. Figures representing five dramatic genres – tragedy, comedy, satire, pastoral and tragi-comedy – stand on a triumphal arch which resembles contemporary processional architecture, monuments and, probably, tiring-house façades. The arch is decorated with Jacobean ideas of classical theatre practice; the theatre itself seems to have a hut for flying mechanisms, and the cart resembles the vehicles which would have been used by Jacobean companies on tour. (By permission of the Syndics of Cambridge University Library)*

It is natural, in any open-air performance, for the audience to form a rough circle, whether that performance be of a busker attracting a desultory stream of passers-by, or a semi-formal spectacle watched by a large crowd. Indoor and outdoor dramatic performances developed in parallel throughout the Middle Ages and the Renaissance, a development emphasized by the fact that Shakespeare's own company had both an indoor and an outdoor house for the last years of his association with them, and had sought such accommodation much earlier. The English-weather argument for explaining the eventual move from outdoor to indoor playing is not perhaps as strong as many American scholars would have us believe – even on the west side of the Atlantic, crowds of thousands (professors of literature among them) will happily sit in the open for many hours on far less salubrious winter afternoons than ever occur in England in order to watch their local football team, and Henslowe's takings at the Rose playhouse show little seasonal variation. The high galleries of the playhouses would have provided shelter from the wind, and the mass of human bodies (far more warmly clad than modern people) would have generated a companionable heat – indeed, the same conditions would probably have made summer performances more unpleasant. The drawbacks of open-air performance were not attracting an audience, but rather the type of audience and the costs of production. In an age of non-fast dyes, with costumes the most substantial expense of any production, foul weather was a deterrent not to the spectators but to the cast, however extensive the protection afforded by the stage-cover, while the greater cost of the indoor houses meant that they attracted a prosperous audience who were more used to indoor entertainments.

The entertainments put on by members of limited and privileged societies, particularly over the period covering Christmas and the New Year, frequently had a mimetic element. These limited societies were not only royal courts or great households. Schools, universities, the Inns of Court and pre-Reformation religious houses all provided hospitality for such entertainments. The forms which the early entertainments took were various. Troupes of professional entertainers, attached to the royal court or to a great household, might put on the equivalent of a modern variety show or cabaret, with music, juggling, comic turns, acrobats and even puppet-shows, as well as mimetic events, either dumb-shows or short spoken dramatic interludes. Far more of these survive in French than in English, but the late thirteenth-century fragmentary *De Clerico et Puella*[11] is a brief farce based on the sexual merry-go-round. John Lydgate wrote some mimetic interludes for court consumption in the early fifteenth century, varying from a commentary to be spoken to a dumb-show to a fully-fledged brief dialogue-form diversion.[12] Courtiers themselves, accustomed to perform in jousts cast in the form of a romance narrative, took part in masques in which they represented other people. These were indoor performances, put on in great halls or great chambers, so there was a strong medieval tradition of both indoor and outdoor drama for the builders of the first Elizabethan theatres to look to.

ACTING AS A PROFESSION

During the reign of Elizabeth, what seems to have been mainly an amateur avocation became a full-time profession. The troupes of entertainers attached to aristocratic households became companies of players, specialists rather than variety artists, although the variety-show element in their performance survived in the form of dancing displays by members of the company, such as that witnessed by Thomas Platter after a performance of *Julius Caesar* in 1599.[13] The earlier leaders of the theatrical world seem to have drifted into the theatre from other professions – James Burbage was a joiner, and Richard Tarlton, the first great Elizabethan clown, was a master of fencing. Even in a later generation, Richard Burbage was skilled enough to paint *impresas* – symbolic pictures on tournament shields – for the Earl of Rutland, which suggests some education in a skill other than acting.[14] Later generations of players tended to come from the children's companies based on the choir schools, or to have been apprenticed to adult actors.[15] The development of an apprenticeship system is a mark of an independent profession.

The early companies which can be traced in records carried the names of the great magnates, like their successors, and there was for a time even a company patronized by the Queen herself, but without permanent bases they tended to be evanescent, to break up and quickly reform. The patrons early in Elizabeth's reign often came from the same families as those who later offered their names to companies with fixed homes. Besides Leicester and Warwick, they included the Earls of Lincoln and Sussex, the family of the Earl of Derby,[16] and Lord Hunsdon, later Shakespeare's patron.[17] What none of these companies seem to have had was a permanent base designed for the production of plays, and the fluctuations observable in the names of the companies may be attributable to the instability produced by the lack of a fixed base.

OUTDOOR ENTERTAINMENT

By the time Burbage built the Theatre, there was a large amount of non-dramatic outdoor public entertainment to which access was open or comparatively cheap. Bear-baitings and bull-baitings were carried on in circular arenas, with tiers of benches or standing places for spectators around the circumference – a modest wooden version of the present bullrings of Spain. Fencing displays were put on both in halls and in outdoor public spaces. Firework displays, water pageants and processional shows were mounted for both court and civic celebrations (surviving as the modern Lord Mayor's Show) and at the more expensive end of the scale, entry to the court tilts was open to anyone who could afford the twelve-pence entry fee at a time when a penny bought a table d'hôte meal in an inn.[18] Sermons were delivered outdoors at Paul's Cross, a structure which was of the same type as those used as a basis for dumb shows in the civic pageants. Even the administration of justice itself became outdoor theatre (an element of which still survives in the public processions of judges and the change of the colour of their robes on red-letter days). In the case of the beheadings of traitors to the state, executions were literally staged (see illustration on p. 57); in the case of the

A crowd watching a combat on foot, c. 1560. (College of Arms MS. M.6, f.62.) The crowd gives an idea of what a theatre audience must have been like. It includes a beggar, an animal trainer with his monkey on his shoulders, and a beer-vendor, as well as family groups. The three-storey gallery for spectators may be related to theatre architecture (note the classical columns flanking the windows). (Reproduced by kind permission of the College of Arms)

The Preaching at St Paul's Cross, c. 1620. *This gives an impression of the sermon as a form of entertainment, and of the appearance of a theatre audience. The gallery in the background may be related to those constructed for the theatres, and also, in the projecting bay in which the royal family sit, to the possible form of the tiring-house façade. (Society of Antiquaries of London)*

punishment of lesser criminals, public example became public entertainment, the central figures frequently recognizing their responsibility in this matter and acting out for the crowd a scaffold repentance, or defiance, or patient suffering of injustice, which they might see elsewhere enacted in fiction on the public stage. The apogee of this spectacle of justice was, ten years after the closure of the theatres, the execution of King Charles I, put on by Cromwell outside the Banqueting House in Whitehall in which the King had acted so many roles in the masques devised for him by Inigo Jones and his collaborators. By being executed outside rather than inside the hall (and, until then, executions by beheading of State prisoners were usually private affairs, either on Tower Green, where access could be restricted, or inside suitable buildings, as was the case with the execution of Mary Queen of Scots in the Great Hall of Fotheringay Castle), the King was forced from the private theatre which the Banqueting Hall represented, on to the public stage. As if he were in fact a participant at a masque, the executioner was masked, and close examination of contemporary pictures of the event shows that his mask is of exactly the same type as those worn at such entertainments. That this theatrical symbolism was deliberate was shown by contemporary recognition of it: Marvell describes the execution in terms of a play, with Cromwell as the author, and the King as the leading tragedian:

> That thence the *Royal Actor* born
> The *Tragick Scaffold* might adorn:
> While round the armed Bands
> Did clap their bloody hands.
> *He* nothing common did or mean
> Upon that memorable Scene.[19]

By the time Charles was executed the fusion of representation and reality, and familiarity with theatrical convention, was such that the mode of the King's death could be used to undermine his kingship – a king on a stage connected to a place of theatrical entertainment is not a true king, but only an actor playing the king. Yet this execution took place within seventy-two years of Burbage's erection of the Theatre.

THE RED LION: THE FIRST LONDON PLAYHOUSE?

Burbage's erection of the Theatre in 1576 has until recently been taken as the first establishment of a purpose-built public playhouse in London. But it has long been known that this was not the first purpose-built permanent structure for acting in London – John Rastell (?1475–1536), who was a lawyer, playwright, publisher of plays and deviser of royal pageants for Henry VIII, and connected by marriage to Sir Thomas More,[20] built a stage of lath and timber in the garden of his property in Finsbury Fields, and had a wardrobe of theatrical costumes which he was prepared to lend out.[21] Nor was the Theatre the first purpose-built public playhouse – the Corporation of Great Yarmouth built a public 'game-house' in 1538/9, and leased it for general entertainment purposes, including plays.[22] The reason for the assumption that Burbage's Theatre was the first purpose-built public playhouse in London is the assertion made in 1635 by his son Cuthbert that his father was 'the first builder of playhowses'.[23] With no earlier record of any purpose-built playhouse associated with the company which Burbage led – Leicester's Men – or with Burbage or any of his family, and with the natural assumption that any structure calling itself 'the Theatre' must be the only one, it was presumed that Burbage's 1576 building must have been the first. But recently evidence has been discovered, in the form of a lawsuit about jerry-building, that Burbage's brother-in-law and partner in the Theatre, John Brayne, had built a playhouse, the Red Lion, in 1567, nearly a decade before the Theatre.[24] The Burbage-Brayne partnership broke up in a welter of family feuding and lawsuits, and part of the Brayne case was that Brayne and his wife had done some of the labouring work on the Theatre, while Burbage's physical input had been minimal.[25] This has been dismissed as special pleading by the party which had lost control of the Theatre in order to establish their right to it, and probably not to be taken too seriously, but James Burbage was not a carpenter, but a joiner, which may mean that he was trained in making small-scale objects from wood, rather than in the construction techniques of timber-framed buildings – and it is possible, in the light of the discovery of Brayne's earlier playhouse, that the Brayne case was in fact correct.

The name of Brayne's theatre – the Red Lion – led many theatre historians, coming upon traces of it in documents, to assume that it was a theatre associated with an inn.[26] But as Janet Loengard points out, in an age of general illiteracy, before the invention of house numbers, all houses were given visually interpretable names. These now survive almost exclusively in the names of public houses,[27] but in the sixteenth century there was no qualitative difference between the names of businesses and private houses. The London theatres – for instance the Swan, the Rose and the Fortune – did not have names specifically linked to the activities carried out inside them. In *The Comedy of Errors* Antipholus of Ephesus lives in a house called the Phoenix (I.ii.75), Antipholus of Syracuse lodges at a house (or inn, or hotel) called the Centaur (II.ii.2), there is an inn (or eating-house) called the Tiger (III.i.95), and the brothel is called the Porpentine (III.i.116). All of these are easily recognizable in visual form, but give no indication of the service provided within. An additional series of visual symbols prevailed to indicate the nature of a business. The two which commonly survive today are the barber's red-and-white striped pole, and the three golden balls of the pawnbroker.

The site of Brayne's exercise in playhouse construction (which, pending further serendipitous discoveries in archives, must be regarded as possibly the first purpose-built London playhouse) was a farmhouse, and the building was erected in its courtyard. It does not seem to have made much use of any existing structures – perhaps Brayne, like Henslowe twenty years later at the Rose, intended to make use of the farm and its buildings as a site for selling refreshments. Brayne's playhouse consisted of a stage 40 feet long on a north–south axis by 30 feet wide east–west, raised five feet above the ground, and containing a trapdoor. On or abutting the stage was a turret 30 feet high from ground level, with a floor in it 7 feet from the top. Around the yard were erected scaffolds or galleries for the accommodation of spectators. There is as yet no information on the dimensions of the theatre apart from the stage and its tower: the

Fortune playhouse, built in 1599/1600, had a stage 43 feet wide by 25 feet deep, set in a yard 55 feet square, within a building 80 feet square. The Rose (1587) had a shallower tapered stage, about 37 feet 6 inches wide, extending into a polygonal yard 49 feet 6 inches in internal diameter, in a polygonal building about 74 feet in diameter.[28] We have no idea of the shape of the Red Lion, nor of the horizontal dimensions of the tower to be erected on or beside the stage.[29]

The lawsuits in which the Red Lion can be traced concern failures by carpenters, and there is no mention of anything other than the stage with its tower, and the spectator scaffolds. There must be a possibility that what is being dealt with here is not a permanent structure but a temporary erection for the accommodation of a specific play, on the lines of the structures needed for the fifteenth-century morality play, *The Castle of Perseverance*.[30] The contract specifies that Brayne must complete payments when the play of Solomon has been once performed in the Red Lion. It has been argued that this was to be the final proof that the playhouse was viable, but the scaffolds and stage may have been only for the performance of this play. Temporary staging and spectator accommodation were erected for tournaments and royal entries: provision was made for spectators for the London mystery-play cycle, which was not peripatetic but performed at a fixed location. If the Red Lion was a nonce construction, this would explain its absence from later records, and vindicate the Burbage claim to be 'the first builder of theatres'.

What is much more certain, since the discovery of the Red Lion lawsuit, is that John Brayne, grocer, has as substantial a claim to be the father of the London theatre as his brother-in-law, James Burbage, actor and joiner. Brayne seems to have been at least involved in the design of the Red Lion, if not its author: it is possible that he, and not, as has always been assumed, Burbage, was the designer of the Theatre. There is no trace of any involvement of Burbage with the Red Lion, although with so partial a record, this cannot be ruled out. When Cuthbert Burbage, seventy years after the building of the Red Lion, spoke of his father as the first builder of playhouses in London, he may have been exaggerating out of filial piety, or unaware of the existence of the pre-Theatre theatre, or lying, or forgetful, or aware that his father had been involved with Brayne in the earlier venture. The history of the Red Lion is patchy and brief. Since the lawsuits in which its existence may be traced are concerned with shoddy workmanship on the part of its builders, who failed to meet Brayne's specifications, it may never have been satisfactory.

INNS AS PERFORMANCE SITES

If the Red Lion was not, as had been assumed until a few years ago, an inn, there were nevertheless plenty of inns providing homes for theatrical performances in sixteenth-century London. The theory that plays were commonly put on in inn-yards has been questioned by some scholars, although it lingers on in popular interpretations. Glynne Wickham pointed out a quarter of a century ago[31] that the yard of an inn is ill-suited to the performance of plays (although single performers, such as jugglers, might manage to do a turn there). The yard is vulnerable to through traffic and noise from

The yard of the Eagle Inn, Cambridge, showing the galleries (c. 1800, but replacing earlier ones). These may give an indication of what playhouse galleries looked like, but their use by audiences during suggested performances in inn-yards would have been impractical, as there would then have been no access to the rooms for those staying at the inn. (Norman Hammond)

adjoining rooms, and to close it off means that the rest of the establishment is inconvenienced. Even allowing for the small scale of sixteenth-century productions, those inn-yards which are held to represent the type in which Elizabethan actors put on their plays – such as the George at Southwark, the George at Norton St Philip or the Eagle in Cambridge, all of which retain their open galleries looking out on to the yard – are all far too small and inconveniently shaped for theatrical use. The acoustics in the courtyard of the Eagle are good, but a play would have disturbed guests in the upper chambers, and use of the balconies for the accommodation of spectators would have blocked access to the rooms while the play was in progress.

In an age when ordinary domestic buildings were far smaller than modern ones, and when public buildings were fewer, a local inn might provide large public rooms. A large village or small town in the sixteenth century would have offered anyone who wished to mount a dramatic entertainment the choice of three indoor locations: the church, the guildhouse (if there was one), built for the meetings of religious guilds, or the large upper room of the inn. Of these, the inn was far more likely to be available for hire than the two religious buildings.[32] The inn-yard theory for the location of dramatic performances presupposes that most inns were built with the external gallery access to the chambers believed to have been copied in the theatres, but the

The tennis court at Hampton Court, showing the spectator galleries. (Interior view, taken in the 1940s before restoration.) (Crown Copyright. Historic Royal Palaces)

architectural feature which they were more likely to share was the large room. Wickham has shown that references to performances in inns are weighted far more heavily in favour of indoor staging,[33] and not all of those records which are capable of bearing the interpretation that the performance was in the yard are unequivocal on this point.

Nor are the types of gallery envisaged as forming an internal feature of the playhouses confined to inns. They are also a feature of, for instance, tennis courts.[34] Although they are only single-storey in this instance, galleries at this date, wherever they are placed, seem to conform to a similar pattern. There seems no reason to confine the model for the galleries in playhouses to those to be found in some inn-yards; they were a common type. The two inn-yards known to have been used to house theatres, at the Boar's Head, Whitechapel, and the Red Bull, Clerkenwell, had permanent playhouses built inside them, with extensive new galleries.[35] The inns offered refreshments and other facilities, but these buildings were essentially inns which had undergone substantial alterations to turn them into playhouses, with permanent companies, rather than providing a temporary home for a visiting company in a busy yard.[36]

Inns are known to have been used for various types of theatrical entertainment throughout the sixteenth century. At the most intimate level they were used by leading comedians for small-scale solo performances, on the pattern of the modern nightclub. The first great Elizabethan clown, Richard Tarlton, was the keeper of an 'ordinary', or eating house in Paternoster Row and a tavern in Gracechurch Street.[37] He was associated with the company known as the Queen's Men, who were licensed to appear at the Curtain playhouse and at two inn theatres, the Bell and the Bull, but he also gave solo performances at banquets at court and in private houses. Tarlton's act was at least partly improvisatory, based on the persona of (usually) a gormless rustic – a clown – who ultimately has enough wit to triumph over his oppressors, even if only fortuitously. For this sort of solo performance no adaptation of the inn's rooms was necessary, nor were any props needed beyond what the performer brought with him.

Those inns which were used for larger-scale theatrical performances must have needed some sort of adaptation for this purpose, even if that only involved clearing out a large room and erecting a temporary stage and seating in it. The attraction for the proprietor of these establishments was not only the rent obtainable from the actors, and

A Marriage Feast at Bermondsey, by Joris Hoefnagel, c. 1570. This shows the essentially rural nature of the settlements on the south bank of the Thames shortly before the playhouses were built. The building used for the supply of refreshments on the Rose site may have resembled the cookshop in this picture. (Courtauld Institute/Hatfield House: by courtesy of the Marquess of Salisbury)

whatever share of the gate receipts he took, but the income from the sale of refreshments to the audience. When the Rose was built, the refreshment concession was an important part of the contract. In addition to half the gate receipts from the playhouse, and ground rent from the site, Henslowe's partner, John Cholmley, was to have the small cottage which stood in one corner of the site to use as a refreshment booth (a cottage adapted as an eating house can be seen in Hofnagel's picture of Bermondsey) and Henslowe guaranteed that no one else would be allowed to sell food or drink on the playhouse site.[38]

INDOOR PERFORMANCE SITES

Although Henslowe was content with his playhouses operating through the winter, despite the climatic drawbacks, the company to which Shakespeare was attached seems from early on to have sought an indoor winter house. The Blackfriars theatre, when they at last entered into possession of it, was used as a winter house, while they returned to the Globe in the summer (and were sufficiently attached to the Globe and its audience to rebuild it after the fire of 1613), and although Schoenbaum makes a case for Burbage's initial purchase of the Blackfriars being an attempt to deal with the difficulties caused by the imminent expiration of the Theatre's lease,[39] the Lord Chamberlain's Men had used the Cross Keys Inn as a winter house in 1594, at a time when they must have had the use of the Theatre.[40] The attraction of the Cross Keys may not have been an indoor playing space but its central position: a visit to the Theatre or its neighbour, the Curtain, involved a long trek out along Bishopsgate, exposed to the weather and to ill-maintained roads, unattractive to foot-passengers in bad weather. The most vulnerable time of year financially was not winter but summer, when an outbreak of the plague was always possible, with consequent enforced closing of the playhouses as a public health measure, and the reduced audience capacity of an indoor playhouse was offset by the fact that entry to the purpose-built indoor playhouses (as opposed to those attached to inns) was substantially more expensive, and the small audience which would turn up on an insalubrious day might be increased by the prospect of sheltered accommodation.

Sixteenth-century London also provided a wide range of private, or semi-private, theatrical entertainment, which was (with the exception of the tournaments and civic ceremonies already discussed) almost entirely performed indoors. The central position of dramatic performance in Renaissance education – acting was believed to increase self-confidence and improve rhetorical skills, as well as promoting facility in the classical languages – meant that the school play has an honourable history stretching at least as far back as the early sixteenth century, and dramas were regularly performed both at schools and at universities.[41] Plays put on by the scholars of Eton, St Paul's and Westminster schools formed a regular part of the semi-public entertainments available in the capital, and, while these institutions never crossed the boundary into professionalism, the children's companies grew from nominally educational institutions.[42] The legitimate schools performed either in their own halls or as visitors at court and great houses,[43] but the troupes based on the choir schools became gradually more commercial, and in 1576 a company which combined boys from the choirs of Windsor Chapel and the Chapel Royal acquired their own playhouse, adapted from rooms in the former ecclesiastical buildings of the Blackfriars. University colleges staged both classical and modern plays for the entertainment of themselves and of distinguished visitors.[44] The Inns of Court had both imported and self-generated dramatic entertainments, ranging from their own Christmas and New Year revels, which might include a command performance at court, to visiting performances staged by major professional companies, such as the Lord Chamberlain's/King's Men, who put on both *The Comedy of Errors* and *Twelfth Night* as visiting entertainers at Inns of Court.[45] Besides this, throughout the sixteenth century there were regular performances at court, either by the monarch's own company of players or by visiting troupes brought in for the occasion. This is beside the regular diet of masques and interludes, which were at least mimetic in form, and by the end of the sixteenth century, had already become the quasi-dramatic entertainments perfected in the next reign by Ben Jonson. All such events were put on in the halls of the various institutions where they took place. Glynne Wickham has pointed out that the bulk of Elizabethan theatrical activities took place indoors. He sees the existence of two separate traditions at this date, the great outdoor amphitheatres being the end of the medieval street theatre which reached its apogee in the miracle cycles, while the indoor theatres, whether purpose-built or occasional adaptations of great halls, were the start of the tradition which was to lead through Inigo Jones to the proscenium arched theatre and thence to modern theatre building.[46]

THE OUTDOOR PLAYHOUSES AND THEIR COMPANIES

It is possible to view the outdoor playhouses as temporary aberrations in the English dramatic tradition, deviations from the norm of indoor performance. They were short-lived: from the building of the Red Lion in 1567 to the closure of the theatres in 1642 is less than eighty years, and few of the buildings themselves existed for more than twenty. The Red Lion disappears from the record before the building of the Theatre (1576), which was itself dismantled in 1598. The first Globe lasted from 1599 to 1613, its successor from 1613 to 1644. The Rose stood (undergoing major modifications at intervals) from 1587 to before 1606 (though no plays are known to have been performed there after 1603), the first Fortune from 1600 to 1621, its successor (the original having succumbed, like the first Globe, to a disastrous fire) until 1642. The Curtain was built in 1577, and proved the most durable of all the playhouses. It was used by a variety of companies until about 1625, after which it was used to stage fights. Sometime after that, it was converted into tenements.[47] The Swan is the only Elizabethan playhouse of whose interior we have any depiction – a copy by Arnout van Buchell of a sketch made by his friend Johannes de Witt, who had visited England in 1596 (see illustration on p. 72).[48] We do not know how accurate (or how accomplished) the original sketch was, or whether it was made on the spot, or soon after de Witt had visited the Swan, or whether it was modified on his return to the Netherlands in an attempt to explain certain features of this peculiarly English form of playhouse to his acquaintance. Scholarly lives have been spent in attempting to tease out this drawing's mysteries. The playhouse which it depicts had the shortest theatrical life of any of the amphitheatres. It was built around 1596, and closed in 1597, and there is no certain evidence that it was ever again used as a playhouse. By 1632 it was ruinous.[49]

Only the Rose and a fragment of the Globe are known to survive archaeologically, although their remains give hope that traces of other playhouses may yet turn up in the course of future building projects on their sites. Certainly in future archaeologists will be looking for them. The playhouses to the north of the city perhaps offer the best prospects, although it is probably too much to hope that the two which did survive to be turned into living accommodation, the Curtain and the Fortune, might survive in fragmentary form, incorporated into later buildings, as has happened at York and elsewhere in London with buildings of even earlier date.[50]

Even though their existence was so short, and perhaps an aberration in the history of the English theatre, the importance of the great playhouses was enormous. For the first time companies of players had a settled, purpose-built, permanent home. While those players retained in royal and noble courts had had a permanent base, they had been dependent on temporary adaptations of existing chambers and halls for the mounting of their plays, and the early independent professional companies had been restricted in size by their peripatetic existence: even after the building of the theatres, companies forced to tour by temporary closure of the playhouses during the plague season cut back their numbers and toured with a minimum number of players. The difficulty of tracing the histories of the early companies and the chaos into which the established companies fell during the long closure of the playhouses from 1592–4[51] shows the lack of stability in companies without a permanent home. A permanent building – controlled, if not owned, by the actors themselves – allowed the players to expand and develop in several directions. Before the advent of permanent playhouses the capital assets of a company of players in the Elizabethan period consisted of their costumes, props and playscripts, in descending order of capital value. The first two of these presented storage problems: it was difficult to accumulate properties and costumes if the company had no permanent home, and therefore no permanent store,[52] and frequent touring meant that baggage had to be kept to a minimum. A permanent home meant that there could be accumulation of capital in the form of costumes and properties, with a consequent enlargement of artistic possibilities.

The actors who were able to accumulate this stock were also able to form themselves into more permanent, and larger, companies. A permanent company, familiar with each other, find it far easier to act together than a small scratch group who have to double in an effort to fill out the parts. This provides the conditions in which authors can write with particular actors in mind. Alleyn provided inspiration for the creation of the great Marlovian roles Faustus, Barabas and Tamburlaine, while senior members of the Lord Chamberlain's/King's Men, notably Richard Burbage and the clowns Will Kempe and Robert Armin, had a part in the genesis of Shakespeare's plays.[53] The establishment of permanent playhouses gave the actors greater input into, and control over, their material. Earlier Elizabethan playwrights, such as Robert Greene, write with bitterness about the way they are exploited by the actors, but by the end of Shakespeare's life the idea of one dramatist having a major attachment to a single company had been accepted, and the permanence of this attachment was felt to be beneficial to both parties. When Shakespeare retired, John Fletcher succeeded him as the King's Men's dramatist-in-residence, and the process of transition may probably be traced in Fletcher's hand in Shakespeare's last play, *Henry VIII*, and in Shakespeare's hand in Fletcher's *The Two Noble Kinsmen*.

The stable relationship of playwright with company was additionally helpful in the context of the intensive repertory system of the Elizabethan playhouses. Their practice was much closer to modern cinema than to modern theatre. Plays were tried out, and were dropped from the repertoire if they failed to attract a substantial audience, Successes were repeated until the audience seemed to be sated. Henslowe's diary records thirty-five performances of *The Jew of Malta* between 26 February 1591/2 and 21 June 1596; the play was still in the repertoire of the Admiral's Men in May 1601, when Henslowe paid for some additional costumes (and possibly properties) for it.[54] *Julian the Apostate*, by contrast, was performed on 29 April and 10 and 20 May, 1596, to rapidly diminishing houses (Henslowe took 47s the first performance, 26s and 14s thereafter) and then disappears from the accounts.[55] Anything with a record of ten to twelve performances might be reckoned a modest hit. The Elizabethan audience demanded novelty from their playhouses.

AUDIENCES AND THE CULT OF THE ACTOR

The establishment of a permanent audience was an important outcome of the construction of playhouses. Until their erection there were no companies permanently based in the capital providing entertainment for anyone who could afford the entrance fee. This was not cheap – a penny, for a standing place, was the cost of a table d'hôte lunch at an eating-house, or a cheap book – so, despite playwrights' complaints about the stinkards who crowded round the stage, it is doubtful if the really poor could ever attend. The apprentices whose masters worried so much about their attendance at the theatre were destined themselves to become pillars of the bourgeoisie on the completion of their training. Audiences were offered occasional plays in a variety of locations by a variety of companies. Those artists who built up a personal following before the erection of the playhouses were comedians like Tarlton – essentially solo performers, although from time to time attached to a company (Kempe was later to break with the Lord Chamberlain's Men and return to solo performance in his morris dance from Norwich to London).[56] The comedian's popularity depends on his comic persona, which remains stable whatever his role; the attraction of the great actor is the multiplicity of his performances – to remark that an actor always gives the same performance is to denigrate him, whereas this is expected of the comedian. It is only the erection of the playhouses, and the consequent opportunity regularly to hear actors in a variety of roles which leads to the cult of the great actor, such as attached to Burbage and Alleyn.

That there were such cults is suggested by contemporary testimony of Burbage's and Alleyn's greatness – tributes after Burbage's death included such lines as

oft have I seene him, play this part in jeast,
soe livly, that Spectators, and the rest
of his sad Crew, whilst he but seem'd to bleed,
amazed, thought even then he dyed in deed.[57]

Though no one seems to have claimed that Alleyn was so moving an actor that he could convince not only the audience but his fellow cast members of the reality of what he played, he was seen as Burbage's equal and rival.[58] Stronger evidence for these cults is provided by the growth of a *mythos* around the great actors. Stories such as the well-known anecdote of Burbage being outmanoeuvred by Shakespeare after making an assignation with a citizen's wife,[59] or Alleyn founding Dulwich College after an encounter with a real devil during a performance of *Dr Faustus*,[60] indicate that there was beginning to be attached to these performers the aura of stardom previously reserved for poets.[61] There is in these anecdotes the blurring, commonplace now, but unusual in earlier theatres, between the player and the part he plays. Burbage is no longer 'he that plays the king' but Richard III; Alleyn not a player representing a magician, but a magician himself. This sort of mystique can grow up only when an actor has a loyal and interested following. The prurient interest in his private life evinced in the Burbage anecdote, the belief that the actor is doing something both powerful and dangerous in the Alleyn one, both depend on a familiarity with the protagonists greater than is possible when actors are sporadic visitors.

THE PLAYHOUSES, ACTORS AND SOCIAL ORDER

The erection of the playhouses under the control of the companies who worked in them also brought problems both for those companies and for the City authorities. Some of the problems seen by the authorities were reasonable points of difficulty, and not necessarily to be traced to hostility to the theatre as a genre. The congregation of large numbers of people in a confined space, many of whom were male adolescents to whom alcohol was freely available, was an invitation to unrest, and unrest did occur.[62] During plague-time theatres were a focus for the spread of disease, and their closure during the recurrent outbreaks seems a reasonable public health measure: theatres were not singled out in such cases – all public entertainments were shut down.[63] Nor do the objections of the inhabitants of the socially élite Blackfriars district to James Burbage's plan to use part of the old priory buildings as a public theatre seem altogether unreasonable: they tolerated its being used by the children's companies, who only performed once a week and catered to a more élite audience. That the objections of Burbage's neighbours to his Blackfriars plans of 1597 were in some measure justified is shown by the fact that in 1633, when the company he founded had for decades been using the Blackfriars as their winter house, it was necessary to impose traffic regulations on the area because of the enormous jams caused by the theatre audience.[64]

Theatres, and related structures, could be dangerous buildings. Put up in most cases by speculative investors who were not averse to cutting corners (or who, like the Lord Chamberlain's Men at the time of the erection of the first Globe, were short of money), they might be constructed from inferior materials, and not satisfactorily maintained. Both the first Globe and the first Fortune were destroyed by fire – in the Globe's case, a fire in the thatch which had formed the roofing material because there was not enough money available to use the more expensive but safer tile. In January 1583 the Beargarden in Southwark collapsed, killing eight people.[65] The theatres and related entertainment houses were notorious for their attraction to pickpockets and similar criminals.[66] Apart from any moral message delivered by such accidents – the collapse of the Beargarden was seen as God's judgement on the profane – there was good reason for civic authorities to regard these buildings with suspicion.

Another problem raised by the existence in London of companies permanently based there and self-controlled was the position of actors in relation to society. The medieval performers who were their forerunners had not posed such problems. Either they were amateurs, whether members of religious orders or laity, and could be defined by their non-theatrical personae, or they were itinerant entertainers, usually travelling in groups under the direction of a minstrel,[67] or they were members of the household of a lord or monarch, retained as private servants, even though they might supplement their income by going on tour.[68] Their place in the social order was definable.

Once the actors set up permanently in London, their social position became much harder to understand. Though still nominally the 'servants' of potentates – the Lord Chamberlain and the Lord Admiral in the case of the two leading companies – they in fact worked for themselves or for middle-class impresarios. What we know of the lives of many of those connected with the theatre suggests that they were models of bourgeois respectability and social conscientiousness. Heminges and Condell were churchwardens. Alleyn married as his second wife the daughter of the Dean of St Paul's Cathedral (John Donne) and founded a great school. Shakespeare became a leading citizen of his home town, as his father had been. But this prosperity was not based upon any tangible commodity, and was inherently divorced from and opposed to the ideally ordered world which contemporary theory demanded. The theatres and those who worked in them earned their income from the presentation of an alternative world to that which existed outside their walls – a world which drew those who should be working away from their work and which provided a focus for other outsiders who preyed on society and threatened good order – prostitutes, pickpockets, and those eager for a fight.[69] In the alternative world within the playhouse walls prevailed an anarchy which was threatening to external society. Men dressed up as women, rebellion triumphed, horrible crimes were committed. All this was performed not by persons who could be defined either as servants – the entertainers traditionally attached to households as jesters, musicians and the like – or as social outsiders – itinerant entertainers who could be regarded as rogues and vagabonds and treated accordingly – but by persons of settled domicile, who served no one and yet manufactured nothing, who were comparatively well-educated in a period when the general standard of literacy was low[70] (literacy was a basic requirement for anyone who wished to advance beyond crowd parts) and yet followed none of the learned professions.

The power for social disruption felt to be inherent in the theatre is exemplified in the episode of the Lord Chamberlain's Men's staging of *Richard II* during the abortive rebellion of the Earl of Essex in February 1601.[71] One of the conspirators, Sir Gelly Meyrick, paid the Lord Chamberlain's Men 40 shillings to perform Shakespeare's *Richard II* the previous afternoon. Summoned to explain themselves to the authorities, Augustine Phillips on behalf of the company pleaded that the play was so old-fashioned that the actors had been reluctant to perform it, and were only seduced into doing so by the large fee offered them. (The play was probably written in about 1594/5, and the Lord Chamberlain's Men were to mount much older plays in the performances at court during the winter of 1604/5 – *The Comedy of Errors* and *Love's Labour's Lost*, both written before 1594, among them[72] – so this plea may have been somewhat specious.) Elizabeth was indignant at the identification made by the conspirators: 'I am Richard II, know ye not that? . . . this tragedy was played 40 times in open streets and houses'.[73] Both parties in the conspiracy – the rebels and those under threat – seem not to have doubted the potential for moral influence in the theatre. Essex and his companions hoped, according to Bacon's prosecution speech, to stir themselves to emulation by witnessing a representation of what they were planning the next day to effect. This may be a motive imputed by Bacon; but they certainly hoped that the representation of a successful *coup d'état* before a popular audience would stimulate those Londoners who saw it to support their cause, or at least to be more sympathetic to it. Elizabeth appreciated their motives in arranging the play's performance, and although the coup failed, does not seem to have doubted its potential effect. Only the Lord Chamberlain's Men seem to have had any doubt about its moral effectiveness, and this was based rather on their doubt that anyone would turn up to see such an ancient piece than on its influence on any who did chance to see it. With such potential potency ascribed to theatrical representation, it is small wonder that the playhouses and those who worked within them were regarded with such suspicion throughout the period.

Modern views of the Elizabethan theatre, which are distorted by the massive shadow of Shakespeare, tend to see the Elizabethan entertainment industry as comprising only the drama. In fact theatre was only one of a wide variety of entertainments on offer in Elizabethan London, with the rest of which it had to compete. Free entertainments included public executions and sermons. Executions are dealt with elsewhere; the quality of the sermon as entertainment may be appreciated by a study of the sermons of one of the great preachers of the age, such as Latimer or Donne.[74] The practice of vernacular preaching has for a long time been regarded as intimately connected with the development of English vernacular drama.[75] Among the entertainments for which charges were made, comparable to the entrance prices at playhouses, were, besides bull- and bear-baiting and cock-fighting, fencing matches, equestrian displays, prize fights and performances by groups of foreign entertainers, both tumblers and acrobats, and actors and actresses.[76] The great Elizabethan playhouses were erected to compete in a crowded market.

CHAPTER THREE

THE THEATRICALITY OF ELIZABETHAN LIFE

LIFE AND DEATH AS A PERFORMANCE

On Ash Wednesday, 25 February, 1601, the Earl of Essex was executed in the Tower of London for treason. For some days before he had given way to hysteria in the face of death, but no sign of this collapse now appeared in his demeanour. Cloaked in black, supported by three clergymen, he ascended the scaffold. Once there, he took off his hat and bowed to those of his peers who had come to witness his private execution. He confessed his sins, lamented his wasted youth and prayed that God might forgive him. He expressed especial regret for the rebellion for which he had been condemned, and prayed for the welfare of the Queen. Prompted by one of the clergymen, he forgave his enemies, then prayed to be strengthened against the fear of death and for all estates of the realm, and repeated the Lord's Prayer. He absolved his executioner of guilt for his death, recited the Creed, and then removed his black outer garments in preparation for his execution. Under them, he was wearing a scarlet waistcoat with long sleeves. He lay down and put his head on the block, said, 'Lord be merciful to thy prostrate servant,' and 'Lord, into thy hands I recommend my spirit,' and then gave the executioner the signal to strike.[1] Among those watching this performance was Sir Walter Raleigh, who seventeen years later on the same spot would act out his own version of heroic death.[2]

Essex's execution, like that of Mary Queen of Scots, was put on for a few privileged spectators. It was, nevertheless, a carefully devised and enacted performance, a moral exemplum of the heroic death of a repentant sinner. Even the costume was carefully chosen. The protagonist started the proceedings as an icon of melancholy: black-cloaked and black-hatted. Black is the colour of death, of mourning, of repentance. Gradually, as he went through the ritual of approaching death, he stripped off his black accretions: first the hat of melancholy, then, after forgiving his enemies, the cloak of mourning, revealing the black doublet which he wore beneath it. The shedding of the outer garments, cloak and hat at this point, as he passed from the public to the private in his penultimate devotions, reduced him to an icon of the private man. Once he had gone through the private devotions – the prayer against the fear of death, and the recital of the Lord's Prayer and the Creed which testified to his orthodox spirituality and assured salvation – he cast off the black garments of mourning altogether and signalled his transition from the earthly to the heavenly in his scarlet waistcoat. Scarlet is the colour of the bloody death which he was about to undergo, but it is also the colour of the saving grace of the blood of Christ, and signified that Essex had been washed in the blood of the Lamb. Scarlet is the colour of martyrdom. Despite Essex's protestations of repentance, his final costume might be read as a signal, not just that he died saved through repentance, but that he died innocent because wrongly accused.[3] Essex's performance demonstrated the virtues of the Christian hero: magnanimity, devotion, despite of worldly values, repentance for the sins of his life. It also managed to suggest that he has attained the greater heroic status of Christian martyr, rather than simply that of Christian knight.

Such transformation of Life (or, in Essex's case, Death) into Performance is an aspect of Elizabethan culture which is essential to an understanding of the theatre of the age. Life is seen as a process which is not simply endured, but which is performed. Essex, who certainly aspired to be the perfect Renaissance aristocrat,[4] was not alone in his determination to act out his life and death. Cranmer, executed for heresy by Mary Tudor, after he had withdrawn a recantation of Protestantism, thrust the hand which had signed the recantation into the fire, so that the most sinful part of him might be first consumed. On the occasion of his martyrdom in Oxford during the same reign, Hugh Latimer pointed out to his fellow-martyr Nicholas Ridley that he was about to physically exemplify his obedience to Christ's exhortation, 'Ye are the light of the world . . . Let your light so shine before men, that they may see your good works and glorify your Father which is in heaven' (*Matthew* 5: 14–16): 'Be of good cheer, Master Ridley, for we shall this day by God's grace light such a candle as shall never be put out.'[5] Even common criminals were not unaware of the drama inherent in their own deaths. But the occasion need not be as vital as an execution. When the transvestite Mary Frith, alias Moll Cutpurse, was sentenced to do public penance, she undermined the dignity of the performance and showed that she was capable of absorbing the law of the country into her own upside-down world by appearing at the penance well fortified with alcohol and amusing those who came to watch with her backchat. They were thus entertained on her terms, rather than edified on the authorities'.[6]

Nor was this sense of performance confined to moments of life-crisis. Any biography of the period astonishes with the sense of how consistently people acted out what they thought was demanded of them. Sir Philip Sidney, one of the central figures in the cult of chivalry at the Elizabethan court, who was seen, and saw himself, as the epitome of Protestant Knighthood,[7] received the wound that was to cause his death because he refused to go into battle with more armour than an older knight and removed his cuisses. In order to settle a quarrel they had had about his marriage, Sir Robert Carey, cousin to Queen Elizabeth I, acted out a scene with her which is worth quoting in full (Sir Robert, with the support of his family had married a virtuous, but poor, gentlewoman; the Queen, who was fond of him, was angry because she thought he should have sought a wealthy wife):

Our first encounter was stormy and terrible, which I passed over with silence. After she had spoken her pleasure of me and my wife, I told her, that she herself was the fault of my marriage, and that if she had but graced me with the least of her favours, I had never left her nor her court; and seeing she was the chief cause of my misfortune, I would never off my knees till I had kissed her hand, and obtained my pardon. She was not displeased with my excuse, and before we parted we grew good friends.[8]

In this little charade, Carey is playing the part of the rejected lover. He claims that he is really in love with the Queen, but as she has rejected him he has been forced in despair to marry on the rebound. The suggestion is grotesque – Elizabeth was twenty-seven years his senior, the cousin (and possibly half-sister) of his father, the Lord Chamberlain, Lord Hunsdon. From Carey's autobiography, it is clear that Elizabeth treated him as a favourite nephew. What both parties in this scene are indulging in is a deliberate charade, but one which permits, under the shelter of their chivalric roles, a degree of plain-speaking. Carey tells the Queen that he would not have left court if she had but graced him with the least of her favours. This is the vocabulary of the rejected lover. But he is also saying that, since the Queen had chosen not to advance his career,[9] she had no right to comment on what he chose to do with his life. The Queen, who understood the coded message, accepted this reply, and they were reconciled. What amounts to a family spat is cleared up by both parties indulging in a performance.

THE CULT OF ELIZABETH I

Carey's scene with the Queen was part of an ongoing theatrical narrative into which the life of the Queen and her court was turned. The narrative, based on the episodic chivalric romances which still formed a large part of popular and courtly reading matter, was based on the premiss that the Queen was a courtly mistress, the love-object and inspiration for a band of knights who were driven by their love for her to perform great deeds in her honour. According to the code of courtly love as interpreted in this cult, the love that the knights felt for their mistress and the moral improvement that it wrought upon them, were their own reward: they could expect for no return from her, except perhaps that of having their service recognized.

The convenience of this fiction for the situation of Elizabeth and her courtiers is considerable. She was the first successful female monarch in English history.[10] In an age in which the inferiority of women and their subjection to men was axiomatic, the presence of a female monarch was difficult to assimilate. The other women rulers of the age either ruled as regents by virtue of their relationship to the monarch (Mary of Guise in Scotland and Catherine de' Medici in France) or married and so acquiesced in assuming the role of queen-consort rather than queen-regnant (Mary Queen of Scots and Mary Tudor). Apart from Elizabeth herself, the successful female rulers were the two regents, rather than the two queens-regnant. For the first two decades of her reign, Elizabeth's administration assumed and, with increasing desperation, hoped that she would marry, surrender the reins of government into the competent male hands of either her husband or her council, and settle down to the Queen's traditional job of producing enough male heirs to secure the succession. These hopes were not finally dashed until Elizabeth was too old to bear children, and the beginnings of her sustained chivalric cult seem to be contemporaneous with the dawning of reluctant realization on the part of her administration that she was unlikely to marry – from the mid-1570s onward. The fiction on which the chivalric cult was based provided a rationale for the fact that a woman was supreme among a group of superior males, and that they voluntarily served her. Even when she was not being treated as a courtly lady from romance, Elizabeth was given personae which provided roles in which her femaleness was compatible with superiority – she was a biblical heroine or a classical goddess (almost invariably a virgin one), and increasingly towards the end of her reign she came to be identified with the Blessed Virgin Mary.[11]

COURT PORTRAITS

The pervasiveness of this habit of self-dramatization; of the presentation of the self to the world in a role in which one wished to be viewed, may be traced in court portraiture. Recent books on Elizabeth I have indicated how much of her wardrobe and jewellery referred to themes which may also be traced in the Court celebrations.[12] Her clothes are embroidered with the spring flowers which refer to her eternal youth;[13] she wears on her arm the ermine which is the badge of chastity;[14] she has jewels representing the phoenix, the unique, self-perpetuating bird to which she is so often compared;[15] the motifs of the armillary sphere,[16] the pillar[17] and the pyramid,[18] which are known to have been emblems in the court cult which surrounded her, appear in her jewels and on the embroidery of her garments. She is the goddess who makes the sun shine,[19] genius of the rainbow which bridges the gap between the heavens and the earth,[20] and the true victor in the strife over the golden apple.[21] Nor is the Queen the only personage to be painted with clothes and jewels which refer to these ceremonials. Ladies who wear such garments in their portraits may, as Janet Arnold suggests, be displaying gifts of clothing which they received from the Queen,[22] but both of the Queen's champions, Sir Henry Lee and George Clifford, Earl of Cumberland, display motifs from the cult in their portraits. Lee, painted by Antonio Mor in 1568,[23] has sleeves embroidered with armillary spheres and true-love knots, while Clifford has armillary spheres and sprigs of laurel embroidered on the lining of his surcoat and the underside of his hat-brim.[24] Lee merely displays the motifs of the Queen's cult, without adopting any identifiable role, but the much later miniature of Clifford (painted by Nicholas Hilliard, *c.* 1590) is fully in the mode of the nostalgic chivalric cult in which he was participating. He wears his armour as Queen's Champion, engraved with suns, and carries the Queen's glove pinned to his hat-brim. He has hung his *impresa* shield in a tree and stands in the wilderness (there is a distant city in the background) on a narrow path, his gauntlet thrown down before him in challenge, his lance in his hand, his helmet ready at his feet, ready to protect the honour of his royal mistress. Other courtiers are shown in equally romance-based poses: in an Arcadian landscape,[25] arming for battle in a tent,[26] or, in the case of Lord Herbert of Cherbury, lying melancholy by a stream, having paused on a quest through an Arcadian landscape, while his page minds his armour and horse in the background.[27]

Such posturings are not restricted for their frames of reference to the world of romance. Many adopt the fashionable posture of melancholy, ascribed to many causes, as Jaques remarks:

> I have neither the scholar's melancholy, which is emulation; nor the musician's, which is fantastical; nor the courtier's, which is proud; nor the soldier's, which is ambitious; nor the lawyer's, which is politic; nor the lady's, which is nice; nor the lover's, which is all these; but it is a melancholy of mine own . . . [28]

Lord Herbert of Cherbury is a melancholy knight-lover, as is, presumably, the young man who sits in the wilderness overlooking a great house and its formal gardens, his hand on his sword, and his black glove thrown down in order to challenge anyone who would dispute his right to be where and who he is;[29] Henry Percy, 9th Earl of Northumberland adopts an identical pose in a garden on a mountaintop, his black and unfastened garments proclaiming his melancholy, but the cause of that melancholy is shown by the accessories and articulation of the picture to be his devotion to scholarship.[30] Another young man is shown naked, his hands crossed over his breast, in what is probably a depiction of religious melancholy.[31]

A Young Woman in Fancy Dress, c. 1590–1600, by *Marcus Gheeraedts the Younger. She is wearing a costume probably designed for a court entertainment – perhaps that at Ditchley in 1592. (The Royal Collection © Her Majesty the Queen)*

The miniature, as much a jewel as a portrait, was an ideal medium for the depiction of the subject in a pose which carried a message about his or her own self-image, but large-scale portraits of this period also display the same desire of the sitter to be depicted in a role. Large-scale portraits of the Queen displaying the accessories of her cult are to be expected, for with the Queen the private and the public aspects of her life are inextricable, but the same seems to have held true for her contemporaries, whose private lives we would not necessarily expect to have been displayed for public scrutiny. The full-scale portrait was a public statement: a formal exposition of the aspect which the private person wished to present to the world. In view of this it is remarkable how many pictures of the age are not simply displays of power, wealth or strength, but carry esoteric messages about the sitter. The most popular artist for the execution of such commissions seems to have been Marcus Gheeraedts the Younger, but examples survive from the hands of all the major painters of the period. At their simplest, such works may be straightforward portraits, with an allegorical inset which makes some statement about the sitter:[32] his devotion to chastity, or to peace; his submission to love, his Christian faith. At their most elaborate, sitters are subsumed into the allegorical world, their costume and gestures echoing their mental and emotional state as they wish the world to perceive it. In the most spectacular surviving example of this type of painting, a lady proclaims the wrongs that have been inflicted on her by a treacherous lover.[33] Wearing the head-dress of a Persian Virgin, and a night gown, she crowns a weeping stag under a tree in which a swallow sits. A sonnet written in the first person proclaims her wrongs, and in its sympathy for the swallow, suggests that the lady in the picture has been seduced with promises of marriage and then abandoned.[34] Even in such an ostensibly private matter as a sexual betrayal, the lady is prepared to make a public statement through a portrait. The first-person sonnet, combined with the emblematic representation of her plight, means that in this picture she acts out a quasi-dramatic scene.

EDUCATION

The basis for this need to act out a public role throughout life may be related to the educational theory of the period. The acting of plays was recommended as pedagogically beneficial: it encouraged self-confidence, 'good behaviour and audacity',[35] it promoted the skills necessary in the orator and it eased the understanding of the classics which formed the sixteenth-century curriculum.[36] The importance and attractiveness of this childish thespian activity is shown by the frequency with which the major schools within reach of court were called to perform there.[37] These are companies quite separate from the professional children's troupes which were coming into existence at the same period. It is a reasonable assumption that attendance at a grammar school at this period would give a boy the opportunity to have some acting experience as part of the normal curriculum. While acting was a calling of theoretically low social status, it was essential that the actor be at least able to read with ease, if not to write, if he had any hope of rising in his profession, and so the fact that a man became an actor implies a certain degree of education. In later life Edward Alleyn was apt, in his dealings with his second father-in-law, the poet John Donne, by then Dean of St Paul's, to speak deprecatingly of his own lack of education,[38] but his desire for immortality was expressed in a munificent educational bequest, and the circles in which he moved (Inigo Jones was one of the witnesses to the foundation of his College of God's Gift in 1618, along with Lord Arundel and Sir Edward Cecil)[39] suggest that he was a man of some intellectual capacity and learning.

If actors were inspired to follow their profession from their experience of drama at their schools, it was an experience which they shared with a great many of the upper classes at this period.[40] The aim of aristocratic education, as practised at the grammar schools and at those households, such as those of Lords Burleigh and Derby, which provided education for aristocratic heirs, was to produce 'a gentleman or noble person in vertuous and gentle discipline',[41] and part of that education consisted of learning to act the role. The training in acting given at school was continued when the young man went to university, or to the Inns of Court. The plays by Terence and Plautus which the boys had acted at school were also put on at university, and just as the importance attached to the performance of classical drama at school was indicated by command performances at court, so its part in the experience of university life was endorsed by the presence of establishment figures at university performances.[42] The university also provided a milieu for the performance of original plays in the vernacular, ranging from *Gammer Gurton's Needle* in *c.* 1563 to the *Parnassus Plays* at the end of the sixteenth century, and for the introduction of foreign vernaculars in translation. The Inns of Court led in the introduction of new forms of drama into England. Both *Gorboduc* (Inner Temple, 1561) and Gascoigne's translation of Ariosto's *I Suppositi* (Gray's Inn, 1566) had their first performances there.[43] These dramas, performed by members of the Inns of Court, were in addition to performances there by visiting professional companies and masques performed by the students over the Christmas and New Year festive season.

The following of this drama-laden curriculum at university was itself seen as a performance: a progress through the stages of education needed to turn a raw boy into a finished gentleman. At Gonville and Caius College, Cambridge, Dr John Caius made his students proceed through a concrete representation of the process of education: they entered the college by the Gate of Humility, proceeded further into its depths through the Gate of Virtue and emerged triumphantly at the end of the educational process to receive their degrees through the Gate of Honour.[44] The gates become progressively more elaborate and splendid: Humility is a comparatively plain affair; Virtue an imposing structure, incorporating a gatehouse, which separates the first and second courts of the college, while Honour is a gloriously frivolous affair, originally coloured and gilded, and topped by a dome. The three arches mark the progress of the student through the college. He enters by way of a detached structure, in humility, for it is not until he has entered that he becomes a member of the college. He passes his time there in virtue – a massive undertaking – and during this virtuous period he is himself part of the college, just as the gate of Virtue is incorporated

The Gate of Virtue, 1567, Gonville and Caius College, Cambridge. The spandrels show figures of Fame and Wealth. (Norman Hammond)

into the College structure. But this virtue has an end, for by exercising it he hopes to attain Fame and Wealth, whose figures are carved into the spandrels of the arch where they will catch his eye each time he walks through it. As he leaves the college, he ceases to be part of it, so the Gate of Honour is another detached structure, through which he may pass out with and to honour.

These three arches are among the very few solid survivors of all the ephemeral processional architecture erected at the time. The *tableaux vivants* which graced the arches in civic pageantry, roles sometimes taken by the greatest actors of the day – Alleyn played the Genius of the City of London on the arch erected at Fenchurch Street for the Entry of James I into London in March 1604, and spoke verses written by Jonson[45] – could not exist on Caius's miniature and permanent structures, but he nevertheless ensured that these could speak to those who had the education to read them. The Gate of Humility carries only its name, Humilitatis, the supreme requirement for the attainment of honour. Virtue again proclaims its name, but carries the images of fame and wealth on its east front; the

The Gate of Honour, 1575, Gonville and Caius College, Cambridge. Together with the Gate of Humility, the Gates of Virtue and Honour represented the progress of the student through his education. The Gate of Honour is a miniature stone version of the temporary pageant architecture erected for ceremonial occasions. (Norman Hammond)

western face shows both in its inscription and by means of a head of the goddess Minerva that the other face of virtue is wisdom: the two are both essential for the attainment of fame and wealth, and all four come together on the path to honour. Honour, like Humility, bears only its name, but it is in the form of a triumphal arch, surmounted with a dome and with obelisks (now vanished) which proclaim fame and immortality, and decorated with the symbols of triumph: flowers, tabernacles, jewelled pedestals for the obelisks. The visual vocabulary here is esoteric, to be read only by the initiate; but the years in college will have provided that initiation for the candidate who leaves in honour. Just as the great civic processions offered to monarchs at the period presented to them an image of their life and their reign, in Caius's architectural vocabulary the life of the student in college is turned into a progress.

The Temple of Janus at Temple Bar, from Stephen Harrison's The arch's of triumph erected in honor of James, the first at his entrance & passage through London *(London, J. Windet, 1604). One of the pageant arches erected for the entry of James I into London on 15 March 1604, this was devised by Ben Jonson and designed by Stephen Harrison. Peace and her handmaids Quiet, Liberty, Safety and Felicity tread the vices of War underfoot. In the centre, the Flamen Martialis and the Genius of the City of London (played by actors) praise James as a peacemaker. (By permission of The British Library G. 10866)*

ROYAL PAGEANTS

The coronation procession of Elizabeth I through the City of London, and the royal entry of her successor James I nearly fifty years later both exemplify the tendency of such events to dramatize the City's vision of history, politics, and the policy which should be followed by the incoming monarch: the reign and life which are to follow become the subjects of anticipatory theatre. Elizabeth was first welcomed to the City, and was then led past a series of pageants which comprised a progressive dramatization of her past, present and future. The first pageant – *The uniting of the two howses of Lancastre and Yorke* – showed Elizabeth's ancestry, the uniting of the houses of York and Lancaster in the marriage of her grandparents Henry VII and Elizabeth of York, and her parents Henry VIII and Anne Boleyn. The emphasis was on her claim to the throne and the historical processes that had brought her to it – she was not only the daughter of a king, but the granddaughter of a marriage which had brought harmony to a land torn by civil war, and, because her mother was sprung from the old English nobility (Anne Boleyn was a Howard), her heritage was predominantly native English. There was an implicit contrast with her half-Spanish elder sister, who had brought division to the country by her religious policies and made a foreign marriage.

History was succeeded by a pageant which showed the proper basis for the establishment of a legitimate regime – *The Seat of Worthy Governance.* Elizabeth was represented by a child, partly no doubt because the use of small, light children made the construction of the arches which supported the *tableaux vivants* easier, but also in an implicit reminder to Elizabeth that she was young, had just come to the throne, and was a child in the process of government and should therefore be ready to receive counsel. The child was supported by four virtues, each trampling its contrary vice underfoot – Pure Religion with Superstition and Ignorance, Love of Subjects with Rebellion and Insolence, Wisdom with Folly and Vainglory and Justice with Adulation and Bribery. While these virtues are predominantly those which Elizabeth is expected to exercise as a ruler, they are also reciprocal, and will produce the same virtues in the subjects ruled according to them, with the consequent destruction of their opposite vices in both people and regime. Love of Subjects is both the love felt by the ruler for the subjects and the love felt by the subjects for the ruler, and Rebellion and Insolence, which it will destroy, relate to both parties – rebellion performed by the subjects, insolence exercised by the ruler. This pageant is an exercise in political theory.

The next – *The Eight beatitudes expressed in the .v. chapter of the gospel of S. Mathew, applyed to our soueraigne Ladie Quene Elizabeth* – was more private in its subject matter, dealing with the personal virtues which Elizabeth must exercise, rather than the virtues of government. It represented the beatitudes from the fifth chapter of St Matthew's Gospel as applied to Elizabeth. The Queen was then presented by the City with a purse with 1,000 marks in gold – a foretaste of the rewards she could expect if she followed the political and personal programme outlined in the last two pageants she had seen.

The next pageant was the most crucial in the whole show, and encapsulated the message of the previous ones, while making explicit what had been implied in their pious generalizations – that the ideal regime which the City was demanding that Elizabeth should exercise must be a Protestant one. Two hills represented a flourishing commonwealth and a decayed commonwealth, with their causes written on each, and from the valley between them Time came out, leading his daughter Truth, who presented the Queen with an English Bible. In this pageant, Elizabeth was presented with a choice of what the future of her kingdom was to be – a flourishing or a decayed commonwealth. The choice would be made in her acceptance or rejection of the English Bible from the hands of Truth, who in this pageant stood for Elizabeth herself. (Elizabeth accepted it.) That Truth is the daughter of Time emphasized the message of the first pageant about the fact that Elizabeth's ascension to the throne was part of an inevitable historical process: her choice was whether to accept or reject her destiny, with the implication that that acceptance or rejection would determine not only her own salvation but the fate of the country to whose throne she had just ascended.

She next heard a Latin oration – a compliment to her renowned learning – and then passed on to a pageant which provided an image of what her regime would be. She was identified with Deborah, the judge and restorer of Israel, and was shown supported by the representatives of the three social orders: nobility, clergy and commons. Having absorbed the messages of the previous pageants she was now revealed as fulfilling her destiny as prophetess/ruler, leader both spiritual and temporal, restoring her subjects to their proper role as God's chosen people. The final events along the route were another Latin oration from a charity-school boy, and the two giant-patrons of London, Gogmagog and Corineus, who held Latin verses in their hands – the boy standing for London's present obligation to the poor and care for them, the giants for London's massive legendary past.[46]

In this series of pageants Elizabeth was presented with images of herself. She is seen in the historical pageant as the product both of her ancestry and of a historical and political progress towards union: she brings union and is the product of it. She is seen as ruler in the pageant of the virtues; as a private individual on that of the beatitudes; as Truth in that of the commonwealth and finally as Deborah, judge and restorer of Israel in the pageant which foretells the political future of her self and the kingdom under her regime.

Elizabeth herself, as well as her mimetic representatives, was present in the pageants. Elizabeth made the occasion a reciprocal drama, as not only did she observe the pageants in which her past, present and future were represented, but she made clear both visually and orally that she understood them and, by her responses, indicated the type of ruler she intended to be. When she was greeted by the people on her first entry into the City, she returned the greeting:

> her grace, by holding up her handes, and merie countenaunce to such as stode farre of, and most tender & gentle la[n]guage to those that stood nigh to her grace, did declare her selfe no lesse thankefullye to receiue her peoples good wyll, than they louingly offred it unto her . . . so that on eyther side there was nothing but gladnes, nothing but prayer; nothing but comfort.[47]

At the pageant of the uniting of the houses of York and Lancaster Elizabeth first demonstrated that she wished to understand its message: she asked for a recapitulation of the parts of the exposition that she had failed to hear because of the noise of the crowd, and she shifted the position of her chariot so that she could see the whole pageant. She then signalled her understanding of and agreement with the message of the pageant by promising that 'she would doe her whole endeuour for the continuall preseruacion of concorde, as the pageant did emporte'.[48] At the pageant showing the seat of worthy governance, Elizabeth promised to maintain the virtues and suppress the vices as the pageant demanded.

Her response at the pageant of the beatitudes was focused on the next pageant, that of Truth the daughter of Time. Catching sight of it ahead, she asked to know its meaning. 'And it was tolde her grace, that there was placed Tyme. "Tyme?" quoth she, "and Tyme hath brought me hether."'[49] This anticipation of the subject-matter of the pageant, in which she identifies herself as Truth the daughter of Time before she has reached the pageant which does so, strongly suggests that Elizabeth was aware of the content of the drama in which she was now both spectator and participant, but it also signalled that that pageant, which was the most controversial in the procession, with its demand that she commit her regime to Protestantism, was welcome to her, and thus relieved the presumed anxieties of those who were responsible for its presentation. That the pageant was indeed welcome was shown by her response when she actually arrived at it. Before that, however, she was given the gift of money by the City, and again took the opportunity of acting in the drama she was moving through, showing that she understood the obligations which were placed on her by her acceptance of the bounty of her subjects – that subjects paid taxes and grants to the regime in the understanding that the regime would provide peace and justice at home, and protection from foreign enemies:

> I thanke my lord maior, his Brethren & you all. And whereas your request is that I should continue your good ladie & quene, be ye ensured, that I wil be as good unto you, as ever quene was to her people. No wille in me can lacke, neither doe I trust shall ther lacke any power. And perswade your selves, that for the saftie and quietnes of you all, I will not spare, if nede be to spend my blood, God thanke you all.[50]

At the pageant of Truth, Elizabeth reinforced her promise at the pageant of the beatitudes: that she would welcome its message. She took the English Bible from Truth, thanked the City for it and said she would often read it; and then, so that her response could be understood even by those parts of the crowd who could only see, being out of earshot, she kissed the Bible and laid it to her breast. She took and kept the oration of the charity-school boy, indicating that she would remember her obligation to the poor. Her final words to the city were, 'Be ye well assured, I will stande your good quene',[51] a reassurance that she had indeed been sincere in her responses to the anxieties and advice from the City expressed in the pageants.

The series of pageants and their success are known to us partly because they were so successful: the events were described in pamphlets published within a few days of the events, so that the audience might be countrywide rather than confined to London, and the slant of the pamphlets is that of the Protestant propagandist; the Queen's responses were felt to be as important as the pageants themselves.[52] The procession and Elizabeth's responses during it show how easily life was conceived of in dramatic terms, and how natural it was felt to be that philosophical and social concepts should be expressed dramatically. Essex at his execution was a private man acting out the role of Renaissance hero; Elizabeth fifty years earlier had acted out the role of a Queen.

James I was greeted with a similar mixture of history, politics, and moral instruction in 1604. As befitted the welcome of a foreign monarch to his new capital, the emphasis was far more international than for Elizabeth, the emphasis on whose Englishness was designed to reinforce the political isolationism which would be forced on her regime by the adoption of Protestantism which the devisers of her pageants hoped for and achieved. He was greeted by the patron saints of England and Scotland, George and Andrew, represented as two armed knights. He then encountered the Genius of the City, and the arch at Fenchurch Street represented the ambience of London. Persons were stationed on it representing Monarchia, Britannica, Divine Wisdom, Genius Urbis (the Genius of the City) and his daughters Veneration, Promptitude, Vigilance, Gladness, Loving Affection and Unanimity. Below were Thames, the Councell of the City and the Warlike Force of the City. This was followed by pageants devised by the Italians and the Belgians, and representing their countries, and then came a pageant, *Nova Felix Arabia*, representing England 'under the shape of Arabia'. The chief figures were Arabia-britannica, Fame and the Five Senses; while there were sleeping figures of Detraction and Oblivion. The three Graces stood opposite Love, Justice and Peace, called the three Hours. Fame and Circumspection addressed the King and, as he approached the pageant, the doleful music which had been playing ceased, the figures brightened and heavenly music began. James, like Elizabeth, was presented with wealth (in the form of gold cups) by the City, and then came a pageant in the form of a summer arbour, *Hortus Euporiae*, the Garden of Plenty, on which sang nine choristers from St Paul's dressed as the Muses. The King then heard an anthem sung from the battlements of St Paul's by its choir, heard a Latin oration and at the next arch was presented with Astraea (Justice) and Virtue, with Envy opposed to them. The four cardinal virtues were paired with the four kingdoms of Britain, and Zeal made the speech explaining the device. At Temple Bar was the Temple of Janus, on which Peace triumphed over Mars; Quiet over Tumult; Liberty over Servitude; Safety over Danger and Felicity over Unhappiness. The Genius of the City appeared again, and offered the heart of the City to the King. The last pageant was in the Strand, and represented a rainbow, with the Moon, Sun and seven Stars. Electra, in the form of a Comet, gave the gratulatory speech.[53]

Perhaps because there was not the desire for a change in the nature of the regime that there had been at the time of Elizabeth's coronation, perhaps because of the number of different writers involved, some of whom were prima donnas, there does not seem to be the progressive coherence in the pageants for James that is evident in the pageants for Elizabeth. The inventions were more spectacular; the sentiments more platitudinous. The sense of historical process so evident at Elizabeth's coronation is absent: apart from the initial appearance of St Andrew there is no sense of James's own background, and there is also none of the uncertainty about the sort of regime he intends that is evident in the pageants for Elizabeth. Instead there is a smug presentation of abstractions related to a generalized idea of good monarchy and the good kingdom, which the devisers of the pageants are sure England is. James's arrival on the scene causes Arabia-britannica to light up: it does not, as Elizabeth's arrival did, change the course of the nation's spiritual destiny. James himself is absent from the pageants, both as a figure on them and as a participant in them. His advent causes a change in the Arabia-britannica pageant, but he is not required to do anything to bring this about. The whole design is splendid, but incoherent and ideologically soft-centred. Nevertheless, although the issues presented are much less engaging, it is still felt to be natural to express James's entry into his capital city in dramatic form.

The public pageantry centred on the court is the medium which links the worlds of learning, the arts and the theatres, whose intermeshing has already been noted in the foundation of Dulwich College. The authorship of the pageants for the coronation of Elizabeth I is not known, but the authors and devisers of those for James I were among the leading writers of the period – Ben Jonson, Thomas Dekker, Thomas Middleton and John Webster – and the physical designs of the arches were by the joiner Stephen Harrison. The number of authors may explain the overall incoherence of the event. The actors who spoke the speeches seem to have come from the same company as Alleyn, the former Admiral's Men, now under the patronage of Henry, Prince of Wales. The leading educationalist Richard Mulcaster was involved, as it was one of his scholars who delivered the Latin oration to the King. Mulcaster was one of the greatest schoolmasters of the age: his pupils achieved very high standards (forty years earlier, one of them, the poet Edmund Spenser, had published verse translations from the French while still at school) and he was a leading exponent of the use of drama in education, presenting plays yearly before the court.[54] In his description of the entry (Jonson and Dekker published independent descriptions of the pageants, in which neither mentions the contributions of the other)[55], Jonson indicates the way in which the pageants were to be seen as a whole, the visual and thematic scheme devised by the poet, as well as the lines actually spoken to the King:

> The nature, and propertie of these Deuises being, to present alwaies some one entire body, or figure, consisting of distinct members and eache of those expressing it selfe, in the [sic] owne actiue sphaere, yet all, with that generall harmony so connexed, and disposed, as no one little parte can be missing to the illustration of the whole: where also is to be noted, that the *Symboles* used, are not, neither ought to be simply *Hierogliphickes, Emblemes,* or *Imprese,* but a mixed Character, pertaking somwhat of all, and peculierly apted to these more magnificent Inuentions: wherein the Garments, and Ensignes deliuer the nature of the person, and the Word the present office. Neither was it becomming, or could it stand with the dignity of the shewes (after the most miserable & desperate shift of the Puppits) to require a Truch-man, or (with the ignorant Painter) one to

write. *This is a Dog; or, This is a Hare*: but so to be presented, as upon the view they might without cloude, or obscurity declare themselves to the sharpe and learned: And for the multitude, no doubt but their grounded judgements gazed, said it was fine, and were satsfied.[56]

The conception of the pageant-arch was emblematic. The emblem, the art form which is perhaps most characteristic of the age, is a multivalent form: a picture and its attendant inscription which symbolically represent an abstract idea or some aspect of the person who carries the emblem and the explanatory verses which accompany them all have equal aesthetic weight. The picture is not an illustration of the verses, nor the verses an explanation of the picture, for the one cannot exist without the other: they are a whole.

It is in the pageant-arches that the closeness of emblem to drama may be seen. Drama, too, is conceived as a whole: what we see presented on the stage makes sense only when it is allied to what is said, and the two go together. It is true that, at this date, the term for attending a dramatic representation was to 'hear' a play; that those attending the theatre are referred to as the 'audience'. Yet Shakespeare addresses them as 'gentle spectators',[57] and the visual dimension of his plays is an important one. They are not radio drama. The play at this date should be read as a narrative emblem, in which speech and spectacle go together.

MONUMENTAL SCULPTURE

Apart from the emblem books, and their use in court-centred pageantry, the principal medium which expressed itself in emblems at this date is monumental sculpture. In the churches of England, contemporaries of Shakespeare offer themselves to us in a frozen drama: posed like the figures in an emblem, their epitaphs explain their actions and their glamorized likenesses justify the sentiments of the words. Shakespeare's contemporaries spent their lifetimes acting out the roles which they thought society demanded of them. Even in their deaths they were not free from thespian obligations. The emblems can be extremely elaborate: in the church of Barnwell All Saints, Northamptonshire, the memorial to the infant son of Lord Montagu, who was drowned as a toddler, shows him standing in a setting of numerous visual and literary allusions to water, which is both the water which drowned him and the water of baptism through which he passed to eternal life. The Montagu child's tomb is a complex image, to be read and understood fully only by Jonson's literate and educated viewer: the understander.

As is suggested by the use of the medium of tombs to express emblems, the emblem was a form that found expression in more contexts than those of the court-centred entertainment or pageant. Nor was it confined to areas of life which may be termed public, such as the educational context in which Dr Caius erected his permanent processional arches of triumph. The works of the devout Roman Catholic Sir Thomas Tresham, who was limited by his religion to a retired and private life, and who bankrupted his estate in erecting them, demonstrate that the habit of externalizing in concrete form the innermost concerns of the individual psyche was not confined to the worlds of the court and of public men. Tresham's triangular lodge at Rushton in Northamptonshire, which expresses in its overall design and its minutest details its builder's devotion to the Holy Trinity and to the idea of man's immortal soul, was designed as a comparatively unimportant element of the Tresham estate – an estate worker's cottage – but the grand overall concept of Sir Thomas's building programme was that every aspect of his life and environment should reflect his devotion to the religion of his ancestors. In the words of John Buxton:

The Triangular Lodge at Rushton, Northamptonshire, built in 1593–5 by Sir Thomas Tresham, to symbolize his devotion to the Trinity. (English Heritage Photo Library)

Sir Thomas was a papist with a special devotion to the worship of the Trinity, which was proper to one whose family name contained the number 3, tres, and whose emblem was the trefoil. This emblematic building was begun in 1593 and completed three years later: it has three sides, each with three gables; three storeys, with three windows in each on each side; the windows are composed of groups of three units, triangles in threes within trefoil frames, or trefoils alone; the central chimney is three-sided. The frieze of the entablature is thirty-three feet long, and the inscriptions on each side contain thirty-three letters. In the trefoil over the door (which necessarily interrupts the symmetry of the building) is the motto *Tres testimonium dant*, from the first Epistle of St John, 'There are three that bear witness'.[58]

Nor was Tresham alone. Other builders determined to make their houses reflect the chief preoccupations of their lives. The well-known (and possibly exaggerated) habit of building houses on the plan of the letter E in honour of the Queen reflects this; on a more complicated level Sir Thomas Gorges, in his trinitarian Longford Castle in Wiltshire, reflects Tresham's penchant for numerical and religious symbolism.[59]

The Elizabethans treated life emblematically, and found it natural to express themselves by means of these devices. In their clothes, in their portraits, in their behaviour and in their monuments they turned themselves into emblems of the roles in which they wished to be judged. On the emblems which were their tombs an individual portrait might, according to these criteria, be unimportant: it was sufficient that the effigy presented the idea of the person as he or she wished to be seen. When the Fermors ordered their tomb in 1582, they were more concerned that their rank be shown accurately than that their features be recognizable to those who had known them during life: the effigies are to be

> a very fair, decent and well proportioned picture or portraiture of a gentleman, representing the said Thomas Fermor with furniture and ornaments in armour . . . [and] a decent and perfect picture or portraiture of a fair gentlewoman with a French hood, edge and habiliment, with all other apparel, furniture, jewels, ornaments and things in all respects usual, decent and seemly for a gentlewoman.[60]

Above all, the Fermors wished to be remembered as gentlepersons. But, having lived out their lives representing that role, they were content that after their death they should be perceived through other representations – stone actors playing their parts for eternity. Provided the actors played the parts correctly, their physical likeness to the deceased was a matter of indifference. The effigies of the children who kneel round the sides of the tomb of the 9th Lord Cobham (d. 1561) at Cobham in Kent do not bear much resemblance to surviving portraits of the children; but they do show that Lord Cobham was the father of an extensive and noble progeny, and that is enough.

JUDICIAL DRAMA – THE EXECUTION OF MARY QUEEN OF SCOTS

The importance which role-playing had for Shakespeare's contemporaries, the extent to which life was seen as theatre, is shown in an earlier execution than that of the Earl of Essex: the beheading of Mary Queen of Scots in the Great Hall of Fotheringhay Castle in 1587. The execution of Essex was essentially a private affair, partly because of his rank, but also because his popularity among the people of London was mistrusted by the authorities, even though the people had failed to answer his call to join him in his rebellion. But the execution of Mary, while for a restricted audience, had something of the air of a private theatrical event, and it was an event which the producers were attempting to make one sort of play while the protagonist was determined to turn it into another. For the English authorities, it was the execution of a traitor and an impostor; for Mary it was a religious martyrdom.

Those who staged the execution were under considerable pressure, for Elizabeth I had only with difficulty been brought to sign Mary's death warrant, and had hinted several times that, if Mary must die, she would prefer it to be at the hands of an assassin rather than as a result of a public judgement made by herself – indeed, Sir Amyas Paulet, Mary's keeper and a man of austere probity, was driven to deliver a shattering snub to the Queen in a letter to Francis Walsingham, in which he made it clear that his duty to the Queen did not include endangering his immortal soul on her behalf.[61] The execution must therefore be done in a way which would as far as possible vindicate the view of Mary as a major danger to the English State, a traitor to her host and cousin Elizabeth, and an impostor with no real claim on the English throne, the pursuit of

The Execution of Mary Queen of Scots, 1587, by an unknown contemporary Dutch artist. This drawing shows a temporary draped scaffold erected for a piece of judicial theatre. (Scottish National Portrait Gallery)

which through numerous conspiracies had led her to the situation in which she now found herself. The scene for Mary's death was therefore prepared as though it were the exemplary final act of a tragedy to be acted on the stage. A scaffold was erected in the great hall of Fotheringay castle, hung with black and railed around. Mary – who had been told of her sentence the previous night, and who had, in the face of all the assertions that she was being executed for the danger she posed to the English State, announced that she was happy to shed her blood for her religion – appeared dressed in black, but her undergarments proved, like Essex's, to be of scarlet silk – the scarlet of martyrdom – attempting to turn her exemplary traitor's death into that of a female martyr.

As with the death of her grandson Charles I some sixty years later, which is probably the last time that the death of a magnate was treated as theatre in quite this way, there was a tension between the exemplary intentions of the executioners and the executed, a tension present in the tragic heroes of the theatre of the age. Is the death of the hero an occasion for regret or rejoicing? Do we pity him or think that he got what he deserved? Are we witnessing the inevitable fate of the great man who has allowed himself to be corrupted by power and pride, or the result of the spite and envy of his underlings? The decision to stage a State execution in the manner of the executions of Mary Queen of Scots and Charles I was a dangerous one. The sense of play, of drama, meant that spectators were invited to interpret the event as either exemplary justice or exemplary tragedy. The enduring power of the glamorous legend built up around Mary Queen of Scots shows that, despite the grotesque details of the aftermath of her execution (when the executioner went to pick up and hold her head by the hair, it fell out of the wig she had been wearing and revealed her cropped grey natural locks), she may have succeeded in making the scenario follow her own script rather than that of her executioners – this was a royal martyr rather than a traitorous impostor. This is despite the fact that she was undoubtedly guilty of high treason, had spent twenty years abusing the hospitality of her cousin by plotting against her, was implicated in the murder of her second husband the Earl of Darnley, and had a far inferior claim to the throne than Elizabeth. Mary's performance was staged in the privacy of a great hall. Charles's, staged as a public spectacle (though to a carefully controlled crowd) in order to show him as a mere player-king, was even more of a triumph. Both executions bore out Elizabeth's wisdom in preferring assassination to judicial drama.

CHAPTER FOUR

THE MAJOR OUTDOOR PLAYHOUSES

SOURCES OF INFORMATION ABOUT THE OUTDOOR PLAYHOUSES

The great public amphitheatres of Elizabethan London, and particularly the Globe, are commonly thought of as being 'Shakespearean theatres'. That there were at the most nine of them, that they were a cul-de-sac in theatre history, while the indoor theatres led on to the modern playhouse, and that we know almost nothing about their interiors, are uncertain about their exteriors and until 1988 knew the shape of only one of them, the first Fortune,[1] does not prevent the existence of a vague national certainty that we know what an Elizabethan playhouse – the Globe – looked like and can recreate the conditions under which Shakespeare staged his plays.

The source of this pervasive, and unfounded, certainty is probably Laurence Olivier's 1944 film of *Henry V*. The Globe in this film was based on the best scholarly research then available; but that research was coloured by an essentially Victorian aesthetic which involved a rejection of many of the most important features of Elizabethan culture. Victorian scholars, in their anxiety to return to the native medieval springs of English art and architecture, effectively sidelined its classical Renaissance aspects. Their preferred view of the Elizabethans was of a nation of jolly Arts-and-Craftsmen, inhabiting stout half-timbered buildings and revelling in their native beer. It is the aesthetic which produced Hood and German's *Merrie England*. Its influence is to be found as late as the reconstruction of the Rose currently on view at Dulwich College.[2] The playhouses which are known to have been amphitheatres are the Theatre (1576), the Curtain (1577), the Rose (1587), the Swan (1595), the Globe (1599 and 1613) and the Hope or Beargarden (1614). The Fortune (1600) was almost certainly purpose-built, but its idiosyncratic square plan and cheap cost suggest that it might have been a conversion of an inn-yard, like the Red Bull and other inn-theatres. The second Fortune (1622) was an amphitheatre. The Red Lion (1567) was possibly an amphitheatre, but its plan is not known. Nothing is known of the early playhouse at Newington Butts used by the Admiral's and Lord Chamberlain's Men in 1594; it may have been either an amphitheatre or a converted inn. Representations of these theatres include several inconsistent views, in panoramas of London, of the playhouses on the south bank, the most authoritative of which is Wenceslaus Hollar's panorama, the *Long View* of 1647, which shows the second Globe and the Hope, but not the Rose or the Swan, which had been demolished by Hollar's time. John Norden's 1600 panorama

Part of Wenceslaus Hollar's Long View of London, 1647, *showing the south-bank playhouses. The labels on the Globe and the 'beere bayting h[ouse]' – the Beargarden, previously the Hope – were interchanged in engraving the plate. (Guildhall Library, Corporation of London)*

shows the four south bank theatres, but while in the panorama they are depicted as hexagons, in the inset map they are shown as circular (the Rose turns out to have been neither). Claes Jan Visscher's 1616 panorama, the most popular source for illustrations of the Globe, particularly in the form of an eighteenth-century forgery based upon it, is highly inaccurate; it presents an improbable view of the playhouses, and it seems unlikely that Visscher had ever visited London.[3] There is one depiction of the northern playhouses, in a panorama of London from the north, which probably shows the Theatre.[4] There is a view of the interior of the Swan and a sketch in the Henslowe papers which may or may not be related to the interior of a playhouse.[5] All other ideas about the interior and exterior appearances of Elizabethan amphitheatre playhouses come from speculation based on building contracts, lawsuits, descriptions by visitors, and what is deduced from the texts and stage directions of the plays performed in them. What the interior of the playhouses were like – the aesthetic impression a visitor would obtain – is a matter for conjecture.

The importance of this can be demonstrated by a more detailed examination of the Globe as presented in Olivier's *Henry V*. The film was made as a propaganda exercise

Part of John Norden's panorama Civitas Londini, *1600, showing the four south-bank playhouses as hexagonal in the main view but circular in the inset map (not shown). (The Royal Library, National Library of Sweden)*

during the Second World War. It excised from the text all those moments where Shakespeare undermines or questions the mythos of Henry as national hero, and it stressed the stalwartness, honesty and general virtue of the British, and the general undesirability of foreigners, against whom Henry is fighting (except the princess whom he will end up marrying, who shows her worthiness by making strenuous efforts to learn English at the earliest opportunity). Olivier put this interpretation on Shakespeare's play without too much straining of the text (it is, among other things, a propaganda exercise), but the film is to be placed in the context of other films of the date, which have a vested interest in presenting the British as the Bulldog Breed, united in the face of a common enemy, an essentially modest people, living without pretension. Olivier desired to set Shakespeare's play (which begins in a supposed replica of Shakespeare's Globe and fades out into the world of the Middle Ages in which it is set) in a similar context: to show the Elizabethans as a united people muddling through and making the best of things in unpretentious surroundings. So the interior of the Globe is an unpretentious affair, and the standard of costume worn by the Lord Chamberlain's Men is that which might be expected in the annual production of the village amateur dramatic society. The whole emphasis is on honesty, wholesomeness, thrift and unpretentiousness – the virtues which were being preached to the film's wartime audience.

CONTEMPORARY DESCRIPTIONS

Contemporary descriptions of the playhouses, whether hostile or friendly, make it clear that thrift and unpretentiousness are the last qualities which should be ascribed to them. Honesty and wholesomeness are a matter of opinion. The playhouses were gaudy, glamorous and extravagant places. The best-known description is that written in 1596 by Johannes de Witt (a copy of whose sketch of the interior of the Swan is the only contemporary representation of the interior of an amphitheatre playhouse):

> There are four amphitheatres in London of notable beauty, which from their diverse signs bear diverse names. In each of them a different play is daily exhibited to the populace. The two more magnificent of these are situated to the southward beyond the Thames, and from the signs suspended before them are called the Rose and the Swan. The two others are outside the city towards the north on the highway which issues through the Episcopal Gate, called in the vernacular Bishopsgate. There is also a fifth, but of dissimilar structure, devoted to the baiting of beasts, where are maintained in separate cages and enclosures many bears and dogs of stupendous size, which are kept for fighting, furnishing thereby a most delightful spectacle to men. Of all the theatres, however, the largest and the most magnificent is that one of which the sign is a swan, called in the vernacular the Swan Theatre; for it accommodates in its seats three thousand persons, and is built of a mass of flint stones (of which there is a prodigious supply in Britain), and supported by wooden columns painted in such excellent imitation of marble that it is able to deceive even the most cunning. Since its form resembles that of a Roman work, I have made a sketch of it above.[6]

In 1599 a German visitor, Thomas Platter, went to the Globe and to the Curtain:

> On September 21st after lunch, about two o'clock, I and my party crossed the water, and there in the house with the thatched roof witnessed an excellent performance of the tragedy of the first Emperor Julius Caesar with a cast of some fifteen people; when the play was over, they danced very marvellously and gracefully together as is their wont, two dressed as men and two as women.
>
> On another occasion not far from our inn, in the suburb of Bishopsgate, if I remember, also after lunch, I beheld a play . . . Thus daily at two in the afternoon, London has two, sometimes three plays running in different places, competing with each other, and those which play best obtain most spectators. The playhouses are so constructed that they play on a raised platform, so that everyone has a good view. There are different galleries and places, however, where the seating is better and more comfortable and therefore more expensive. For whoever cares to stand below only pays one English penny, but if he wishes to sit he enters by another door, and pays another penny, while if he desires to sit in the most comfortable seats which are cushioned, where he not only sees everything well, but can also be seen, then he pays yet another English penny at another door. And

during the performance food and drink are carried round the audience, so that for what one cares to pay one may also have refreshment. The actors are most expensively and elaborately costumed; for it is the English usage for eminent lords or knights at their decease to bequeath and leave almost the best of their clothes to their serving men, which it is unseemly for the latter to wear, so that they offer them for sale for a small sum to the actors.[7]

English descriptions of the playhouses are mainly hostile, deploring their extravagance and the immoral ends which it serves. John Stockwood, in a sermon preached in 1578, says:

I know not how I might with the godly learned especially more discommende the gorgeous Playing place erected in the fieldes, than to terme it, as they please to have it called, a Theatre.[8]

William Harrison in the 1570s considered that it was 'an evident token of a wicked time when plaiers wexe so riche that they can build such houses'.[9] These were luxurious buildings, as was appropriate to their escapist purpose, and worthy predecessors to the gaudiest Victorian theatres or twentieth-century picture-palaces.

It is unfortunate but inevitable that the fullest descriptions of the theatres come from foreign visitors: if one is familiar with a type of building, one does not describe it. Only someone who had never before been to a cinema would feel it necessary to describe one. What seems to be common to both foreign and English witnesses is that the theatres are described in terms of classical culture. Stockwood can find no worse word to describe a playhouse than to call it a theatre, thus linking it with the pagan culture of the Greeks and Romans, associated with luxury and vice. De Witt finds it natural to describe the Swan in terms of the classical theatres with which he was familiar through his education. When Jonson illustrates a Roman theatre on the title-page of his *Workes*, he gives it a heavens such as the playhouses which he wrote for are known to have had. The Elizabethans regarded their theatres as buildings in the same idiom as those of the venerated classical dramatists Plautus and Terence.

CLASSICAL INFLUENCES AND THE ENGLISH RENAISSANCE

It has for many years been the critical fashion to stress the continuity of English culture through the Middle Ages and the Renaissance. The attitude expressed at its most extreme by the reported remark of C. S. Lewis: 'I have just decided that the Renaissance did not happen in England, and if it did, it did not matter,' has permeated criticism of both literary and visual art. England has been seen as cut off from Continental Europe by the sea and by its own internal political obsessions, so that Renaissance influence, when it did arrive, was diluted by and absorbed into an essentially continuous medieval culture. Spenser is seen as the heir to medieval popular romance,[10] rather than as the author of a Renaissance epic like Ariosto and Tasso. The greatest of the native-born painters, Nicholas Hilliard, is viewed as the successor of the medieval manuscript illuminators rather than as the forerunner of Samuel Cooper.[11] The amphitheatre playhouses are seen as the end of the medieval theatrical tradition, rather than as the beginnings of modern British theatre.[12]

This is not how the Elizabethans viewed their own art or their own era. Where we see continuity, they saw change, disruption and, usually, amelioration. Even Harrison, who is apt to regard any change from ancient custom as one for the worse, sees a break in continuity in architectural tradition which took place in the reign of Henry VIII as an improvement (although he does not feel that it is an improvement which has been sustained):

> thus much I will say generally of all the houses and honours pertaining to her majesty, that they are builded either of square stone or brick, or else of both. . . . Those that were builded before the time of King Henry the Eighth retain to these days the shew and image of the ancient kind of workmanship used in this land; but such as he erected after his own device (for he was nothing inferior in this trade to Adrian the emperor and Justician the law-giver) do represent another manner of pattern, which, as they are supposed to excel all the rest that he found standing in this realm, so they are and shall be a perpetual precedent unto those that do come after to follow in their works and buildings of importance. Certes masonry did never better flourish in England than in his time. And albeit that in these days there be many goodly houses erected in the sundry quarters of this island, yet they are rather curious to the eye like paper work than substantial for continuance: whereas such as he did set up excels in both, and therefore may justly be preferred far above all the rest.[13]

A study of surviving buildings bears out Harrison's perception of a break in English architectural tradition at the time of Henry VIII. He is probably wrong in ascribing its origins to the King – Cardinal Wolsey was more influential, and Henry benefited from his ideas at Hampton Court and in London – but a new architecture comes into England with the new learning. If one compares great houses built at the beginning of the sixteenth century, such as Thornbury Castle or Compton Wynyates, with Hampton Court, one realizes the extent of the break. Thornbury and Compton Wynyates are still essentially Gothic in their aesthetic vocabulary: a playful Gothic, with the defensive detail which had been necessary to earlier magnates now transformed into decorative *jeux d'esprit*, but Gothic nonetheless. Hampton Court is a Renaissance palace, proclaiming in its classical detail its rejection of the medieval past. The modern visitor looking at the façades of Wolsey's palace sees a medieval outline, battlemented, with the imposing gatehouse and pointed arches of the medieval great house. But the façade has three storeys, in a reflection of the three orders of classical architecture, and the decorative detail is classical: roundels containing the heads of Roman emperors and a coat of arms enclosed in a frame with Corinthian columns and with the supporters naked putti of an unmistakably Renaissance idiom.

The break between the late-medieval and Henrican architectural styles is apparent in

One of eight roundels of Roman emperors by Giovanni da Maiano, purchased in 1521 for Hampton Court. Architectural decoration was one of the means of the diffusion of the classical style through the country. (Crown Copyright. Historic Royal Palaces)

the Chapel of King's College, Cambridge. Here, the discontinuity is marked by the great Renaissance screen, the building is split between the contemplative plainness of the chapel and the Renaissance secularity of the decoration imposed on the antechapel. The king's beasts who support the coats of arms come from medieval tradition, but it is medieval tradition interpreted in a Renaissance idiom. The screen and the stained glass windows are purely Renaissance.

It was through the parish churches that Renaissance art forms were disseminated throughout provincial England. These monuments to medieval art were invaded by the

The monument (erected in 1573) to John Harford in Holy Trinity Church, Bosbury, Hereford and Worcester, by John Gildon of Hereford, showing knowledge of classical style by provincial craftsmen. (RCHM England)

monuments of the sixteenth-century nobility and gentry, and in the process even the most remote village might learn something of the new art. Even more than the great houses of the time, these monuments were a means of disseminating the new vision around the kingdom. When the Harfords of Bosbury, Herefordshire, erected their monuments in 1573 and 1578, they used a local craftsmen, John Gildon of Hereford, who produced works which were provincial in execution, but recognizably Renaissance in their vocabulary.[14] These monuments were erected at the same time that James Burbage was building the Theatre. If the people of a remote village in Herefordshire found the Renaissance interpretation of classical motifs the natural idiom for artistic and monumental expression at this date, it must have been far more familiar to craftsmen based in the capital, where there was access to Renaissance art works as diverse as Hampton Court Palace and Somerset House and Pietro Torrigiano's monument to Henry VII in Westminster Abbey. The prevailing artistic mode in London at the time that the Elizabethan playhouses were built was Renaissance – classical detail reinterpreted by contemporary artists. It was commonplace for writers of the time to use classical culture as a standard of reference and identification. Even so patriotic and insular a writer as Harrison explains the England of his day in terms of classical culture:

The monument to Henry VII (d. 1509) and Elizabeth of York (d. 1503) by Pietro Torrigiano, in Westminster Abbey – an Italian Renaissance monument in the heart of London. (By courtesy of the Dean and Chapter of Westminster)

The barony or degree of lords doth answer to the degree of senators of Rome (as I said) and the title of nobility (as we used to call it in England) to the Roman *Patricii*. Also in England no man is commonly created baron except he may dispend of yearly revenues a thousand pounds, or so much as may fully maintain and bear out his countenance and port. But viscounts, earls, marquesses, and dukes exceed them according to the proportion of their degree and honour. But though by chance he or his son have less, yet he keepeth this degree: but if the decay be excessive, and not able to maintain the honour (as *Senatores Romani* were *amoti a senatu*), so sometimes they are not admitted to the upper house in parliament, although they keep the name of 'lord' still, which cannot be taken from them upon any such occasion.[15]

Francis Meres in *Palladis Tamia* is determined to show that contemporary English literature is a modern version of that of the Greeks and Romans:

As Plautus and Seneca are accounted the best for comedy and tragedy among the Latins, so Shakespeare among the English is the most excellent in both kinds for the stage.[16]

The format and presentation of Edmund Spenser's *The Shepheardes Calender* is designed to claim that English is a language as capable of producing a great poet as are Greek or Latin, and that in Spenser it has produced him, while Sir Philip Sidney's argument, in *A Defence of Poetry*, is that the language has already produced its equivalent of the early classical poets in Chaucer, and that the duty of modern poets is to complete the task which Chaucer began, albeit in a time very different from his.[17] Elizabethans proclaimed in their art, their literature and their architecture that they regarded themselves as living in a new Classical Age.

WHAT WE KNOW ABOUT THE OUTDOOR THEATRES

Those who have attempted theoretical reconstructions of the interiors of Elizabethan playhouses have implicitly acknowledged that the style of decoration would probably be Elizabethan neoclassical. Their range of reference has, however, tended (with the honourable and distinguished exception of C. Walter Hodges, who made use of Elizabethan domestic interior design)[18] to be restricted either to views of the interiors of theatres (the Swan drawing, some designs by Inigo Jones for indoor private theatres and some title-page vignettes from published plays illustrating scenes from the dramas, together with any work which includes the word 'theatre' in its title) or to rooms in which plays are known to have been performed (the Banqueting House in Whitehall; the great halls of the Inns of Court).[19] Before proceeding to examine in greater detail an area which has been comparatively neglected as a source for such studies, I would like to recapitulate what we do know about the Elizabethan amphitheatre playhouses. I shall mention the Rose only briefly in this study, since I will deal with it in detail in a separate chapter.

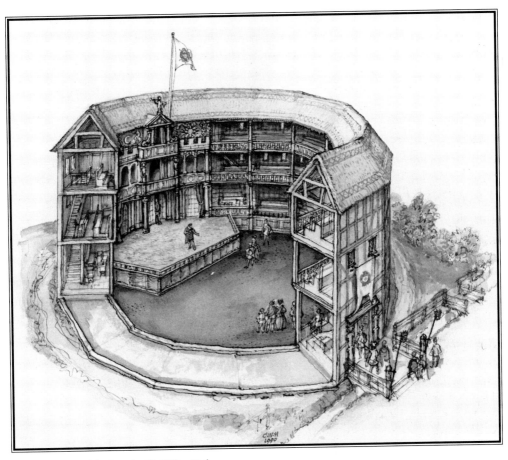

A reconstruction of the Rose by C. Walter Hodges.

THE RED LION

Of the Red Lion (1567) we know the dimensions of its stage (30 feet by 40 feet by 5 feet from the ground), that it had a trapdoor, that there was a turret 30 feet high from the ground with an interior floor 7 feet from the top erected on or abutting the stage, and that the whole was set in a yard around which scaffolds were to be erected for the accommodation of spectators. We do not know the shape of the yard, nor the height of the scaffolds, nor the form or horizontal dimensions of the turret. It is not certain that the Red Lion was a permanent building. The constructors were William Sylvester and, subsequently, John Reynolds, fulfilling the orders of John Brayne, but their work was so unsatisfactory that it led to lawsuits.

NEWINGTON BUTTS

The playhouse at Newington Butts was probably constructed in about 1575 on the orders of Jerome Savary, leader of the Earl of Warwick's Men, but whether it was a new structure or a conversion of an existing one, such as an inn, is not known. It was used by the Admiral's and Lord Chamberlain's Men in 1594, and was gone by 1599.[20] De Witt, writing in 1596, does not list it among the amphitheatre playhouses, which may mean that it had been demolished already, or that it was disused and so far out of town that he never learned about it, or that it was not an amphitheatre playhouse.

THE THEATRE

The Theatre (1576) was built by John Brayne and his brother-in-law, James Burbage. Since, when it was demolished, its timbers were used to construct the first Globe, and the second Globe was rebuilt using the foundations of the first Globe, John Orrell has argued that the Theatre, and both Globes had the same dimensions – an external diameter of about 100 feet.[21] But De Witt writes that the Swan was the largest theatre in London at that date, accommodating 3,000 people, with the implication that the other theatres he mentions (the Theatre, the Curtain and the Rose – which was, indeed, much smaller) were not of the same size. He says that the Rose, as well as the Swan, was more magnificent than the two northern playhouses. At the time he visited London the Theatre and the Curtain were about twenty years old, and the Rose had been renovated some two years previously, while the Burbages knew that their lease on the Theatre was coming to an end, so it may have been becoming shabby. On the basis of Platter's general descriptions of the London playhouses (although by the time he visited London the old northern Theatre had become the new southern Globe), and a description by another German traveller, Samuel Kiechel, who came to London in 1584 –

> there are some peculiar houses, which are so made as to have about three galleries over one another, inasmuch as a great number of people always enters to see such an entertainment[22]

– as well as the fact that its frame was incorporated into that of the first Globe, it seems that the Theatre had three galleries. If the Theatre is the Shoreditch playhouse represented in the anonymous *View of the Cittye of London from the North towards the South*,[23] and that view is an accurate representation of the playhouse, then it had two external staircase towers, like those shown by Hollar on the second Globe, a substantial hut, or cover for a stage-tower or heavens, big enough to incorporate machinery for flying, and a small battlemented turret or similar structure surmounted by a flagstaff. It is also known from documentary sources that the Theatre had 'lord's rooms' or private boxes in the galleries nearest the stage.

THE CURTAIN

The Curtain was built by a speculator called Henry Laneman in 1577. It seems to have been used by the Lord Chamberlain's Men between 1597 and 1599, and it may be the structure described in the prologue to *Henry V* as a 'cockpit' and a 'wooden O'. It is possible that the substantial ridged roof surmounted by a flagstaff on the right of the view of Shoreditch belongs to the Curtain. Since the Theatre and the Curtain were the only playhouses known to be amphitheatres and known to be in use in 1584, it seems from Kiechel's description that it had three galleries. The Curtain was the northern theatre visited by Thomas Platter in 1599.

THE ROSE

The Rose was built by Philip Henslowe, in partnership with John Cholmley, a citizen and grocer of London, in 1587. It was the first of the theatres erected near the river on the south bank of the Thames. De Witt describes it as being more sumptuous than either the Theatre or the Curtain, although neither as large nor as splendid as the Swan. It may have been built initially as a multi-purpose entertainment complex, with facilities for animal-baiting as well as playing, and only later have been dedicated completely to the performance of plays.

THE SWAN

The Swan was built around 1596 by Francis Langley, who called himself a draper and goldsmith, but was in fact a moneylender (which activity he shared with Henslowe). It is the only amphitheatre of whose interior we have any representation. But 'To say that a number of the features illustrated by de Witt are debatable is to put it mildly'.[24] The sketch appears to show a building with a curved interior, and three galleries whose heights diminish from top to bottom, whose roofs are supported by cylindrical, or perhaps bulging, columns, with similar columns decorating their fronts. In the galleries are stepped ranks of seating. There are entrances (marked 'ingressus' on the drawing) consisting of flights of steps going from the yard into the lowest gallery, but these seem to have been added after the drawing of the galleries, because the rows of columns continue above them with no break. It is possible that what appear to be steps are in fact removable bars across a recessed entrance. (A flight of steps with bars across sketched among the Henslowe papers[25] may represent an entrance of a similar type. This, too, appears to have a permanent bar across the centre of the bay, if what is represented is a playhouse gallery bay, which is uncertain – the Dulwich papers show that Henslowe was a doodler.) The roofs of the playhouse and the over-stage hut seem to be thatched, that of the heavens over the stage tiled or shingled. Into the yard of the amphitheatre projects a large rectangular stage, apparently longer than it is wide, labelled 'proscænium' on the drawing. It is either borne on two oddly-shaped supporting trestles or, as Gurr suggests, is hung with curtains, like the scaffold erected for the execution of Mary Queen of Scots.[26] The stage is partially covered by a roof, which seems to slope down from the rear (in an arrangement which would guarantee the actors getting soaked on a rainy afternoon) and to be carried by two round columns with bulging profiles, with Corinthian capitals but Doric socles, resting on cubic or rectangular plinths with stepped or sloping bases and decorated with diagonally-crossed squares in relief. At the front of the stage, and unprotected by its roof, three figures are grouped around a bench.

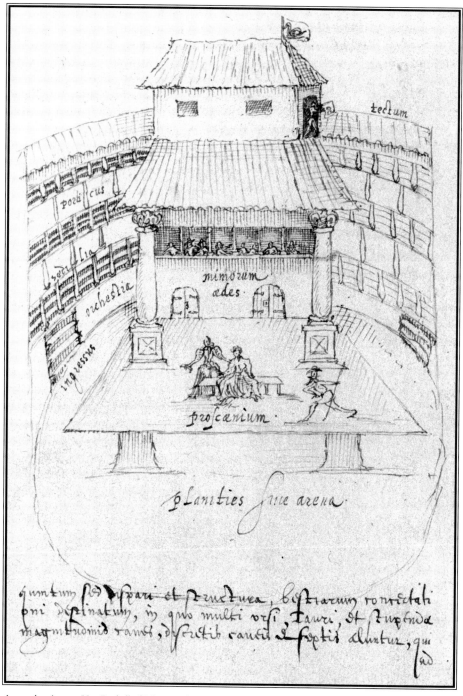

A copy by Arnout Van Buchell of Johannes de Witt's drawing of the Swan. This presents many problems of interpretation. (Bibliotheek der Rijkuniversiteit, Utrecht)

The problems of interpretation raised so far are as nothing to those of de Witt's depiction of the tiring-house façade or *frons scenae* – the rear of the stage. It is not clear whether this, labelled 'mimorum aedes' ('the actors' building'), is continuous with the front of the galleries, projects forward from it, or cuts horizontally across a segment of the circle formed by the amphitheatre. De Witt's drawing seems to show it projecting, but this raises problems with sight-lines (everyone in the theatre was supposed to have a good view), and the standard of drawing elsewhere is not such as to produce absolute trust in de Witt as an accurate visual reporter, or in van Buchell as a copyist. The tiring-house façade contains a gallery, either fronted by a line of columns such as those which face the galleries round the amphitheatre or divided into individual boxes, and within this are seated figures. Below them, and improbably small in proportion to the figures in the gallery, and improbably distant in proportion to the figures on the stage, are two pairs of double doors, apparently made out of wood, with heavy ironwork and large fastenings or locks. The tops of the door arches are semicircular. The scale does not permit much detail of the façade to be shown, but it looks as though the columns of the above-stage gallery have bases and capitals. No indication is given of either hangings or decoration in this area.

The drawing seems to imply a considerable vertical area above the second gallery and concealed by the stage roof, but, as has already been indicated, the proportions in the drawing must be unreliable. The stage roof appears to project at a lower level than the eaves of the roof of the topmost gallery, while the stage gallery appears to be lower than the second seating gallery, but higher than the lowest one. Above the stage gallery, with the stage roof running down from its base, is a substantial hut, with a thatched roof, two small windows looking out over the stage, and a large opening in its returning side, out of which a man is blowing a trumpet which has a banner representing a swan attached to it. Another swan-banner flies from a flagpole – situated at one end of the ridge of the hut's roof, with no indication of how access would be obtained to it by anyone not an expert climber. Again, there is difficulty in interpreting the perspective and scale of the sketch: there is no indication of what happens below the returning wall with the opening for the trumpeter in it, and, while the hut appears to project from the roof of the surrounding amphitheatre on this side, on the other it appears to be contiguous to it. The question of whether the tiring-house façade projected from the surrounding amphitheatre structure might have been expected to be settled by the Rose excavation, but unfortunately was not: there is no indication of foundations for a projecting tiring-house façade, but their absence does not mean it was not there; it may have been built on the stage, as in one interpretation of the Red Lion contract. On the other hand, so substantial a building as that implied in the Swan drawing, if it does indeed represent a projecting structure, would surely have been too heavy to have been carried on the stage alone, and one would have expected that separate foundations for it would have been essential.

The drawing gives no indication of exits or entrances, except those from the yard to the galleries, and no indication of how access was obtained to the gallery above the stage (the contract for the Hope theatre, which refers to the Swan, shows that the Swan had two external stair-towers, such as are shown on the Theatre and the second

Globe). Nor is it informative on the use of the gallery above the stage: the figures in it may be spectators (but there are none in the amphitheatre galleries), musicians (some of their postures might indicate that they are bowing stringed instruments), other actors in the play or, if no play is taking place, theatre hangers-on.[27]

Of the exterior of the Swan, there is no reliable view;[28] de Witt says that it was the biggest of the amphitheatres in existence at the time of his visit, and that it was built of 'a mass of flint stones'. Presumably de Witt was observing an exterior covered with knapped flints, a common practice in domestic and sacred building in the south-east of England at this period, rather than a wholly flint construction. Although the Swan seems to have had only intermittent use after its enforced closure in July 1597 following the production of the 'seditious' *Isle of Dogs*, its design was considered successful enough by Henslowe for him to use it as the basis of the Hope, when that structure replaced the old Beargarden.

THE FIRST GLOBE

The next playhouse to be built on the south bank was the first Globe. It is possible that this playhouse tends to be given too much importance in its relationship to Shakespeare's plays: he wrote exclusively for it for only ten years of a writing career spanning twenty-five years, but it is the house for which his most important works were written. It was built using the timbers of the old Theatre by a carpenter called Peter Street,[29] for a syndicate which included the two sons of James Burbage, Richard and Cuthbert, and other members of the Lord Chamberlain's Men including William Shakespeare. If John Orrell is right and the Theatre and both Globes, being built first with the same timbers,[30] and then on the same foundations, were the same size, at least as far as plan goes, it was a very large playhouse, perhaps as much as 99 feet in diameter. The capacity of the second Globe was estimated by contemporaries as over 3,000; even if the seating capacity of the galleries was increased in the second Globe, the first cannot have held many fewer than this. The first Globe seems to have had a single-gabled hut, and a roof made of thatch, rather than the more expensive tile (an economy responsible for its ultimate demise). Internal evidence from plays known to have been put on there seems to demand two stage entrances and a possible space for 'discoveries' (which may have been simply another use for one or other of the stage doors), and some sort of playing area 'above', which need not have been extensive. Apart from this, everything else about the playhouse remains conjecture: any reconstruction must be very speculative.

THE FORTUNE

The advent of the Globe seems to have made Henslowe decide to abandon the now decrepit Rose on the south bank and to move away to the north of the City, although in a different area from Bishopsgate, where the old Theatre had been, and the equally old Curtain still was, situated. He possibly did not want to risk theatregoers who had decided to spend an afternoon in the Rose finding that the neighbouring Globe was offering more attractive fare. He hired Peter Street, who had constructed the Globe, to erect his new playhouse, the Fortune, and the building contract and specifications for this survive. In the contract the Globe is used as a point of reference and comparison, which is unfortunate, because instead of illuminating both theatres, this tends to cloud our knowledge of both. Except where specified, everything is to be 'like the Globe': but we have no idea what the Globe was like. The contract is dated 8 January 1599 (1600), and the cost is £440.

Phillipp Henslowe & Edward Allen, the daie of the date hereof, Have bargayned, Compounded & agreed with the saide Peter Streete ffor the erectinge, buildinge & settinge upp of a new howse and Stadge for a Plaiehouse in and uppon a certeine plott or parcell of ground appoynted oute for that purpose, Scytuate and beinge nere Goldinge lane in the parishe of Ste Giles withoute Cripplegate of London, To be by him the saide Peeter Streete or somme other sufficyent woorkmen of his provideinge and appoyntemente and att his propper Costes & Chardges, for the consideracion hereafter in theis presentes expressed, Made, erected, builded and sett upp In manner & forme followinge (that is to saie); The frame of the saide howse to be sett square and to conteine ffowerscore foote of lawfull assize everye waie square withoute and fiftie five foote of like assize square everye waie within, with a good suer and stronge foundacion of pyles, brick, lyme and sand, bothe withoute & within, to be wroughte one foote of assize att the leiste above the grounde; And the saide fframe to conteine Three Stories in heighth, the First or lower Storie to Conteine Twelve foote of lawfull assize in heighth, the second Storie Eleaven foote of lawfull assize in heighth, And the Third or upper Storie to conteine Nyne foote of lawfull assize in height; All which Stories shall conteine Twelve foote and a halfe of lawfull assize in breadth througheoute, besides a Juttey forwardes in eyther of the saide Two upper Stories of Tenne ynches of lawfull assize, with ffower convenient divisions for gentlemens roomes, and other sufficient and convenient divisions for Twoe pennie roomes, with necessarie Seates to be placed and sett, Aswell in those roomes as througheoute all the rest of the galleries of the saide howse, and with such like steares, Conveyances & divisions withoute & within, as are made & Contryved in and to the late erected Plaiehowse On the Banck in the saide parishe of Ste Saviours Called the Globe; With a Stadge and Tyreinge howse to be made, erected & settupp within the saide fframe, with a shadowe or cover over the saide Stadge, which Stadge shalbe placed & sett, As alsoe the stearecases of the saide fframe, in such sorte as is prefigured in a Plott thereof drawen, And which Stadge shall conteine in length ffortie and Three foote of lawfull assize and in breadth to extende to the middle of the yarde of the saide howse; The same Stadge to be paled in belowe with good, stronge and sufficyent newe oken bourdes, And likewise the lower Storie of the saide fframe withinside, and the same lower storie to be alsoe laide over and fenced with strong yron pykes; And the saide Stadge to be in all other proporcions Contryved and fashioned like unto the Stadge of the saide Plaiehowse Called the Globe; With convenient windowes and lightes glazed to the saide Tyreinge howse; And the saide fframe, Stadge and Stearecases to be covered with Tyle, and to have a sufficient gutter of lead to Carrie & convey the water frome the Coveringe of the saide Stadge to fall backwardes; And alsoe all the saide fframe and the Stairecases thereof to be sufficyently enclosed withoute with lathe, lyme & haire, and the gentlemens roomes and Twoe pennie roomes to be seeled with lathe, lyme & haire, and all the fflowers of the saide Galleries, Stories and Stadge to be bourded with good & sufficyent newe deale bourdes of the whole thicknes, wheare need shalbe; And the saide howse and other thinges beforemencioned to be made & doen To be in all other Contrivitions, Conveyances, fashions, thinge and thinges effected, finished and doen, accordinge to the manner and fashion of the saide howse called the Globe, Saveinge only that all the princypall and maine postes of the saide fframe and Stadge forwarde shalbe square and wroughte palasterwise, with carved proporcions called Satiers to be placed & sett on the Topp of every of the same postes, And saveing alsoe that the said Peeter Streete shall not be chardged with anie manner of pay[ntin]ge in or aboute the saide fframe howse or Stadge or anie parte thereof, nor Rendringe the walls within, Nor seelinge anie more or other roomes then the gentlemens roomes, Twoe pennie roomes and Stadge before remembred. Nowe theiruppon the saide Peeter Streete dothe covenante, promise & graunte ffor himself, his executours and administratours, to and with the saide Phillipp Henslowe and Edward Allen and either of them, and thexecutours and administratours of them and either of them, by theis presentes In manner & forme followeinge (that is to saie); That he the saide Peeter Streete, his executours or assignes, shall & will att his or their owne propper costes & Chardges well, woorkmanlike & substancyallie make, erect, sett upp and fully finishe In and by all thinges, accordinge to the true meaninge of theis presentes, with good, stronge and substancyall newe Tymber and other necessarie stuff, All the saide fframe and other woorkes whatsoever In and uppon the saide plott or parcell of grounde (beinge not by anie aucthoretie Restrayned, and haveinge ingres, egres & regres to doe the same) before the ffyve & Twentith daie of Julie next Commeinge after the date hereof; And shall alsoe at his or theire like costes and Chardges Provide and finde All manner of woorkmen, Tymber, Joystes, Rafters, boordes, dores, boltes, hinges, brick, Tyle, lathe, lyme, haire, sande, nailes, leede, Iron, Glasse, woorkmanshipp and other thinges whatsoever which shalbe needefull, Convenyent & necessarie for the saide fframe & woorkes & everie parte thereof; And shall alsoe make all the saide fframe in every poynte for Scantlinges lardger and bigger in assize Then the Scantlinges of the timber of the saide newe erected howse Called the Globe; And alsoe that he the saide Peeter Streete shall furthwith, aswell by himself As by suche other and soemanie woorkmen as shalbe Convenient & necessarie, enter into and uppon the saide buildinges and woorkes, And shall in reasonable manner proceede therein withoute anie wilfull detraccion untill the same shalbe fully effected and finished.[31]

The principal difference between the Fortune and the Globe was that of shape: the Fortune was a square measuring 80 feet on the outside and 55 feet on the inside. This, combined with the comparatively low cost of its erection, suggests that the first

Fortune may have been not an independent structure but a conversion of an existing inn, like the Boar's Head, although the shape may simply have been conditioned by the plot of land that Henslowe had available – it is clear that the shape and size of the Rose was affected by its plot. In other points the contract is ambiguous. The stage and tiring house are to be erected 'within' the seating framework, which suggests the sort of arrangement found at the Red Lion, where the turret may have been put up on the stage, but the contract does not list the tiring house as a separate unit in the specifications for the roof tiling, whereas it does list the staircases, thus suggesting that the tiring house was incorporated into the frame, while the staircases were protruding external structures such as may be seen on the Hollar engraving of the second Globe (see illustration on p. 60). The iron fencing to be erected on the interior face of the lower storey of the frame suggests that there was to be no internal access from the yard into the galleries, and that every effort was to be made to prevent those in the yard entering the galleries – something which again points to protruding staircase entrances. Other differences from the Globe are implied in the contract: the stage may have been a different shape, conditioned by the shape of the arena – although de Witt's drawing suggests that the Swan had a rectangular stage, excavations have revealed that the Rose's stages were trapezoidal, and this would seem to be a more suitable shape for a polygonal building. Further excavations on the Globe site might reveal the shape of at least the second Globe's stage.

The reference to the posts also suggests that those of the Globe were a different shape; perhaps turned and cylindrical (again, a standard feature of galleried structures at this date). The carved figures on the posts are another familiar motif. The Globe may have had similar figures: in its case, perhaps of Hercules carrying the world, which it is thought was the theatre's emblem. But the Fortune was not built with the same eye to economy as the Globe: the timbers were more substantial, and the Globe may have lacked such refinements of interior decoration as carved figures on the posts. John Orrell believes that the Fortune was a Serlian structure, with classical proportions, its satyr-terms proclaiming its origins to the cognoscenti.[32] If he is right, the Fortune would replace Inigo Jones's Banqueting Hall in Whitehall as the first building in England which certainly shows an understanding of classical architectural principles. It is more likely that the Serlian proportions Orrell perceives were co-incidental, and the satyrs classicizing decoration: as Malcolm Rogers remarks,

In their approach to such detail the Elizabethans were far more eclectic than their contemporaries in Italy

A bracket in the form of a satyr, from a seventeenth-century house. Similar carved brackets may have been used in the Fortune. (Museum of London)

Supporters in the form of wild men or satyrs, on the tomb of John Osbaldeston, d. 1614, at Burford, Oxfordshire. This is a provincial interpretation of the motif that Henslowe introduced at the Fortune. Note the classical pillars that flank the supporters. (Norman Hammond)

and France, where there was a concerted attempt to re-create the architecture of imperial Rome, both in detail and in principle. The English way was altogether more superficial, and the use of detail decorative rather than organic.[33]

When the first Fortune burnt to the ground in 1621 (fire was a constant hazard in a city of timber buildings, with naked flames providing both light and heat), it was replaced with a brick-built circular amphitheatre, possibly the only one of the Elizabethan and Jacobean playhouses to be truly circular, since it is now accepted that timber-framed construction methods meant that a wooden playhouse could not be an O but had to be a many-sided polygon.[34] This survived until 1649, when it was probably dismantled, although traces of its site are still to be found in the street-names where it stood – Fortune Alley and Playhouse Yard. In the late eighteenth century the building was believed to survive:[35] it is one of the playhouses for whose traces it is possibly worth digging.

THE HOPE

In 1613–14 Henslowe and Alleyn decided to resume theatrical production on the south bank of the Thames, a decision probably connected with the destruction of the first Globe by fire in 1613. The Hope, as the new entertainment complex was called, replaced the old Beargarden (or Paris Garden), which had been used primarily as a location for animal baiting, although some jigs and interludes had been staged there. With the Hope, Henslowe returned to the idea he may have originally used at the Rose: he constructed a building which could be used both for the baiting of animals and for the production of plays. The Hope therefore had a revolutionary design for the heavens: these were to be supported without any pillars on the stage, which was itself removable.[36] Once again Henslowe used an existing playhouse for his model. In this case the building upon which the Hope was to be based was its near neighbour the Swan. It was to have two external staircases (like the Swan), a tiring house, a removable stage to be carried on trestles, three galleries and two gentlemen's rooms in the lowest storey, and it was to be built substantially, using oak rather than pine for at least the visible timbers. The decorative posts were to be turned.[37]

The problem with the Hope seems to have been that, as anyone who has visited a zoo will appreciate, animals are noisome neighbours. Jonson's *Bartholomew Fair*, written for the new playhouse, includes references to the dirt and odours produced by the animals, and the stage-keeper is accused of deliberately delaying the start of the play so that he may gather the apple-cores thrown by the audience to signify their disapproval of being kept waiting for 'the bears within'.[38] The Hope was eventually used only for animal-baiting, and became known by the name of its predecessor, the Beargarden. It can be seen, mislabelled as the Globe, on Hollar's panorama (see illustration on p. 60) – its original unsupported heavens traceable in the distinctive shape of its roof.[39] Henslowe's last exercise in the erection of buildings for entertainments thus went the opposite way to that of his first, the Rose, where the players soon ousted the animals.

THE SECOND GLOBE

At the same time as the Hope was being built, the Lord Chamberlain's Men were replacing their own house, which had been burnt to the ground at a performance of Shakespeare's *Henry VIII*, with the second Globe. This was rebuilt on the foundations of the first, and so must have shared its horizontal dimensions, but contemporary reports describe it as being 'fairer' than its predecessor: it was tiled, rather than roofed with the previously disastrous thatch, and, if Norden's representation is to be trusted in this (see illustration on p. 61), the design of the heavens was changed, the distinctive double gable and lantern of the playhouse shown by Hollar replacing a more conventional single-gabled structure. Something of the effect of a stage lantern may be gauged from a sixteenth-century altar in Toul Cathedral in France, which appears to represent a theatre with a lantern over the stage. The extent of the heavens represented by Hollar would seem to make extra external lighting imperative for so shadowed a stage, and the suggestion that the lantern represented on the Hollar engraving provided such illumination is compelling. Shakespeare wrote no plays for the second Globe (the extent of his contribution to Fletcher's *The Two Noble Kinsmen* is a matter of speculation) – the conflagration in which its predecessor perished seems plausible as the occasion for his retirement to Stratford, but the excellence of the Hollar engraving

A Renaissance altar at Toul Cathedral, France, in the form of a stage lit by a lantern. (Norman Hammond)

and the studies which have been made of it mean that this is the theatre which, externally at least, has to a great extent now risen in reproduction on Bankside, near to where its original stood.

If it is possible, thanks to the accuracy of Wenceslaus Hollar and the ingenuity of John Orrell,[40] to reproduce the exterior of the second Globe, for a reconstruction of its interior we are dependent on the internal evidence of the plays put on there and in its predecessor. What theatre historians have been able to deduce from these is admirably summarized by Andrew Gurr.[41] The first Globe had a tiring-house façade with a small upper-acting area, a stage extending into the middle of the yard (although the wording of the Fortune contract and the excavations at the Rose make it more questionable than was previously thought whether that stage was either rectangular or projected as far into the yard as did that of the Fortune). There was a trapdoor in the stage, large enough to take two men, two pillars supported the heavens, and there were at least two doors on to the stage. Several of the plays staged at the first Globe seem to require what is now generally known as a 'discovery-space' – a smallish area which could be set with a scene, such as someone writing in their closet, and revealed by the opening of doors or the withdrawal of a curtain. Gurr describes the problems attendant on this area:

> Such a feature would represent a major departure from the Swan's stage, of course,
> and we have no pictorial evidence for what it might have looked like, or even
> where it might have been located. Was it a recess in the tiring-house façade

between the two doors, a booth or curtained scaffold built out on the stage in front of the façade, or simply one of the entry doors, double like those of the Swan, opened out and curtained across? On this, and on the parallel question of the playing-area 'above', which might have been a gallery, 'tarras' [upper acting-area], chamber or window, an enormous body of argument has built up, with few positive answers coming out of it. The design of the whole tiring-house façade remains a matter for conjecture.[42]

The most important work done on theoretical reconstructions of the tiring-house façade in both indoor theatres and outdoor amphitheatres has been based on the design of great hall screens.[43] These fulfill the basic requirements of what we know of the tiring-house façades, providing usually two substantial entrances, certainly extensive enough to contain a small discovery-scene, and also an area above which could be used for acting, for the accommodation of musicians, or for members of the audience (although the view of anyone seated there would not be entirely satisfactory, as the geography of the playhouses meant that the action would necessarily be directed forwards and sideways – they were not theatre-in-the-round). However, it should be remembered, even in the cases where a particular play is known to have been performed in a particular hall, as is the case with two of Shakespeare's plays – *The Comedy of Errors*, put on at Gray's Inn on 28 December, 1594, and *Twelfth Night*, put on at the Middle Temple on 2 February 1602 – that it is only an assumption that they were staged using the hall screen as a make-shift tiring-house façade, an assumption which is contradicted by the records of the staging of plays in halls where the location of the stage is known.

The most important evidence we have for the staging of a play in a similar hall is the proposal drawn up, but rejected, for the accommodation of the court on a visit to Oxford in 1605 (see illustration on p. 137). Here the audience was to be placed on a sloping scaffold, abutting an arched portico, with more accommodation for spectators on its top, which is described in the proposal as a 'skraene'. The stage (which was raked) was to be erected at the upper end of the hall. It is certainly plausible that the great hall screen would provide a satisfactory backing for the action of the play, especially before the advent of a strong Italian influence in theatre architecture, but the only certain piece of evidence we have shows that on that occasion the stage was placed at the opposite end of the hall from the normal position of the screen (Christ Church Hall does not have a screen).[44] When Elizabeth I was entertained with a play in King's College Chapel on her visit to Cambridge in 1564 the stage was built on an east–west axis, at right angles to the great screen, and close to it, with the *frons scenae*, entrances and tiring-house itself being provided by two side-chapels. The screen could have been used to form the back of the stage, but it was not.

TOMB-SCULPTURE AND THE THEATRE

There is a major area of Elizabethan culture which has been comparatively under-used as material which may provide the basis for theoretical reconstruction of the interior of

Elizabethan playhouses and of their staging practices. This is the monumental architecture of the period. The Elizabethans continued their practice of enactment past the end of their earthly lives and into their tombs, and the churches of Britain present an array of sculptured representations of the acting-out of various presentations of the deceased – as dynast, as centre of a family, as matriarch, as innocent victim, as devout Christian. These are frozen, eternal dumb-shows, and their settings are often suggestive of what we know of theatre practice at the period.

It would not be going too far to say that monuments at this period formed part of the entertainment industry. They were there to be looked at, to be read, their epitaphs studied, their meanings – together with the implications of the posture of the effigies, their costumes, and the symbolism of any subsidiary decoration, – pondered. They were speaking pictures – emblems grown large and petrified. They were viewed and visited, searched for their messages, for their information, for what might be gained from them by the pensive visitor. If their main purpose was to proclaim the affluence and influence of those who could erect such massive and expensive works, they also invite contemplation, edification – even amusement. Lady Margaret Hoby visited the tombs in Westminster Abbey in 1600, and a contemporary writer on church monuments, John Weever, writes about the

> concourse of people who come daily to view the lively Statues and Monuments in Westminster Abbey . . . a sight which brings delight and admiration, and strikes a religious apprehension into the minds of the beholders.[45]

The vocabulary in which Weever expresses the reaction which he expects his contemporaries to have to church monuments is close to that in which supporters of the theatre explained the reaction of audiences to stage plays. These, too, produced delight, admiration and apprehension. They were monitory: speaking pictures. The emblematic aspect of Elizabethan theatre is perhaps under-emphasized in general treatments of the subject, but it is a strong one: Hamlet, dressed in black, with his explanation to his mother of the precise nature of his melancholy –

> 'Tis not alone my inky cloak, good mother,
> Nor customary suits of solemn black,
> Nor windy suspiration of forc'd breath,
> No, nor the fruitful river in the eye,
> Nor the dejected haviour of the visage,
> Together with all forms, modes, shows of grief,
> That can denote me truly; these indeed seem,
> For they are actions that a man might play:
> But I have that within which passeth show;
> These but the trappings and the suits of woe.[46]

– inhabits the same visual world as those of Shakespeare's contemporaries who have themselves portrayed in the fashionable posture of the melancholic. What is presented

The monument to Sara Latch, d. 1644, in the Church of St John the Baptist, Churchill, Avon. Her husband is parting his dead wife's shroud to take a final glimpse, or kiss, of her. (RCHM England)

on the Elizabethan and Jacobean stage and in contemporary visual art uses the same vocabulary. The mourners at the deathbed of Edward West, on Epiphanius Evesham's brass to him at Marsworth, Bedfordshire, are exhibited in the postures of grief and melancholy which Hamlet delineates. For them, as for Hamlet, the postures and trappings of woe reflect a true grief, rather than the affectation of a currently fashionable mood, although the manifestations of both psychological states may be indistinguishable. The monument to Sarah Latch at Churchill, Avon, shows her husband performing a parallel act to that of Laertes taking his last embrace of Ophelia's corpse (or, more repellently, Vindice's retention of the skull of his murdered mistress in Tourneur's *The Revenger's Tragedy*)[47] as he parts the shroud covering his wife's face to take a last glimpse, or kiss, of her. Sir Francis Vere is shown on his monument on Westminster Abbey in civilian dress, but attended by four soldiers, who bear his armour above him in a composition similar to that of the last moments of *Hamlet* as the prince is carried like a soldier off the stage by four captains.[48]

The ways in which the figures of Elizabethan and Jacobean tomb-sculpture may point in both their costume and their gesture to the presentation of contemporary drama will be dealt with in the next chapter. It is the architectural settings against which the frozen dramas of the dead are acted out, and their possible relationship to contemporary theatrical architecture, that I wish to examine here. Tombs at this period are of several types: the most familiar is that usually described as the four-, six- or eight-poster, which represents the funeral ceremonies common at the time, in which the body of the deceased, or an effigy of it, was laid in state under a canopy before the actual interment. Effigies from this type of funeral still survive. The tomb thus represents either the deathbed or the catafalque, the line between representation and reality blurring in those cases where the canopy used for the lying-in-state is transferred to the permanent memorial. Figures of the family may attend such stone deathbeds, in the place of mourners at the lying-in-state; or the family gathered round to witness the demise of their relative.

Another group of tombs, usually smaller and cheaper wall-monuments, show the family at prayer, kneeling on either side of a prie-dieu, the emphasis here being on the unity and holiness of the family during life, rather than on its separation by death. There are, however, tombs which fit into neither of these categories, which frame an action performed by the petrified representations of those commemorated, and in which the architectural setting is important in delineating the nature of the action depicted by the artist. It is in these tombs that we see most clearly the idea of sculpture as drama.

The worlds of tomb-sculpture and of entertainment were closely connected, geographically and professionally. Much has been written about the lawless character of Southwark – its supply of brothels, bear-baiting houses, and other aspects of the entertainment industry which made it appropriate as the site of playhouses. Equally important was Southwark's role as a centre of artistic activity. The same restrictive practices which forced the playhouses into areas outside the control of the City of London authorities forced the refugee families, mostly of Low Country origin, who dominated the London artistic world at this period to situate their workshops in areas which were not controlled by the trade guilds: the principal such area was Southwark. Shakespeare's own funeral monument (see illustration on p. 105) was made within a few hundred yards of the Globe theatre. Even before the influx of refugees, Southwark had been a centre for artists and craftsmen, which is probably why the refugees were attracted there. The windows of King's College Chapel, Cambridge, were made close to St Mary Overies (now Southwark Cathedral) – the masterpieces of what is known as the 'Southwark School'.[49] The men of the theatre may have been attracted to Southwark not because they were outlaws but because they were artists.

The same artists were engaged in the manufacture of permanent stone monuments in churches and in the evanescent pasteboard monuments erected for civic pageantry. The most notable example of the worlds of tomb-sculpture, entertainment and theatre overlapping is in the case of the Cotton monument designed by Inigo Jones[50] but other, less well-known artists, were more frequently engaged in both areas. The Christmas family – leading monumental sculptors – were also renowned for their pageant designs.[51] A comparison of the design of some tombs with surviving records of pageant-arches shows how similar the conceptions were. The tomb was frequently conceived as a triumphal arch, marking the passage of the deceased from earth to heaven, and yet celebrating his secular triumphs and ancestry. A great Elizabethan tomb was expected to be read in exactly the same way as a triumphal arch on a royal entry: the only difference was that the epitaph was a permanent record of what, on the entry arch, would be spoken by a performer. The tomb of Shakespeare's patron, the Lord Chamberlain, Lord Hunsdon, in Westminster Abbey (1596), provides an easily accessible example.[52] The tomb-chest itself, flanked at the corners by four obelisks decorated with shields displaying the Carey ancestry and connections, is placed inside an arch with a coffered vault, the back of which is also embellished with strapwork ornament, heraldic devices and winged books representing the Scriptures. Further obelisks, standing forward of and surmounting the general structure, display more heraldry and achievements of arms. At the very top is a lantern, resembling that which may be seen in Hollar's engraving of the second Globe. The arch is surmounted by an achievement of arms, flanked by obelisks which stand on bases decorated with Carey beasts, urns and fruit. The inscription, in the back wall of the arch, celebrates Hunsdon's career and achievements. The imagery of the whole monument celebrates his descent (he was Elizabeth I's closest living relative), his career as a soldier, a Christian and a cultivator of the arts of peace, and, in its lavishness, his wealth.

The monument to Henry Carey, Lord Hunsdon (d. 1596), in Westminster Abbey. Hunsdon, Lord Chamberlain, was patron to Shakespeare's company, and his monument would have been made close to where the Globe was built. Note the lavish decoration and lantern over all. (By courtesy of the Dean and Chapter of Westminster)

It is conceived in the same mode as the arches erected to welcome James I into the City of London in the next decade, which likewise celebrate his ancestry, achievements and wealth, but Lord Hunsdon's lapidary inscription is designed to have a longer life than the oration spoken by Edward Alleyn to welcome the king.

Until inflation and the gradual comparative impoverishment of the nobility curtailed the custom the ceremony of the aristocratic funeral partook of the character of a royal entry, with equal emphasis on the triumphant crown of a virtuous life in the entry of the deceased into salvation and on the nobility of the deceased himself. In place of the numerous pasteboard arches of the royal entry, however, the funeral culminated in the single stone triumphal arch which was to be the deceased's permanent resting-place.[53]

The tomb of Lady Savile, d. 1631, at St Nicholas Hurst, Berkshire, probably by James White of Long Acre (Dr G.F. Fisher, personal communication). The scene of Lady Savile and her family at prayer is 'discovered' by two angels who draw back curtains. (Conway Library, Courtauld Institute of Art)

But Elizabethan and Jacobean monuments have closer affinities with the world of the stage than the fact that they were made by the same artists and to similar designs as the temporary structures erected for court pageantry. The purpose of the monument was to provide a representation of the deceased. It functions as a three-dimensional stone emblem, with the architectural surround, the effigy of the person commemorated and the text of the epitaph intended to be read as an organic whole: no one of the three elements can be fully understood without the other two. There are monuments which represent the deceased as in life, at prayer as a member of a family, taking part in a conversation with his or her spouse, or bidding a last farewell to a well-beloved corpse. In such moments we are presented with a dramatic representation of the deceased's life. The sense of our being spectators at a dramatic scene is highlighted in a group of monuments in which the scene is 'discovered' for us by attendants – usually angels, but occasionally armed men – pulling back a curtain. Even the multi-poster type of monument may become a representation of a particular moment: when the tomb-chest is surrounded by the figures of the family of the deceased, it becomes a

The tomb of Robert Cecil, 1st Earl of Salisbury, d. 1615, by Simon Basil and Maximilian Colt, at Hatfield, Hertfordshire. The effigy rests on the shoulders of the cardinal virtues – Temperance, Justice, Fortitude and Prudence – and is borne above a skeleton. (Conway Library, Courtauld Institute of Art)

representation of the wake, as the family pray beside the deathbed; or the moment of the funeral at which the bier is lowered so that the corpse may be laid in the ground is conveyed by the effigy resting on a stretcher borne on the shoulders of supporters. Such supporters may be personified virtues, representing the qualities shown by the deceased in life or they may be more concrete, so that the tomb, when the supporters of the bier are armed men, can represent the moment when the body of the hero is borne off the field of battle. In these cases the tomb has moved from the area of commemoration into that of drama – psychological or social.

The tomb of Robert Cecil, 1st Earl of Salisbury at Hatfield, where the corpse of the deceased is carried on the shoulders of four virtues above a skeleton, is a petrified allegorical drama on several levels. On the most obvious, the presence of the skeleton represents what is in fact going on in the tomb itself – it is as though the sides of a tomb-chest on which lies the effigy of the deceased as he was in life, have been taken away, showing the process of dissolution which is proceeding beneath it. On a higher level, the monument shows how Salisbury's virtues enable him to triumph over Death: he will be remembered as he was in life, even though his body has rotted, because the virtues which he displayed ensure that his fame will survive him. On the subtlest and highest level of allegory, the monument shows how Salisbury's immortal, spiritual body has been separated from his earthly body by his practice of heavenly virtues: the earthly body returns by dissolution into the earth from which it was made, while the heavenly body (represented as floating above the earth on the shoulders of the personified virtues) is borne up to heaven.

Other forms of tomb are more explicitly dramatic in their conception, showing, either as the overall conception of the tomb itself or as a subsidiary part of it, scenes from the life of the deceased. The tombs of Sir Thomas Lucy at Charlecote, Warwickshire, and of Edward West at Marsworth, Bucks, both incorporate scenes from the life of the subject. Lucy's tomb shows him engaged in his favourite pastime, hunting, while the Marsworth tomb depicts the subject on his deathbed, surrounded by his household, while Death either reveals the scene by pulling back a curtain or draws the mortal curtain which will separate West from his family for ever.

The presentation of the tomb as a dramatic event is particularly characteristic of Epiphanius Evesham, in his more common sculptural monuments as well as in the Marsworth brass. In the monument to Lord Teynham (d. 1622) at Lynstead, Kent, the whole family, although treated on different scales, are incorporated into an overall act of mourning. The tomb is surmounted by a triumphal arch, surmounted by statues of virtues, within the frame of and in front of which a representation of another ambiguously exemplary deathbed scene is enacted. Like Edward West, Lord Teynham is armed (and clothed in his peer's robes) and holds his sword. He lies supine, his open eyes directed upwards, while beside and behind him at a prie-dieu kneels his wife in her widow's weeds. Below, on the sides of the tomb-chest itself kneel groups of sons and daughters executed on a smaller scale, but still part of the monument's overall conception. The separation of the three components of the family suggests their differing status: Lord Teynham, dead, whose thoughts are now fixed only on heaven, to which his eyes are directed, and where his existence must henceforth be; Lady

The tomb of the 2nd Lord Teynham, d. 1622, by Epiphanius Evesham, at Lynstead, Kent. The different effects of Teynham's death on himself, his wife and their children are dramatized in the sculptural treatment of the different members of the family. (A. F. Kersting)

Teynham, spending her life in prayer and grief, tied to him in spirit (and therefore on the same level and scale in the monument) although separated by death (and therefore represented on the monument on a different plane and within a separate setting, although the overall design encloses and unites husband and wife), and the children, whose everyday lives have been disrupted by grief and by contemplation of their father's exemplary deathbed and their mother's devotion to him, but in whose lives this is only an interruption, and who will eventually return to their ordinary lives, and who are therefore shown on a different scale, in a different place and in a different form (bas-relief) from the life-size sculptures in the round of their parents. The bas-reliefs are also uncoloured, in contrast to the naturalistically painted figures of Lord and Lady Teynham. The whole monument becomes a three-dimensional emblem which dramatizes the family's experience of death.

What is often thought of as the most formal of all the English Renaissance tomb-types – the family lined up at prayer, usually on either side of a prie-dieu – is, in fact, one of the most informal and intimate. Such tombs represent the family not on public display, but at their private devotions, exposed only to their God. The articulation of such tombs may also be used to make important visual statements about family cohesiveness; on many of them the inclusion of both dead and living family members, several sequentially-married spouses with their respective offspring, means that the family is portrayed as it exists spiritually and will exist when reunited after death, but can never have existed on earth.

The architectural settings for these dramatic monuments may lead us to some ideas about the appearance of that area of the Elizabethan playhouse for which there is least evidence – the tiring-house façade. The similarity in form between monuments, on which frozen drama is staged, and the triumphal arches of royal entries, which formed the setting for a related form of emblematic drama, has been noted. The style of the monuments is that which was associated at the time with the setting for drama. Most modern hypothetical reconstructions of Elizabethan playhouses recognize this. Basing themselves on contemporary architectural style, and with the evidence of the Fortune contract, with its classical motifs of the pilasters and satyr-posts which formed part of its integral decoration, and the related evidence that the interior of the Swan was painted to look like marble, another element in the classicizing style of the period, they have abandoned the timber-framed rusticity of earlier reconstruction attempts and produced an interior of Elizabethan-classical style.

Some monuments may be of more specific help than in giving indications of the overall style which was associated with dramatic shows at this date. A group of them – probably from one atelier – seems to be related to one of the most disputed areas of English Renaissance drama – the discovery, in which an inset scene was revealed by the drawing-back of curtains or opening of doors. Such scenes, combined probably with a misunderstanding of the vista-stage of early perspective theatres, led early historians of the playhouse to posit the now-rejected 'inner stage'. Since its abandonment, argument has raged over whether, in addition to the two doors shown on the Swan drawing, there was a central section in the tiring-house façade which could be used for such revelation scenes; whether, as some authorities have argued, all such scenes were executed by means of substantial scenic elements moved on to the stage, or whether one of the double doors shown on the Swan façade might also double as a location for discoveries, the scene being set up behind it and either the doors opened, or a curtain drawn back, in order to reveal the spectacle. The monuments, of which one of the most substantial is the monument to Lady Savile (see illustration on p. 86), seem to show a discovery as it might have been staged in a playhouse, and may therefore show how this part of the tiring-house façade appeared. Lady Savile and her family kneel at prayer against a three-bay architectural façade, set on a platform at about head height (in terms of the scale of the monument) from the floor. This intimate moment of family piety is revealed or discovered by a pair of angels who draw curtains, which are carried on a projecting ovoid bay and are also looped over the heads of cherubs which top the pilasters dividing the façade into bays. The form of the façade, with the projection from which the curtain is suspended, is not dissimilar to some of the façades known to have been used on Netherlandish stages, and the façades in the tantalizing title-page vignettes to *Roxana* and *Messallina* (see illustration on p. 150), thought possibly to represent the interior of private indoor playhouses, also seem to be projecting in

The title-page of Roxana tragaedia *(London, A. Crook, 1632), by William Alabaster, the lower central vignette of which may represent the tiring-house façade of a private indoor playhouse. (By permission of the Syndics of Cambridge University Library)*

form, and to be covered with curtains.[54] A façade of this form would provide both a flat background with two entrances, as shown on the Swan diagram, and, with the curtains closed, accommodation for a discovery, whether or not the discovery space was accessible from the rear. If, by being based on curtains hanging from a projecting bay, the discovery-space could incorporate some of the stage, the amount of back-stage accommodation used for the discovery-space, if there was access to it from the façade, would be reduced. The Savile family are presented as a discovery: it seems possible that the background against which they are shown echoes the discovery-space of contemporary theatres.[55]

Two other monuments related to that of Lady Savile are further suggestive of the possible nature of the discovery space. They have discoveries made within oblong frames, again with curtains drawn back by supporters. That to Sir William Clarke

The monument to Sir William Clarke, d. 1625, in St Mary's, Hitcham, Buckinghamshire. Two soldiers draw back curtains to reveal a narrow rectangular discovery-space. (RCHM England)

The monument to Ninian Burrell, d. 1628, at Cuckfield, Sussex, showing curtains suspended over a small discovery-space. (Norman Hammond)

(d. 1625) at Hitcham, Buckinghamshire has the curtains drawn back by figures of soldiers, revealing a narrow rectangular discovery-space, such as might have been produced by the arrangement of rear-stage hangings shown on the *Messallina* vignette. Both the title-page vignettes show the curtains suspended by a series of integral loops which would allow for a substantial pole to support them, and split in the middle to allow access to the stage, but they do not give any indication that they could be moved horizontally along their support. The curtains on the Savile tomb are pulled back and up by the flanking angels, and do not give any indication of horizontal movement. At Cuckfield in Sussex, however, there is a discovery-monument which illustrates in some detail how curtains might be suspended and drawn back; it shows curtains sewn over a pole, and pulled back along it, enclosing a small discovery-space, such as might have been set up either within an entrance-door or within a specially-constructed space on a tiring-house façade. A discovery-space constructed on this model would presuppose a jettied tiring-house façade, but, judging from the Fortune contract, the galleries of the playhouses were jettied in any case, and Hodges posits a projecting upper-storey for the façades in his Rose reconstructions exhibited at the Museum of London in 1991, although he also includes a recessed discovery-space, rather than one simply formed by the suspension of curtains from the projecting portion of the façade, as shown on the monuments.

The monument to Richard Boyle, Earl of Cork, d. 1643, by Alexander Hills of Holborn, at Youghal, Ireland. This shows human beings placed against a three-level façade. (Photograph courtesy Bord Fáilte)

The Savile tomb suggests other possible affinities with the tiring-house façade. The relative heights of its three elements – base, three-section background to the kneeling figures, and third storey – may indicate the proportions of the architectural backdrops against which the human figure was expected to be viewed. The third storey of the monument, which is used for a display of an achievement of arms, is centrally placed, and in the situation of the hypothetical gallery of the Renaissance playhouse. Other monuments display the same proportions and three-level structure. The tomb of Richard, Earl of Cork, at Youghal, Republic of Ireland, uses the third storey (which it shares with contemporary tombs) for the display of figures. It seems that this architectural proportion was thought at the time to be that against which the human figure might correctly be displayed. It is unlikely that theatre designers would differ from sculptors on this matter.

The tiring-house façade can itself become a monument. In *Antony and Cleopatra* (IV.xv), the dying Antony is hoisted aloft to Cleopatra, who is on the upper stage level, representing an opening in the façade of her monument. Theatre historians have been intrigued by the ways in which the scene might have been staged,[56] but if, as has been suggested, the façade against which the scene was played resembled a contemporary monument in its construction, then Antony and Cleopatra, displayed on it in the postures adopted by the deceased and bereaved on tombs, would become their own monument.

DISSEMINATION OF THE CLASSICAL STYLE

The three-bay façade with a triple opening is, indeed, a common feature in material remains contemporary with the great playhouses, and provides suggestive material on which to base playhouse reconstructions. It was through smaller, comparatively portable, artefacts, such as monuments and items of furniture, rather than through the great prodigy houses which were erected at this period, that the Elizabethan classical style was first disseminated, not only geographically but also socially; furnishings are available to the prosperous middle classes when prodigy houses are not. The erection of the public playhouses, revolutionary as they seem to have been architecturally, took place in the context of an unprecedented frenzy of construction and reconstruction among all classes from the yeomanry upwards,[57] and they should be placed in a context in which new building and new movements in architecture and arts were being embraced by all social classes. A chest in Southwark Cathedral provides a good example.[58] It is thought to have been executed about 1585 in Southwark by immigrant German and Flemish craftsmen, who had settled in the area for the same reasons that those concerned with the entertainment industry chose to erect their buildings there – to evade the restrictions imposed by the City of London. These were craftsmen working in a classical style in precisely the same area and at the same time as the great playhouses were being built. The chest shows a monumental three-bay façade.[59] The visual language here is again classical; the conception of the central massive arch similar to that of the Hunsdon tomb. It is perhaps to works such as this rather than to hall screens that we should look in order to see how Shakespeare's contemporaries

A chest, c. 1588, in Southwark Cathedral, bearing the arms of Hugh Offley, from a Southwark workshop, other products of which survive at Hardwick and Arundel. (Jarrold Publishing)

conceived a three-opening façade, and therefore how the tiring-house façades of their playhouses may have looked.

Although there is only the Swan drawing of the tiring-house façade of a playhouse, there is a consistency in contemporary depictions of the architecture which was conceived suitable for the display of human figures and actions. The title-page to Ben Jonson's *Workes* of 1616, which is packed with visual allusions to both ancient and contemporary theatre, is conceived as a triple-bayed monument in which figures of Tragedy and Comedy stand in front of curtains draped across the front of niches on either side of a central space in which is situated the title of the book (see illustration on p. 22). Above are further figures, Satire and Pastoral, the whole composition surmounted by the crowned figure of Tragi-Comedy. The central opening is covered by a canopy borne on columns, although the stage in front of it is recessed to provide accommodation for the printer's trade-mark, and the upper corners are surmounted by laurel-wreathed obelisks.[60] There are three representations of what were conceived to be the forms of ancient theatre: a Greek amphitheatre, a players' cart, and a Roman theatre, in which, as has been frequently pointed out, there is visible an Elizabethan stage-hut, carried on columns above the stage. The similarity between this monumental title-page, funerary sculpture and the temporary monuments erected for pageants is clear: here the action (the title of the book) is raised up on a stage, and the two levels on which action takes place are clearly delineated by the figures of the various types of drama to be found in the book. The curtains draped across the niches behind Tragedy and Comedy are interesting in view of the suggestions that the discovery-space may have been achieved by means of a concealing curtain.

This type of title-page seems to be particularly associated with works which have or claim dramatic associations. The title-page of John Speed's *The Theatre of the Empire of Great Britaine* (1616) again adopts the form of a monument against which the various actors in the drama of the historical formation of the British people are displayed. The triple-bayed façade, in which the text that explains the action is centrally placed on a stage under a canopy, supports major figures – Roman, Saxon, Briton, Dane and Norman, all in carefully distinguished costumes. There are upper and lower levels on which the figures are placed. Subordinate elements in the design relate to the prosperity and martial history of Britain, to its learning, power and fame. This title-page is both a celebration of the history and ancestry of the British and a warning: a monitory monument.

The title-page of John Speed's The Theatre of the Empire of Great Britaine *(1616), showing a monumental façade. (By permission of The British Library G. 7884)*

WORDS AND IMAGES

There is a consistency of vision in what was conceived of as monumental at this date. Title-pages, funerary sculpture and the less permanent structures which welcomed and celebrated royalty on their progresses are all conceived in identical visual language, form and imagery. The same language may be seen in chimney-pieces, often a medium for the display of dynastic triumphalist images in the houses of the upper classes. These vehicles all have in common the fact that they are envisaged, to a greater or lesser extent as 'speaking pictures': images which are to be read, both verbally and visually, in order to achieve a full understanding of their import.

The title-page of Jonson's *Workes* makes claims about his own rootedness in the traditions of classical theatre; about his status as a poet who should be measured with the great masters of Greece and Rome; about the comprehensiveness of his achievement, his mastery of all dramatic genres, and, through the linkage with the literature of the ancients, about the status of English as a language and the British as a people, who should also be grouped with Greece and Rome. This impression, gained from the visual elements of the design, is reinforced by the Latin labels and quotations, and by the title of the book – the only English poet whose complete works had previously been published was Chaucer; otherwise the distinction was reserved for classical authors. Speed's title-page conveys a similar, but even more complex message. Its title indicates that the book is to be a display of the islands which go to make up Great Britain, and its figures, and other subordinate visual elements in the design, indicate that the display of Great Britain will not be simply geographical, but that the atlas is also a historical enterprise. As with Jonson, there is an element of classicizing patriotism in the work: it is a celebration of the antiquity as well as the present glory of the British Isles, and the presence of the Roman on the title-page indicates that Great Britain is the direct descendant and equal of ancient Rome. The title pages proclaim the content of the books, which are themselves speaking pictures: Speed's maps, inset vignettes and commentary combine to provide a comprehensive geography and history of the British Isles. The texts of Jonson's plays are designed to form the spoken part of the ultimate development of the spoken picture: the contemporary theatre.

The vision of the organic combination of words and pictures as being essential to the integrated art form is most clearly apparent in an area of entertainment in which Jonson felt that words eventually lost out to pictures – the court masque. Jonson's *An Expostulacion with Inigo Jones* includes, among all its vituperation, a lament for the supremacy that the pictures have gained over the speaking:

> What is the cause you pompe it so? I aske,
> And all men eccho, you have made a Masque.
> I chyme that too: And I have mett with those
> That doe cry up the machine, and the Showes!
> The majesty of Juno in the Cloudes,
> And peering forth of Iris in the Shrowdes!
> Th'ascent of Lady Fame which none could spy,
> Not they that sided her, Dame Poetry,
> Dame History, Dame Architecture too,
> And Goody Sculpture, brought with much adoe
> To hold her up. O Showes! Showes! Mighty Showes!
> The Eloquence of Masques! What need of prose
> Or Verse, or Sense t'express Immortal you?
> You are the Spectacles of State! 'Tis true
> Court Hieroglyphicks! and all Artes affoord
> In the mere perspective of an Inch board!
> You aske noe more then certeyne politique Eyes,
> Eyes that can pierce into the Misteryes
> Of many Coulors! read them! and reveale
> Mythology there painted on slit deale!

> Oh, to make Boardes to speake! There is a taske!
> Painting and Carpentry are the Soule of Masque!
> Pack with your pedling Poetry to the Stage!
> This is the money-gett, Mechanick Age!
> To plant the Musick where noe eare can reach!
> Attyre the persons as noe thought can teach
> Sense, what they are! which by a specious fyne
> Terme of the Architects is called Designe!
> But in the practisd truth Destruction is
> Of any Art, besyde what he calls his! [61]

Jonson is lamenting the impoverishment which he sees as coming from the domination of designer over poet. The allegories have to be unsubtle and obvious (Juno; Iris; the Arts) or their meaning will escape the spectators (no one can understand the costumes). Instead of being educated by a complex politico-religious argument, the spectators are left to be amazed by expensive but shallow transformation scenes and other effects. Even the music is so subordinated to the exigencies of Design that it has to be situated where the audience cannot hear it. Ben Jonson's argument is based on a good deal of personal rancour, but the importance he places on the word is not invalidated by this. If Jones dismisses poetry to the public stage, and is endorsed in his efforts by the private court, where he now dominates, then the court is condemned as shallow, mercenary and base.

PLAYHOUSE DECORATION

But before the triumph of the mere show, at the period of the building of the great playhouses, and their private equivalents the visual incorporated the verbal: later generations' assertions that the playhouses were plain refers more to the absence of elaborate scenic effects, such as may now be seen in the wonderfully preserved Swedish court theatre at Drottningholm, rather than to any primitiveness in their decoration. The visual language of art, architecture and craftsmanship at the time of the building of the playhouses was elaborate

Painted sky decoration from the western gallery of Rycote Chapel, Oxfordshire – perhaps an indication of how the 'heavens' of playhouses were decorated. (English Heritage Photo Library)

The tomb of Sir Robert Dormer, d. 1552, at Wing, Buckinghamshire, showing plasterwork beneath the canopy and a cover carried on pillars. (Conway Library, Courtauld Institute of Art)

and complex: there is no reason to doubt that the playhouses – described by their contemporaries, used to an elaborate visual language, as 'gorgeous' even by their own standards – were built using the same vocabulary. The place to look for the style in which the theatres must have been built is not only in the Swan drawing and other scanty records, but in the show art and architecture of the period. We will learn far more by looking at structures such as Hunsdon's tomb than by looking at Anne Hathaway's cottage.

The tombs may give an idea of the style of decoration which was being practised in Southwark at the time that five of the major amphitheatres were built there, but one must not carry these parallels too far. John Orrell suggests that the decoration of the heavens, or stage-cover, may have been of elaborate plaster-work, such as may be seen in the ceilings of great houses or the coffering of contemporary tombs.[62] Elaborate plasterwork was extremely expensive, and weighty, although its intricate surface would have improved the quality of the heavens as a sounding-board. If the stage-cover was decorated as a literal heavens – either with a zodiac or with a representation of the sky – and this is only an assumption, based on what may be an over-literal reading of contemporary playtexts – then the sort of decoration visible in the western gallery of

Rycote Chapel, Oxfordshire seems more likely than the sort of elaborate plaster programme visible at a house such as Blickling Hall. If plaster decoration was used, then it is more likely to have been of the restrained type visible under the canopy of the tomb of Sir Robert Dormer at Wing, Buckinghamshire[63] – another example of the pure classicism which was available in the country at this date, and which provides a potential model for the pillar-carried stage-cover of the playhouses.

Our view of Elizabethan decorative schemes is coloured by the way that we now perceive them: frequently stripped of their original paint by the chaster taste of later generations, the wood weathered and faded by age, or blackened with the accretions of centuries. Hunsdon's tomb seems unacceptably gaudy. But the playhouse Hunsdon's players built was almost certainly as gaudy as their master's tomb, and the tasteful wood-tones in which the panelling of Elizabethan interiors is

Internal porch from Montacute House, Somerset (c. 1590), showing a three-bay façade. (Norman Hammond)

now presented should not make us believe that they were always so quiet. In houses such as Hardwick, where the original decorative schemes have in part survived, they indicate that the temporal houses of the Elizabethans were just as gaudy as their eternal ones.

The decorative schemes of great houses may help with the theoretical reconstruction of now vanished buildings. Montacute in Somerset, begun in about 1590, has an internal porch in its first-floor library.[64] On each of its three sides above the doorway is represented the typical three-bay façade of the period, with a pair of doors flanking, in this case, a central square space. These spaces each bear the words, 'Hoc Age' – which may be translated as 'Act this' or 'Perform this'. Why the builder of Montacute, Sir Edward Phelips, Speaker of the House of Commons and Master of the Rolls, should have wished to include this decoration in his house, and what significance its injunction had for him, is unknown, but it must be added to the number of possible contemporary representations of the façade of a contemporary playhouse – the doors representing the entrances, and the central square the space which might be used for discoveries but which in any case would be the area against which the principal action would have been played.

The sixteenth-century western gallery at Bishop's Cleeve, Gloucestershire, showing the construction of a scaffold or seating gallery. (Norman Hammond)

The façade of a house in Bridge Street, Cambridge, showing three-storey jettying, as specified in the contract for the Fortune. (Norman Hammond)

The tiring-house façade was common to both public and private playhouses, although not necessarily identical, and the three-bay façades shown in the Southwark chest, the Montacute doorcase, and a number of church monuments, as well as the discovery scene shown on Lady Savile's monument and those related to it, accord well with the more substantial evidence available about the appearance of the stage in the later private playhouses.[65] Both types of playhouse included a great deal of woodwork, and the principal source used for reconstruction of this aspect of the buildings has been the hall screens of great houses. But again the interior of ecclesiastical buildings may provide a wider body of examples of contemporary woodwork, in forms which would have been needed in playhouse construction. The church at Bishop's Cleeve in Gloucestershire has a Jacobean musicians' gallery, which is an example of the 'scaffold' put up for the accommodation of spectators and closer to the Swan drawing than reconstructions which are essentially based on contemporary house façades with galleries inserted in the place of windows. The screen at Holdenby in Northamptonshire (1580) uses the Netherlands-classical vocabulary of contemporary monumental sculpture, but in a refined and restrained form: it provides as valid a model for playhouse

The 1580 screen at Holdenby, Northamptonshire, showing a restrained interpretation of the classical style in woodwork. (Norman Hammond)

woodwork as the heavily encrusted and elaborate screens of places such as the Middle Temple.

The great playhouses were built at considerable cost, as we know from Henslowe's accounts; they were condemned for their lavishness, and must have been decorated in a florid style. The prodigy houses of the sixteenth and seventeenth centuries are examples of public art – but the public art of the aristocracy, not of the classes who were involved in playhouse construction. Public art on their more modest scale can be found in ecclesiastical buildings, and it is there that we should look for parallels to what was being done in the playhouses of the time.

CHAPTER FIVE

COSTUME

The major expenditure for any Elizabethan theatre company, and its major assets apart from its playbooks (unless it owned its own playhouse), were its costumes. When the Globe burnt down in 1613, the King's Men's major loss, apart from the playhouse itself, would have been the costumes accumulated over the previous twenty years. The playbooks, or at least some of them were saved, or duplicate copies existed, as the publication of Shakespeare's *Works* proves, but if the costumes were stored in the Globe, and were not rescued in time, then a major capital asset had gone. The performance conditions in the playhouses meant that illusions attempted by the substitution of cheap for more expensive materials were unlikely to be particularly convincing, and clothes, as labour-intensive manufactured products, frequently using imported materials, were very expensive.[1] When Henslowe was consistently paying more for a single costume than for a new playbook[2] it is not surprising that the worst sin in the hired man's potential repertoire was leaving the playhouse wearing a costume, or letting any other member of the company do so. The fine for this was £40 compared with 10s for turning up drunk for a performance.[3] Foreign visitors were credibly informed that the theatre provided a market for the cast-off clothes of the aristocracy.[4]

Nor was it only on stage that the gorgeousness of the players' costumes was noted. Despite the fact that most surviving portraits of players show them in the clothes of the wealthy citizen or the scholar, hostile report credited them with sumptuousness in their attire.[5] For the contemporaries of the Elizabethan actors, such finery was subversive and threatening. The multiplicity of attempted sumptuary legislation[6] reflects the anxiety of a changing age that social barriers were being broken, that it was no longer possible to distinguish the gentleman from the common man by clothes, that the luxurious prerogatives of the aristocracy were being usurped by the merely rich. The rich clothes of the players reflected their marginal status: unclassifiable in terms of social station, obtaining their living not from rents, nor from trade, nor from manufacture, but from pretending to be what they were not; they emphasized their falsely-derived status by wearing their borrowed robes outside as well as inside the playhouse. As nominally gentlemen's servants, they should have worn their livery. When Shakespeare's company received the patronage of the King, livery was one of the rewards of that strengthened its position. The presentation of actors in their portraits as either respectable rich citizens or men of letters may be seen as an affirmation of their true social status in the face of public disparagement and distrust.

The knowledge that the players purchased discarded aristocratic wardrobes, together with various anachronistic references to details of contemporary costume in plays set in the classical past has led to the assertion that Elizabethan costuming was contemporary,

The monument to William Shakespeare, d. 1616, by Gerard Johnson the Younger, in Holy Trinity, Stratford-upon-Avon. Shakespeare is depicted in the dress of a scholar. (Conway Library, Courtauld Institute of Art)

no matter what the ostensible period of the play in production. The true situation is more complicated.

THE USE OF CONTEMPORARY DRESS

The dearth of illustrations of contemporary plays, and the fact that the bulk of those illustrated were set in contemporary imaginary kingdoms, means that most of the illustrations that exist show Elizabethan actors in Elizabethan costume. Even in these plays, visual classification by costume takes place. Costume is used to proclaim social status (in *Twelfth Night* the gradations of Olivia's household – mistress, waiting-gentlewoman, jester, servant, poor relation, steward, and social-climbing hanger-on – are all proclaimed through costume) and to announce avocation. Shakespeare's plays contain cardinals (*Henry VIII*), friars (*Romeo and Juliet*), bishops (*Richard III*), archbishops (*Henry V*), scholars (*The Taming of the Shrew*), shepherds (*As You Like It*), reapers and nymphs (*The Tempest*), seamen (*Hamlet*), soldiers (*Henry VI*), nuns (*Measure for Measure*), conjurers (*The Comedy of Errors*), schoolteachers (*The Merry Wives of Windsor*), doctors (*Macbeth*), and a host of other professions. Just as in a modern play a postman is proclaimed by his uniform, a doctor by his bag, in a visual shorthand which saves time on exposition, so the Elizabethan playhouse, whatever the chronological setting of its offerings, had a great need for a wide variety of vocational costumes. These needs can be seen being met in Henslowe's 1598 inventory of his company's costumes.[7] They included costumes for senators (presumably, since there were caps with them, Venetian, rather than Roman, senators), janizaries, soldiers and friars, Danes and shepherds, some no doubt made or bought for specific plays, but all instantly recognizable by the audience, labelling the actors who wore them without the need for further explanation.[8]

Besides these there were in Henslowe's possession a great many costumes of unspecified purpose – the contemporary clothes which we associate with our idea of Elizabethan stage production. A 'murey lether gyrcken' and a 'white lether gercken' were costumes for general use, as were 'ij black saye gownes, and ij cotton gownes, and j rede

The title-page of Thomas Kyd's The Spanish Tragedy *(rev. edn, London, Augustine Mathewes, 1633: first published 1592), showing actors in contemporary dress. (By permission of the Syndics of Cambridge University Library)*

saye gowne'. More interesting are costumes linked with specific roles and plays. There was a group of green costumes for the Robin Hood plays (Antony Munday's *The Downfall* and *The Death of Robert Earl of Huntington,* which were a hit for the Admiral's Men in 1598). Henry V's doublet and his velvet gown were missing from the costume store, along with eight other items, but there were costumes for Merlin, Will Somers (as well as other clowns' and fools' costumes), 'Eves bodeyes' (perhaps a leather suit representing the naked body of Eve before her fall), hose for the Dauphin, a pair of hose and a jerkin for Vortigern, and 'ij leather anteckes cottes with basses, for Fayeton'. These were in addition to what might be classified as monster costumes, such as a firedrake's suit, a costume for Neptune, animal skins, and a robe for to 'goo invisibell'. They are not simply costumes for particular actors (some of these do appear in the inventory, attached either to the 'leading lady', John Pigg, who was still a child, or to other actors, who may have been difficult to fit) but seem to be specific costumes for specific parts. With production costs confined to costumes and portable properties, such as those also itemized in the 1598 inventory, it was through costumes that theatrical illusion must principally have been created and maintained.

The nature of the characters for whom the specific costumes are itemized is interesting: they are not solely the sort of parts to be played by Alleyn or Pigg, the company's leading man and lady. The large number of green costumes for the Robin Hood plays shows that the Lincoln-green costume so irrevocably associated with the Robin Hood legend was reproduced on the stage, even though the plays purported to be the Elizabethan equivalent of historical docu-drama, giving the real story of Robin Hood, stripped of the accretion of popular legend. Merlin presumably needed a special costume because he was a wizard, although there were enough magicians and enchanters in Elizabethan drama for it to have been worthwhile for the companies to carry a generalized enchanter's costume as part of their stock, if costumes were arranged on a contemporary basis.

ATTEMPTS AT HISTORICAL ACCURACY

The costumes for Henry V, for 'Longshanks' (also lost) and for Vortigern suggest that, rather than putting kings into contemporary costume, there was an attempt at historical authenticity. Illustrations to contemporary history show that the Elizabethans did not

A tomb to a medieval member of the Poyntz family, at North Ockenden, Essex, put up in 1606, showing a version of medieval costume (but note the Ionic columns). (Conway Library, Courtauld Institute of Art)

'A woman nighbour [sic] to the Pictes', by John White, from Theodore de Bry's America *(Frankfurt, 1590), shows that the New World influenced White's conception of the British past. (By permission of the Syndics of Cambridge University Library)*

envisage their ancestors wearing the same clothes as themselves. They were aware that the armour and costume of the past were different from those which they wore, although they may not have got the details correct. A group of tombs put up to ancestors, real or imagined, provide examples of contemporary antiquarian imaginings. In his *The Theatre of the Empire of Great Britaine*, John Speed distinguishes between the costumes worn by the various ancestors of the modern British, and, although his depictions lack historical correctness, they are not merely Jacobean dress. The image of Henry V known to Speed and his contemporaries was widely popularized through royal portrait sets.

The input of contemporary anthropology into historical imaginings is well-known: John White's studies of the New World indigenes were translated into pictures of the early inhabitants of the British Isles, who were assumed (correctly) to have been a society at a parallel stage of development. When Speed illustrated Boudicca and her Roman opponent, he gave the Roman classical armour while putting Boudicca into a plausible version of what a barbarian warrior-queen might have worn at that date: she has a plainer version of the Roman body-armour, but her bare legs and feet proclaim her barbarity. A contemporary image of an Amazon, while obviously related to the image of Boudicca, looks different: she is shod, her armour is more elaborate, she is coiffed and decorated. The image of Boudicca has been pared down to the essentials of warrior-womanhood, without the veneer of civilization.

Even when Boudicca is shown in a costume closer to that worn by the Elizabethans, there are still some adaptations: her costume bears some relationship to the coronation robes of a sixteenth-century queen, as reconstructed by Janet Arnold,[9] but the flowing garments, not to mention the pet hare, all mark this woman out as a barbarian queen, one who lived in a period in which the flowing line of the clothes echoed the unrestricted nature of the passions. Boudicca is not simply seen as a sixteenth-century English queen: her costume is not historically accurate, but it is carefully differentiated from that of the period which is depicting her. This is what the Elizabethans thought the Iceni looked like: that they were wrong does not mean that there was no attempt at authenticity or use of historical imagination. Historical costumes as interpreted

A Roman and Boudicca, from John Speed's The Theatre of the Empire of Great Britaine *(London, John Sudbury and George Humble, 1611), showing contemporary ideas of Roman and barbarian costume. (By permission of the Syndics of Cambridge University Library)*

through the nineteenth and twentieth centuries have remained firmly of their period, even while they have striven for authenticity: we no longer dress our Robin Hoods in the lines worn by Errol Flynn, though the Lincoln green has remained constant since Henslowe's time.[10]

PERFORMANCE PRACTICE – THE PEACHAM SKETCH OF *TITUS ANDRONICUS*

The rapid turnover of plays in the Elizabethan playhouse (between 31 May and 18 July 1596, Henslowe put on twenty-two different plays at the Rose)[11] meant that costumes for an entire production were impractical: most subsidiary characters would be dressed out of the playhouse stock. But it does appear from Henslowe's diary that the principals in plays where contemporary dress was not appropriate were given special costumes, and occasionally (as with Munday's Robin Hood plays) a large number of costumes would be made for a single production. The audience would be presented with an eclectic group of costumes, in which the principals were appropriately dressed but the rest of the cast wore an assortment of more or less appropriate garb. That this

The title-page of Sir Philip Sidney's The Countess of Pembroke's Arcadia *(London, William Ponsonbie, 1598), showing Pyrocles disguised as an Amazon to the right of the title. His cousin Musidorus, disguised as a shepherd, stands to the left. (By permission of the Syndics of Cambridge University Library)*

was the case is confirmed in the one contemporary drawing of a Shakespearean play: the sketch, ascribed to Henry Peacham, which illustrates an extract from *Titus Andronicus* (at one point in its history among Henslowe's productions at the Rose).

This drawing presents problems. It is dated to about 1595, at the time when the play was in the repertoire at the Rose. The scene as illustrated, however, does not appear in the text as printed, and the passage it illustrates is a hybrid drawn from both the first scene of the play, and from Act V, Scene i – set-piece speeches, consisting of Tamora's plea for her son's life and Aaron's credo of evil. It may not reflect an actual performance, but be an imaginative response by the copyist to extracts from a contemporary hit.[12] The male principals in the scene – Titus, Aaron and the two of Tamora's three sons shown – wear variations on a version of Roman armour (Henslowe's inventory contained an 'antique' costume for Phaethon). Titus's costume looks overall the most authentic. He wears a square-shouldered corselet over what may be either bare arms or a short-sleeved shirt, buskins on his feet and calves, a cloak draped toga-wise across

his body and a conqueror's laurel wreath. His lower body is hidden by the cloak, but the other male characters are wearing the paned skirts associated with Roman armour: this is presumably also Titus's costume. Of the other characters, Tamora's fairer son seems to be wearing a costume similar to Titus's, but without the laurel wreath, while the darker son has his Roman corselet and skirt over what may be a doublet with striped sleeves or may be meant to represent contemporary plate armour, which he may also be wearing on his legs and feet. Parallels for both these costumes may be found in Speed's title page and his picture of Boudicca's conqueror. Aaron is wearing black face and body make-up,[13] and his costume is more barbaric. He wears a full-sleeved shirt under his Roman corselet and buskins on his bare legs. A scarf is tied round his head. Tamora wears a crown on her loose hair, and a loose garment with embroidered sleeves and spotted, split hanging sleeves, possibly belonging to an

Boudicca, from Raphael Holinshed's Chronicles of England, Scotlande, and Irelande *(London, L. Harrison, 1577). Boudicca's costume has elements both of sixteenth-century coronation robes and of barbarian costume. (By permission of the Syndics of Cambridge University Library)*

A drawing c. 1595, attributed to Henry Peacham, illustrating extracts from William Shakespeare's Titus Andronicus. *The principals are in Roman dress; the minor characters are dressed more haphazardly. (Longleat House: Reproduced by permission of the Marquess of Bath, Longleat House, Warminster, Wiltshire)*

overgown. Her costume bears no resemblance to contemporary female outer garments, and must symbolize her barbarity. The major characters in this scene are all costumed appropriately for roles in a play which deals with conflicts between ancient Romans and barbarous Goths. But the minor characters – two soldiers who stand behind Titus – are dressed in contemporary soldiers' costumes, with bonnets and armour, such as one would expect the wardrobe of a playhouse to provide. (This anachronistic mixing of costume styles is the strongest argument in favour of the drawing's reflecting actual playhouse practice.)

THE EVIDENCE OF MASQUES AND PORTRAITS

The principal sources that have been searched in an attempt to discover how Shakespeare's plays might have been costumed in his theatre have been the masque designs of Inigo Jones and those portraits of Shakespeare's contemporaries which show them wearing either masque costume or fancy dress. Jones's designs show many parallels with the classicism of the Titus drawing, but a better idea of what contemporary ideas of Roman dress were may be gained from the Holles monuments in Westminster Abbey. The dead men are commemorated in the guise of antique Romans, and are wearing the same costume as that shown in the Jones designs and the Peacham drawing.

It has been the custom to celebrate Jones's innovation as a theatre designer, and to emphasize his reliance on various pattern-books that illustrated costumes of different countries and periods.[14] In fact Jones was working, at least as far as costume design goes, within a tradition which was already well-established in England, dating back to at least the early years of the reign of Elizabeth I. In the picture *Queen Elizabeth and the Three Goddesses*, by the monogrammatist HE, the goddesses spring from the same idea of the classical tradition as many of Jones's Jacobean designs, a tradition observable in *Allegory of the Tudor Succession*. The corselet over the flowing skirt, the sandalled or buskined

Inigo Jones: Knight with Impresa shield – a seventeenth-century version of classical costume. (Devonshire Collection, Chatsworth. Reproduced by permission of the Chatsworth Settlement Trustees)

feet, the helmet or elaborate headgear are visible in these pictures, and reappear in Jones's designs. They are also the stuff of the allegorical figures on many church monuments. This tradition in art in England goes back at least as far as Holbein,[15] and is still visible in the early designs of Inigo Jones. We should envisage the costumes worn on the Elizabethan stage as falling, where appropriate, within this tradition.

It is a commonplace of the history of theatre design that, however much one strives for authenticity, the period at which the production must be dated is given away by the shape of the underclothes. The human body is moulded to fit the fashions of the era, and no Victorian in medieval costume can ever disguise a basic nineteenth-century silhouette. The same is true of English Renaissance art which depicts fantastic or classicizing costume. The supernatural figures in both *Allegory of the Tudor Succession* and *Queen Elizabeth and the Three Goddesses*[16] show an essentially sixteenth-century silhouette, with a tightly-fitting bodice over padded hips. Both Peace in the *Allegory* and Juno in the *Three Goddesses* have their skirts pinned up to form a padded roll in a manner which is visible in various pictures of ladies wearing wheel farthingales two decades later.[17] Peace's jacket is related in its flaring shape to the short jackets worn by ladies in some contemporary pictures. Her head-dress, with veil dependent from a caul, is like

The monument to Francis Holles, d. 1622, by Nicholas Stone, in Westminster Abbey. Holles's costume, equating him with classical heroes, is similar to those in the Peacham and Jones drawings (see illustrations on pp. 111, 112). (By courtesy of the Dean and Chapter of Westminster)

that of Elizabeth I herself. Plenty wears a more authentically classical costume as she juggles with her cornucopia and Elizabeth's train, but, despite her bared breast and fluttering draperies, she shows the bulging outline at the hip which is so characteristic of women's costume at this date. Mars, attendant on Mary I and Philip of Spain, wears the same version of classical male costume, apparently with leather cuirass and bases,

Queen Elizabeth and the Three Goddesses, by monogrammatist HE. The goddesses – from left to right: Juno, Minerva and Venus (with Cupid) – are defeated by Elizabeth. (The Royal Collection © Her Majesty The Queen)

visible in the Holles monuments and the *Titus Andronicus* drawing. The *Three Goddesses* gives some idea of how Tamora's costume may have been made up. Venus has discarded an embroidered smock, usually worn as an undergarment or for moments of relaxation.[18] Although there is a portrait of a pregnant lady wearing such a garment under a gown,[19] the usual associations of such garments in art are with unrestrained passion, and it would be appropriate for the rapacious Tamora to be thus costumed. Her crown is like that worn by Juno in the *Three Goddesses*, and is part of the conventions of role-playing costume at the date, since it bears no resemblance to contemporary royal crowns, of which Elizabeth I is herself wearing an example in the picture.

The loose mantles worn or discarded by the three goddesses are the stuff of contemporary masquerade rather than a feature of everyday clothing, and seem to be frequently – though not invariably – associated with classical or classicizing settings. Pyrocles disguised as an Amazon wears one both in his portrait on the title-page of Sidney's *The Countess of Pembroke's Arcadia*, and in Sidney's description of him, which it is worth quoting in full:

Allegory of the Tudor Succession, *attributed to Lucas de Heere. Mars follows Philip II and Mary Tudor on the left, while Elizabeth ushers in Peace and Plenty on the right, as Henry VIII hands his sword to Edward VI. (National Museums and Galleries of Wales (on loan to Sudeley Castle))*

Well might he perceive the hanging of her hair in fairest quantity in locks, some curled and some as it were forgotten, with such a careless care and an art so hiding art that she seemed she would lay them for a pattern whether nature simply or nature helped by cunning be the more excellent: the rest whereof was drawn into a coronet of gold richly set with pearl, and so joined all over with gold wires and covered with feathers of divers colours that it was not unlike to an helmet, such a glittering show it bare, and so bravely it was held up from the head. Upon her body she ware a doublet of sky-colour satin, covered with plates of gold and, as it were, nailed with precious stones that in it she might seem armed. The nether part of her garment was so full of stuff and cut after such a fashion, that though the length of it reached to the ankles, yet in her going one might sometimes discern the small of her leg, which with the foot was dressed in a short pair of crimson velvet buskins, in some places open, as the ancient manner was, to show the fairness of the skin. Over all this she ware a certain mantle made in such manner, that coming under her right arm and covering most of that side, it had no fastening on the left side but only upon the top of her shoulder, where the two ends met and were closed together with a very rich jewel. . . . On the same side, on her thigh she ware a sword which, as it witnessed her to be an Amazon or one following that profession, so it seemed but a needless weapon, since her other forces were without withstanding.[20]

Sidney's novel is set in an imaginary ancient Greece, and its characters are clothed in the classical style thought appropriate to such settings. What is described in the picture of the Amazon is a young man engaged in a masquerade, wearing a costume rather than authentic garments. The rich materials which he wears – velvet, jewels, gold wire – combine to form the appearance of armour, but it is armour of the type which would be worn for a fancy-dress party, rather than a battle.

There exist a number of portraits of this date in which the sitters are wearing fancy dress or masque costume, and they share the characteristics of the illustration to the *Arcadia*, the *Titus Andronicus* drawing and the two allegorical royal pictures. The sitters wear an Elizabethanized version of what was conceived to be appropriate wear for whatever role they wished to be seen as adopting. The *Rainbow Portrait* of Elizabeth I should be compared with Sidney's description of Pyrocles as an Amazon. Elizabeth's wig, part curled, part allowed to flow in loose ringlets, matches his. Her head-dress (based on a picture from a costume-book) is constructed on a wired framework. Her mantle, passing over one shoulder and under the other arm, reflects the line of that described as being worn by Pyrocles. Other aspects of Elizabeth's costume are more clearly of their date: the elaborate ruff and veil flowing from its wire frame, the embroidered bodice, the emblematic jewels, the line of the farthingale showing under the folds of the cloak over the Queen's right hip.[21] The mantle worn across the body seems to be a marker of a masquing costume: it occurs in portraits by both Gheeraedts and Larkin where the sitters are in masque costumes, short petticoats convenient for dancing topped with embroidered jackets, rather than elaborate gowns.[22] Masque costumes are marked by their comparative brevity, observable in both Inigo Jones's designs, and in the paintings of ladies wearing the costumes made from them. Jones's early designs often combine these short dresses with diagonally draped mantles. The diagonal mantle is featured in the *Titus* drawing, and a related motif, of a mantle cast round the shoulders, is observable in some portraits where the sitters may be intending to suggest antique costume, indicated by the low necklines and absence of shirts.

Other portraits of Elizabethans and Jacobeans wearing fancy dress show the same adaptation of alien costume to contemporary native shapes. Lady Elizabeth Pope is probably intending to be an Indian maid wearing a sari, but she misunderstands the nature of the garment, turning herself into an Amazon, her naked left breast concealed under her flowing hair, and wearing a version of the masculine turban. The feather motif embroidered on the material and stuck into her turban suggests that there may have been a confusion between subcontinental and American Indians, so that she is indeed intending to be a New World Amazon, the feathers-and-sari combination implying both. Her flowing hair, while appropriate to an unmarried young woman, suggests the unrestrained passions of the barbarian or noble savage appropriate to her forest environment.[23]

Another young woman lost in the heart's forest appears in the picture at Hampton Court of a young woman in fancy dress (see illustration on p. 44). The source of her

ION SINE SOLE
IRIS.

The Rainbow Portrait of Queen Elizabeth I, *by Marcus Gheeraedts the Younger, showing the type of costume worn in masques before Inigo Jones is known to have been involved in their design. (Courtauld Institute/Hatfield House: by courtesy of the Marquess of Salisbury)*

Lucy Harington, Countess of Bedford, in masque costume, *attributed to John de Critz.*
The costume is believed to be for the masque Hymenaei, *performed on 5 January 1606.*
Portraits are extant of two other ladies in the same costume. (By kind permission of the
Marquess of Tavistock and the Trustees of the Bedford Estate)

costume is known to be the figure of a Persian virgin from Robert Boissard's *Habitus Variarum Orbis gentium* (Antwerp, 1581), but it is too simple to describe her simply as a Persian virgin.[24] It is tempting to associate the picture with the Ditchley entertainment put on by Sir Henry Lee in 1592 for Elizabeth I, with which the *Ditchley Portrait* of Elizabeth, now in the National Portrait Gallery, is usually connected. The Hampton Court picture has a riddling sonnet inscription in the same style as that on the Ditchley picture, and part of the entertainment involved Elizabeth interpreting a series of allegorical pictures hung in a pavilion in order to free a group of enchanted knights and ladies, trapped by inconstancy. Inconstancy is the theme of the sonnet on the Hampton Court picture: the lady has been deserted for another by an inconstant lover. It may be that both the Hampton Court and Ditchley portraits were among the enchanted pictures

Lady Elizabeth Pope, c. 1615–20, attributed to Robert Peake the Elder. She is dressed as an Amazon, and may be intended to personify America, but her costume contains elements taken from India. (Tate Gallery)

which Elizabeth was invited to interpret.[25] It is possible that the lady is intended to be pregnant, but more likely that the line of her gown reflects the fact that under it she is wearing the padding for a farthingale. Only her head-dress in fact closely resembles the Persian virgin's, and that only in overall conception: it follows the general shape, and has the hanging veil, but is covered with the type of gauze puffs which may be seen on the Queen's costume in the Ditchley portrait. Her long gown does not look like that of the source, and seems to be a long, loose version of the embroidered jacket (perhaps a dressing-jacket) worn by the Countess of Southampton in the Boughton House, Northamptonshire, informal portrait of her at her toilet.[26] It is the lady's shoes which point most clearly to this being a true masque picture: they are unlike any shoe known to have been worn as part of normal attire, but strongly resemble some of those in early designs by Inigo Jones. The picture depicts a costume which comes from sources outside the classicizing tradition.

Another fancy-dress picture which falls into this category is that of Thomas Lee as an Irish knight.[27] Lee's costume is, like that of the Persian Virgin, based on an engraving by Boissard,[28] and, like the other costume, heavily adapted to Elizabethan tastes. The wild Irish knight went bare-legged in his shirt, and was armed with the circular targe and spear, such as Lee carries, but Lee's embroidered shirt is an English courtier's garment, and rather than hanging loose, it is gathered into the shape of trunk hose. He wears a contemporary jerkin, rather than an Irish mantle. His costume is intended to mark him down recognizably as Irish, rather as the kilt serves as a marker for the Scot today, and raises the question of whether Captain Macmorris, in Shakespeare's *Henry V*, written shortly after this picture was painted, would have worn a national costume of this type. A parallel to Lee's costume exists in a late masque design by Inigo Jones:[29] it is a sketch, but shares the conception of Lee's costume. Jones's Irishman also carries a mantle, and has shaggy hair, like the wild Irishman in Speed's atlas, whereas Lee tops off his barbaric costume with a neat Elizabethan haircut. The companion figure of the Scotsman in Jones's sketch, apparently wearing kilt and plaid, may give some idea of how Captain Jamy in *Henry V* might have been costumed.

The classicizing costume which served for both Romans and their barbarian enemies, and for the inhabitants of an ancient Greece of the imagination, seems also to have been adapted for the heroes of the Bible, and even for those of the European Middle Ages. The nine armed men who embellish the garden front of Montacute House in Somerset are all identically clad in the familiar Elizabethan-classical style, but they represent the Nine Worthies. Examples of art from the earlier part of the century, such as the windows of King's College Chapel, Cambridge, show this tendency to express the past in a more or less fantastic version of the costume known from Roman remains[30] – in the case of Biblical figures, often with the addition of elements of costume associated with the contemporary Levant, such as turbans. The classical-cum-

Macbeth and the Witches, from Raphael Holinshed's Chronicles of England, Scotlande, and Irelande *(London, L. Harrison, 1577). The witches are dressed in a combination of classical and Eastern styles. (By permission of the Syndics of Cambridge University Library)*

eastern style may also be associated with the supernatural, as in the picture from Holinshed's *Chronicles* of Macbeth's encounter with the three witches.

This type of costume, which should perhaps be described as 'classical-cum-eastern', may have been adopted in plays dealing with the Levant. A portrait of Tamerlane from Richard Knolles' *The Generall Historie of the Turkes* (1603) is no longer accepted as representing Edward Alleyn in the role of Marlowe's Tamburlaine,[31] but is consistent with other contemporary depictions of Levantine costume, such as that of Ptolomy on the monument to Sir Henry Savile in Merton College Chapel, Oxford. Gurr describes the picture as showing Tamerlane wearing 'an Elizabethan doublet and jerkin', but although the sleeves of the costume do indeed follow a contemporary pattern, the doublet looks as though it is skirted below the waist, and resembles elements in Vecellio's and Boissard's pictures of Turkish costume.[32] The loose coat which Tamerlane wears over his

Tamerlane from Richard Knolles's The Generall Historie of the Turkes *(London, A. Islip, 1603). Once believed to represent Alleyn as Marlowe's Tamburlaine, this shows the type of costume which the actor might have worn in the role. (By permission of the Syndics of Cambridge University Library)*

doublet is an element which seems to have been particularly associated with near-eastern costume,[33] while the elaborate cut edges of the over-sleeves and front of the garment are elements more often found in contemporary masque costume than in everyday dress.

THE EVIDENCE OF TOMB-SCULPTURE AND CARVINGS

Although, with the exception of Jones's festival designs, visual evidence for quasi-dramatic costume at this era is scanty, funerary monuments provide a body of material evidence for the presentation of figures clothed in costume other than that worn in ordinary life. As has already been noted, the worlds of funerary sculpture, court entertainment and the theatre were interconnected. The Christmases were responsible both for church monuments and for the triumphal arches erected for royal entries into the City of London.[34] Inigo Jones designed at least two church monuments still extant,[35] and was responsible for the design of a screen for Winchester Cathedral, with figures by Hubert le Sueur. Although the figures on the tomb of the first Earl of Salisbury at Hatfield, Hertfordshire, are by Maximilian Colt (see illustration on p. 87),

The monument to Sir Henry Savile, d. 1622, in the chapel of Merton College, Oxford. The four attendant figures – St John Chrysostom, Ptolomy, Euclid and Tacitus – show early seventeenth-century conceptions of early Christian, Eastern, Greek and Roman costume. Note the similarity between Ptolomy's costume and that of Tamerlane (see illustration on p. 121). (Norman Hammond)

it was ordered from Simon Basil, who is now believed to have been responsible for the design of a theatre erected in the great hall of Christ Church, Oxford.[36] Jones was one of the trustees of Edward Alleyn's foundation at Dulwich College,[37] and Alleyn himself took part in the welcome for James VI and I on his entry into London in 1603 and in 1622 discussed the designs for the second Fortune playhouse with the great art-collector, Thomas Howard, 2nd Earl of Arundel, another of the Dulwich trustees.[38] Richard Burbage and William Shakespeare were both involved in the design and execution for *impresas* for knights taking part in tournaments.[39] Peter Street supplied equipment for the construction of the 1606 Banqueting House in Whitehall, and early in his career, Nicholas Stone worked on the Banqueting House designed by Inigo Jones which replaced it, and was later involved in the manufacture of Charles I's costume for the masque *Cælum Britannicum*.[40] With this intersection of the artistic worlds in contemporary London, it seems illogical to suppose that the commercial theatre would have operated in a different visual world from everything that was going on around it.

Part of the difficulty in appreciating how consistent that visual world was is the dispersal of the evidence, particularly the material survivals. Jones's greatness as an artist is recognized because it has proved possible in the last twenty-five years to mount several spectacular exhibitions of his work, close to, and in one case in, his architectural masterpiece, the Whitehall Banqueting House.[41] For Epiphanius Evesham and Nicholas Stone there can be no such collection: their *œuvres* can be studied only in photographic archives or by means of extensive cross-country travel. The guidebooks provided in many churches do not necessarily name the sculptors of monuments, even when these are known, so casual visitors may not know what they are looking at when they admire a particular monument. To see it, one has to know that it is there, and what it is: there are few chances for the serendipitous discovery of the works of our two major native

Allegorical figures from the tomb of Sir Laurence Tanfield, d. 1625, Burford, Oxfordshire. (Norman Hammond)

Prudence, from the monument to Ludovic Stuart, Duke of Richmond and Lennox, d. 1624, by Hubert le Sueur, in Westminster Abbey. (By courtesy of the Dean and Chapter of Westminster)

seventeenth-century artists. The work of lesser sculptors is doomed to even greater neglect; probably the only work of funerary sculpture familiar to most people is Shakespeare's monument by Gerard Johnson (see illustration on p. 105), which is an unimpressive piece (the monuments at Bottesford to the Earls of Rutland from the same workshop are much finer), and probably not in its original form.[42] Visitors to Westminster Abbey tend to pass through too quickly for them to be able to appreciate the quality of the sculpture when they view the royal tombs, although these have been a major tourist attraction since at least the sixteenth century.

Although the persons commemorated on sixteenth- and seventeenth-century tombs tend to be depicted in contemporary costume, as they would have appeared in life,[43] the overall style and iconographic accessories of funerary sculpture are closely associated with the style which may be described as English Renaissance Classicism. These attendant figures are most usually virtues: the theological virtues Faith, Hope and Charity, with additions where a fourth is needed to make up the number (Truth in Westminster Abbey); or the cardinal virtues Temperance, Justice, Fortitude and Prudence, as on the tomb of the 1st Earl of Salisbury at Hatfield (see illustration on p. 87). They may be

Zenobia, Queen of Palmyra, *from* The Masque of Queens *(1609), by Inigo Jones. (Devonshire Collection, Chatsworth. Reproduced by permission of the Chatsworth Settlement Trustees)*

deities, or generalized mourning supporters, as on the monument to Henry Fryer (d. 1631) at Harlton, Cambridgeshire. The Fryer monument shows how clearly the allegorical figures (Faith, Hope, Charity; two Fames, two cherubs, and the mourning male and female caryatids) are distinguished by dress from the subjects of the tomb, naturalistically presented in contemporary costume. The real people are separated from the theoretical shadows by those abstract concepts being clothed in the classicizing conventions which are apparent in Jones's costume designs. The effect of these tombs is allied to that of the court masque, particularly the moment at the end when the masquers dance with the audience. The masquers, frequently representing allegorical or abstract concepts, are separated by their costume from the real world of the audience even while they are joined with them in the overall design/pattern of the dance.[44]

Nor is it simply allegorical figures that may be shown on tombs. Two monuments by Nicholas Stone, in Southwark Cathedral and at Writtle in Essex, show figures of harvesters.[45] Tombs at Burford and Ickford, Buckinghamshire, show New World Indians.[46] Other tombs show figures as diverse as a miner (Newland, Gloucestershire),[47] a gamekeeper (Hunsdon, Hertfordshire),[48] and a sexton (Peterborough Cathedral). Tomb sculpture records not simply the contemporary dress of the affluent classes, but a wide variety of other costume, both for persons who are not usually represented in portraiture, and for creatures of the imagination, who must still be portrayed in a manner recognizable to contemporaries if the emblematic programme of the tomb is to have any effect.

As with tombs, so with interior decoration. The coincidence of the manufacture of tombs and of chimney-pieces is well known, and the designs are often similar. Overmantels are frequently furnished with the same figures of virtues as tombs, and executed in the same convention. Even chimney-pieces which show mythological scenes, such as the Apollo piece at Hardwick adhere to the conventions of this genre. Mythological figures are not simply presented as contemporaries in extra-pretty dresses with a few mythological details stuck on, as is the case with the masquers in the Sir Henry Unton biographical portrait in the National Portrait Gallery. They are dressed in a manner which separates them from the contemporary era and makes reference to the costume of the ancient world, even if that costume is, in the light of modern studies, misunderstood, and is distorted by the underlying sixteenth- and seventeenth-century body shape. What is shown in the Unton picture is a small-scale domestic masque, which (insofar as it is possible to impose a coherent scale on a confusingly composed piece) looks as if it is being performed by children. The little pairs of cherubs who act as torchbearers are clearly naked except for the black body make-up worn by one of each pair, and have scarves round their heads. The rest of the masquers wear red masks, and have appropriate head-dresses. What is shown is a private celebration, and not necessarily one in which one would expect a great deal of expenditure on

The monument to Sir Edward Pynchon (d. 1627), by Nicholas Stone, at Writtle, Essex, showing figures in agricultural costume. (Norman Hammond)

costume. When Lord Norris entertained Elizabeth I at his home at Rycote in 1592, he laid on an entertainment which was essentially informal (he performed it himself, with the aid of some servants playing messengers) and involved no expenditure on costumes, setting and properties. The tone of the visit and the little entertainment they put on was that of private enjoyment. On the same progress Elizabeth had visited Lady Russell at her home at Bisham. Lady Russell was anxious that Elizabeth should take her daughters as maids-of-honour to court. She was not a member of Elizabeth's inner circle, and the entertainment she laid on, in contrast to that provided by Lord Norris, was lavish, and involved expenditure on costumes for mythological beings, and elaborate props.[49] The visit to Bisham was essentially public, that to Rycote private.

The Unton picture shows a private masque, at an event which forms one of the scenes from Unton's private life, as opposed to his public role as ambassador to France. The expenditure on such an affair would not be on the lavish scale of a more public entertainment. But the worlds of monumental sculpture, court masques, civic pageantry and the theatres are all public ones, and the evidence we have of the ways in which events in their spheres were presented suggests that wholly different conventions apply. A small private masque put on for an educated group of friends needs no

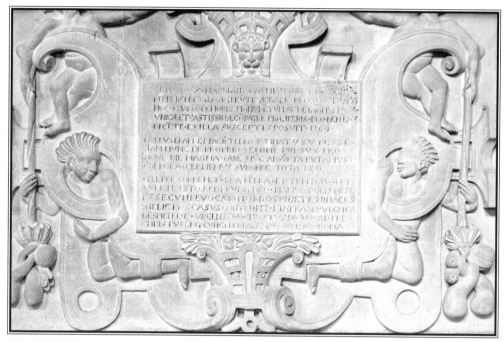

New World Indians, from the monument to Edmund Harman, d. 1569, at Burford, Oxfordshire. (Norman Hammond)

Apollo and the Nine Muses, c. 1570–80, a chimney-piece in the withdrawing-chamber at Hardwick (originally at Chatsworth). (Norman Hammond)

elaborate explication – it is obvious that little naked boys are cupids, that a lady with a crescent moon in her hair attended by other ladies carrying bows and arrows is Diana and her train of nymphs, that a messenger with wings in his hat and on his feet is Mercury. A public world with a larger audience demands a different, more elaborate, set of conventions, and this is what the classicizing style observable in monuments and masques, and, probably, the theatre, provided. Jupiter in Shakespeare's *Cymbeline* is most unlikely to have been presented as a Jacobean gentleman who just happened to drop in on his pet eagle.

COSTUME AS SYMBOL

Although treatments of costume in the staging of Renaissance plays mention the importance of such aspects as colour symbolism and the wide variety of costumes available in Henslowe's inventory,[50] costume tends to assume a minor part in books devoted to the subject.[51] M. C. Linthicum's *Costume in the Drama of Shakespeare and his Contemporaries*[52] deals only with contemporary costume, rather than with the range which must have been used, and sources for its reconstruction. Even if one ignores the plays of his contemporaries the clothing of Shakespeare's plays is a major factor in their dramatic impact, and not solely because the audience was intended to be overwhelmed by the gorgeousness of the players' costumes. Just as in monuments, costume is used to delineate different spheres of existence.

As You Like It, a play which would have been performed in contemporary costume, provides an example. It is a play about convention, and the different conventional worlds in which each of the characters' lives are defined by the characters' dress. Few of them wear the rich court costumes which are usually treated as the staple of Elizabethan theatre: these are confined to Act I, and to the court of Duke Frederick. The two heroines signal their escape from the stifling conventions of the court by changing their clothes. Humble clothes – the clothes of outsiders to society – mean freedom, but there is a variety in the humble clothes which indicates that the characters who wear them inhabit various gradations of the world into which they have escaped. Oliver's redemption is signalled by the ruin of his fine clothes on his journey into the forest in search of his brother. This world is the pastoral, the humble vein in which poets find freedom; but within the pastoral and the romance conventions of the play characters from different worlds mingle with each other, and their clothes signal the appropriateness of their individual situation. Orlando, deprived by his brother of the rich clothes which are his birthright, spends Act I, in which he is dealing with his well-dressed brother and the court, obviously morally misplaced. As soon as he enters the pastoral world of the forest of Arden, his costume is appropriate and signals his right to be there. The two princesses, having been appropriately dressed for the court, disguise themselves as a shepherd boy and his sister to enter the pastoral world, and again change their clothes for the final wedding masque, when the world of mythology enters the play with Hymen. The protean nature of Rosalind and Celia, and their ability to adapt at will to all the worlds of the play, is indicated by the fact that they are the only characters who are always appropriately dressed. In the pastoral world there are several gradations: the professional shepherd Corin, the pretty and comparatively prosperous lovers Silvius and Phebe, and the squalid rustics Audrey and William. The banished Duke and his followers are outlaws. At the end of the play, the need for the court characters to move back to their courtly milieu, itself necessitating a change of costume, is signalled by the arrival in the forest of the third son of Sir Rowland de Boys, wearing court costume, and standing out as much among the rustically clothed participants in the last act as did Orlando, in his rustic clothes, against the sophisticatedly-clad court in Act I.

In addition, part of neither court nor forest, there are moving through these sartorially-designated spheres two characters who display the characteristic garb of totally different conventions – Jaques and Touchstone. Touchstone is a court fool, but the fool is, by definition, not part of the court whom he entertains, being set apart by either inferior or superior intelligence, a person who spends his life as a performer. The melancholic Jaques, his black clothes the mark of his perpetual mourning for his view of the world, is also self-separated from his fellows, and certainly has no part in the pastoral tradition, whose essence is a celebration of harmony and the fundamental innocence of mankind. Pastoral is holiday: Jaques moves through it not as just another of the banished Duke's followers who happens to be rather more miserable than the others, but as a creature who inhabits a different moral universe. Though Touchstone and he are visual opposites – the one an icon of celebration, brightness and folly, the other an icon of world-weariness and mourning – the Duke recognizes their fundamental kinship (as they do themselves) and treats them alike as sources of entertainment.

A third world enters *As You Like It* in the final scene, when the gods come down to earth in the wedding masque. No explanation is given for the sudden irruption of Hymen into the play – it is not clear if he is meant to be played by another character (one of the Banished Lords or Corin, for example) – or whether his entry is to be viewed as a moment of supernatural intervention, like the descent of Jupiter and visitation of Posthumus by the ghosts of his family in *Cymbeline*, or the animation of Hermione's statue in *The Winter's Tale*.[53] Hymen is an iconographically recognizable being, whose typical costume, of the classicizing type accorded to other deities, marks him out as inhabiting a different realm from the mortal characters in their contemporary costume, be it courtly, pastoral, melancholic or foolish.

With only one character who is not in contemporary dress, *As You Like It* nevertheless has a complex iconographical programme dependent on costume – and this examination does not take into account the depth which might have been added by the use of colour symbolism.

A play with a far more complicated programme, where the role of costume in defining the moral and physical worlds of the various characters is paramount, is *The Tempest*. This was written eight years after the earliest costume designs by Inigo Jones which survive – years which were spent by Shakespeare's company as the personal servants of the same monarch for whom Jones was making his designs. *The Tempest* displays a wide variety of characters, including seamen, Stephano, described as a drunken butler and therefore presumably marked out by some sort of livery, and the jester Trinculo. The main divisions are between Prospero and his daughter Miranda – the magician and his child who have been living for twelve years on an island supported by his enchantments – the magician's preternatural servants, and the courtiers who are shipwrecked there. Prospero has a magic gown, and, since Ferdinand believes Miranda to be a goddess when he first sets eyes on her, her costume must be other than courtly dress as worn by Ferdinand and his companions. Within the realm controlled by Prospero, there are other divisions: his servants include Ariel, an airy spirit; Caliban, a semi-human monster who is partly the offspring of the devil; and spirits in the form of grotesque creatures, nymphs and harvesters, and classical deities. There are a number of designs by Inigo Jones which are suggestive of how some of these might have been costumed, but for the reapers at least, we may look to works like the Southwark and Writtle tombs of Nicholas Stone.

COSTUME AND ARTISTIC EFFECT

The intervening centuries of post-Inigo Jones theatres, in which a great deal of the effect of the drama depends on transformation scenes, elaborate stage machinery and sophisticated lighting effects, are apt to blind us to the extent to which the visual effect of Shakespeare's theatre depends on costume. A limited number of effects were possible – *The Tempest* itself contains a vanishing banquet; there was the possibility of flying in characters on thrones – but the definition of the magical, the strange or the unnatural is achieved by the means of costume. Jones's first audiences did not understand the elaborate visual effects he created with his machinery – they literally could not read them. Jonson describes thus the setting for the first masque known to have been designed by Jones:

> an artificial sea was seen to shoot forth, as if it flowed to the land, raised with waves which seemed to move, and in some places the billows to break, as imitating that orderly disorder which is common in nature. In front of this sea were placed six tritons in moving and sprightly actions . . . Behind these a pair of sea-maids, for song, were as conspicuously seated; between which two great sea-horses, as big as the life, put forth themselves, the one mounting aloft and writhing his head from the other, which seemed to sink forwards . . . The masquers were placed in a great concave shell like mother of pearl, curiously made to move on those waters and rise with the billow . . . [54]

Sir Dudley Carleton, who was present at the masque, saw this:

> There was a great Engine at the lower end of the Room, which had Motion, and in it were the Images of Sea-Horses with other terrible Fishes, which were ridden by Moors: the Indecorum was, that there was all Fish and no Water. At the further end was a great Shell in the form of a Skallop, wherein were four Seats; on the lowest sat the Queen . . . [55]

The Elvetham entertainment, 1591, showing the crescent-shaped pond made for a water-pageant in honour of the Queen's visit, from The honorable Entertainement gieven to the Queenes Maiestie in progresse, at Eluetham in Hampshire, by the . . . Earle of Hertford *(London, John Wolfe, 1591). (By permission of the Syndics of Cambridge University Library)*

Carleton saw nothing new in Jones's visual programme for the masque – only an inferior version of what had previously appeared in court entertainments. (It is possible that the execution of Jones's designs did not match up to the conception – the portraits of the *Hymenaei* masquers show costumes far less imaginative and exotic than Jones's contemporary designs.) Sea-maids had appeared in court masques as early as Leicester's Kenilworth entertainment for Elizabeth I in 1575; tritons had been seen at Elvetham in 1591[56]; seahorses were forming part of Gerard Christmas's designs for the Lord Mayor's Show a decade later. The revolutionary nature of Jones's designs is frequently stressed, but they may be seen as part of a continuous entertainment tradition. Jones is usually treated as being a member of a younger generation than Shakespeare, but this is a misleading assumption, based on the scant records of his early life: he was born in 1573, only nine years after Shakespeare, and is known to have been a painter before his foreign travels. He was thirty-two in 1605, the year of the first masque which he is known to have designed.[57]

Even in Jones's masques, the major part of the artistic effect is produced through the costumes. It is the costume designs, rather than those for the sets, which are now remembered – even though they did not always please contemporaries. Dudley

Carleton was as unsympathetic to the costumes in the *Masque of Blackness* as he was to the machinery – again on the grounds of indecorum:

> Their Apparell was rich, but too light and Curtizan-like for such great ones. Instead of Vizzards, their faces, and Arms up to the Elbows, were painted black, which was a Disguise sufficient, for they were hard to be known; but it became them nothing so well as their red and white, and you cannot imagine a more ugly Sight, than a troop of lean-cheek'd Moors.[58]

The setting for Jones's masques takes on its meaning only from the characters displayed against it; even in *Oberon, The Fairy Prince* – the greatest and best-integrated of all the masques, with text, costumes and setting all combining to form a complete harmony – Oberon's palace makes sense only when it is viewed in the light of the Arthurian theme in both the text and the costumes (and even so, it is not clear that spectators understood it).[59] In plays produced without the benefit of scenery, even in the private theatres, visual effect was produced only by means of costume.

The number of surviving garments from the sixteenth and early seventeenth centuries is small. They range from a wonderful embroidered panel at the remote church of Bacton, Herefordshire, which is thought to have belonged to Queen Elizabeth I, to a pathetic knitted child's vest in the collection of the Museum of London. Many of the pieces of fabric which survive do so because they were embroidered but never made up, or were never completed, and so are unworn. Nothing survives which can even plausibly be said to be a stage costume, although the Swedish Royal Collection contains ceremonial costumes from the first half of the seventeenth century which give some idea of the richness with which court masques, at least, must have been dressed.

Perhaps because of the paucity of evidence, there has been no concerted historical movement in the theatre in the manner of the early music movement. There have been several attempts, more or less successful, to reproduce Elizabethan playhouses. There have also been attempts to produce medieval plays in what is believed to have been their original style, as well as attempts to update them for modern audiences. There is evidence of some interest in the acting styles of former generations,[60] but there have been few serious attempts to mount plays in a reproduction of the manner in which they were first staged. In part this is because the plays of Shakespeare's age still form part of a living theatrical tradition, unlike those of the Middle Ages, and historical exploration can seem a deadening way of dealing with them when they contain live issues to be explored. When plays by Shakespeare and his contemporaries are set (with less and less frequency in recent years) in the period at which they were written, there tends to be a blanket style imposed on the costumes, with none of the gradation and stylistic differences which were used by their author to make important visual points. If *As You Like It* were costumed authentically, it would need an educated eye to distinguish the subtle variations – so important to the Elizabethans themselves – in its Elizabethan costume. The differences between rich imprisonment and poor freedom, the distinctions between the different pastoral types, the anachronistic styles of both Jaques and Touchstone, the irruption of the supernatural with Hymen are best appreciated by a modern audience if the play is performed in modern dress. Nevertheless, as has been done for some early opera, it is possible to go some way to recreating the style of costume which would probably have been adopted on the Elizabethan stage. In the absence of all but a very few representations of plays of the period, it is to the general cultural heritage that we must turn, and the material remains, in the form of tomb-sculpture and other carvings, have often as much to tell us as easel pictures and masque designs.

CHAPTER SIX

THE INDOOR
THEATRES

Parallel with the development of the great amphitheatres ran the evolution of permanent indoor venues for the performance of plays. In 1576 were built both the Theatre and Richard Farrant's first Blackfriars playhouse, the first permanent indoor venue for plays in London. Although one strand of the medieval theatrical tradition – the great mystery cycles – had been concerned with open-air performance (in the height of summer), a parallel tradition had developed which used indoor locations. The entertainments linked with seasonal winter festivals had always been performed in the settings of halls, and other court entertainments were also staged inside. The central role of drama in Renaissance education meant that plays were frequently mounted by educational institutions, and these took place in the setting of the school or college hall. The plays performed by the boys at Eton and Westminster became so institutionalized that the performances, attended by members of the court, became in effect, semi-public events – the audience was invited, but the event was public in its nature. It was this educational strand which was to be developed and commercialized into the childrens' companies when a number of unscrupulous operators moved in on the choir schools, turning them from educational establishments which produced plays into professional theatrical troupes.

PERFORMANCES IN GREAT HALLS

In some ways the material remains of the private indoor playhouses are more extensive than those of the public ones. Many of the places which we know to have been transformed – at least temporarily – into theatres have survived. The hall of Christ Church, Oxford; the chapel of King's College, Cambridge; the Middle Temple Hall; the Banqueting House in Whitehall – all of which are known to have been used as theatres, with the erection of temporary stages – are still standing more or less unaltered. In the case of the Oxbridge colleges, we are able, with the aid of contemporary plans and descriptions, to reconstruct the theatres. There are surviving designs by Inigo Jones and John Webb for private theatres, to be erected either in the royal palaces, for the personal use of the monarch, or as commercial ventures. But of the nine commercial private playhouses known to have been adapted from existing buildings in the Elizabethan and Stuart period none survives, and the fact that they were altered from existing buildings, rather than being built *de novo*, makes their archaeological survival more improbable (although few thought that the Rose and Globe could have survived archaeologically until they proved to have done so). The

The hall of the Middle Temple, London, where Shakespeare's company performed Twelfth Night *in February 1602. (Country Life)*

playhouse which was eventually to become the winter home of Shakespeare's company, the second Blackfriars playhouse, converted out of the upper floors of an old ecclesiastical building, can never be recovered.

As with the amphitheatres, there are more views than there are scholars about the form of the indoor theatres. To modern eyes it seems obvious that hall screens should have provided the backing for the plays: a screen supplies at least one entrance, and often two; the gallery above may be used for music, extra audience accommodation or scenes needing an upper stage level, just as the tarras or above-stage gallery in the commercial theatres is believed to have been used; the screens passage provides space for changing and other necessary backstage accommodation, and the screen is situated at the end of the hall opposite the high table, so that the great and the good are already installed in the optimum seats. When plays are staged in such locations nowadays, they are invariably set against the screen.[1]

The 1622 Banqueting House, Whitehall, designed by Inigo Jones for the performance of court masques. (Crown Copyright. Historic Royal Palaces)

The evidence for the placing of stages in these buildings in the Renaissance does not show the screen being used. When Elizabeth I saw a play in King's College Chapel on her visit in 1564, the stage was built across the antechapel, in front of the screen; the Queen's throne was put on the stage itself at the end opposite the actors (the Queen witnessing the play was part of the performance);[2] two of the side-chapel doors provided entrances and exits, the side-chapels themselves giving adequate backstage accommodation; and the audience was situated on top of the screen or at the foot of the stage on its antechapel side. In the theatre built in Christ Church, Oxford, for King James I, the stage was built at the upper end of the hall.

In an age in which ceremony was theatre, the focus of the hall was not the screen, but the drama enacted at the opposite end, at the high table. The screen was an important feature of the Hall, part of the general conception which was designed to provided a fitting setting for the court life which went on in the room and, as is the case with rood screens in churches, a ceremonial marker which separated one area from another. (In the church, the screen separates the chancel or chapel proper – the area of the initiate (which is itself subdivided by the sanctuary into which only the priest may enter) – from the antechapel, or nave, the area of the general public.)[3] In the hall the screen separated the public area of the court from the areas which serviced it – the kitchens and other offices. To pass through the screens passage into a palace hall was to become an initiate, a member of the household, rather than a member of the public or a menial, but a further degree of initiation was needed before one might pass through the doors at the other end of the hall which led from the dais area into the private apartments of the household. The focus of life in the hall was the high table, at which the head of the household and his or her family sat. Meals were served with elaborate ceremony, and, in royal households, the meal itself became an elaborate ritual even when the royal personage was not present at it:

> When the Queen is served, a great table is set in the presence chamber near the Queen's throne. The cloth being laid, a gentleman and a lady come in, walking from the end of the room with the course, and making three reverences, the one by the door, the next in the middle of the chamber, the third by the table. Then they set down the course and the lady tastes the food. The guards bring in the meal in the same manner then the lady tastes the food with a piece of bread and gives it to the guards. Such food as she wanted was taken into the privy chamber.[4]

The area of the hall most associated with display was the high table, not the screen, and it would not necessarily seem that the obvious place to site a stage was against the screen. The screen provided access to the catering facilities of the great house, and to use it for the performance of plays would impede such access.

SIMON BASIL'S CHRIST CHURCH THEATRE

The most interesting document related to the creation of a temporary indoor theatre from the period is the plan for the transformation of Christ Church hall in order to put on a play for the visit of James I to Oxford in August 1605. The proposed plan for this by Simon Basil, who would the following year become Surveyor of the King's Works, survives. Oxford was determined both to be innovatory in its dramatic offerings and to display its classical scholarship. Four plays were acted during the visit: a satyr play, a tragedy, a comedy and a pastoral. The stage and settings were designed by Inigo Jones, and his work is available through eyewitness accounts – one enthusiastic, from Oxford, and the other rather cooler, from Cambridge. Jones evidently designed a raked stage with spectacular sets, based on the Vitruvian *periaktoi* (triangular machines which might be revolved so that each face showed a different scene), and which presented a perspective scene to the audience, the ideal viewing point of which was where Basil's design specified that the King's chair should be placed. There were also moving clouds. The scenes changed for and within each play.

To accommodate the audience for this avant-garde feast, Basil intended to transform the hall of Christ Church into a U-shaped auditorium with steeply raked rows of seats. These were supported on temporary wooden scaffolds which were designed to focus attention both on the stage and on the King, sitting on a raised platform in front of it, the cynosure of the perspective set as well as of the noble and learned audience. Unfortunately for Jones and Basil the learned and avant-garde was met with

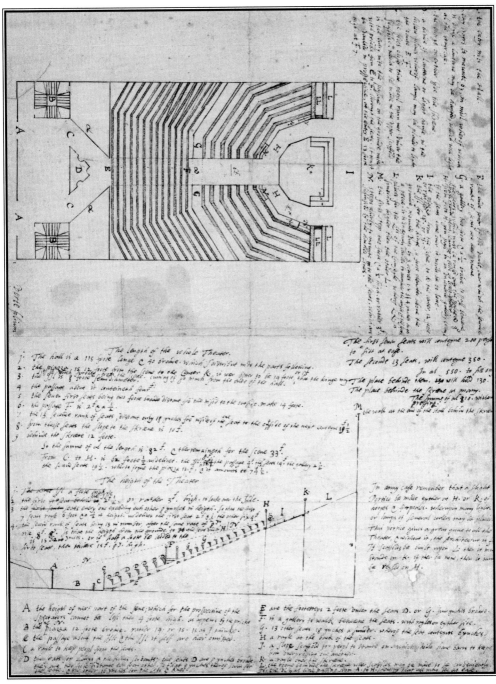

Simon Basil's projected theatre for the hall of Christ Church, Oxford, in 1605. (By permission of the British Library Ms. Add 15505)

establishment incomprehension and disapproval. When courtiers were sent down to check the arrangements made for the King's entertainment, they objected to the fact that the King would not be more visible – he, and not the drama, was the real focus of the occasion. Despite the arguments of the university authorities, backed up by their Chancellor, Thomas Sackville, Earl of Dorset (the author, with Thomas Norton, of *Gorboduc*, the avant-garde sensation of 1561), the Earl of Suffolk insisted that the King should be raised higher and made more visible. The design for the hall was altered, the King's chair was set further back from the stage, with the result that he could not easily hear the words spoken by the actors, and the grand design of the hall, with both auditorium and stage set focused on the King, was lost.

The Christ Church design is one of the principal sources for calculations of Elizabethan playhouse capacity, giving the inch-to-bottom ratio allowed. The most important members of the audience, after the King, are allowed 24 inches of front-to-back space; the ladies of the court and King's servants who were to sit behind were allowed only 18 inches. As the patella-to-spine measurement of a man of 5 feet 9 inches is about 24 inches, and that of a woman 5 feet 2 inches about 20 inches, the audience must have been considerably cramped, even allowing for body sizes about 10 per cent smaller than today's, and an estimated side-to-side allowance of 18 inches seems ludicrous when the width of contemporary fashion is taken into account. Court masques were notorious for the amount of overcrowding. Orazio Busino, the chaplain to the Venetian embassy, who attended a masque at Whitehall in 1618, remarked on the crush:

> we . . . entered the usual box of the Venetian embassy, where, unfortunately, we were so crowded and uncomfortable that had it not been for our curiosity we must certainly have given in or expired . . . Then there was such a crowd; for though they claim to admit only those favoured with invitations, nevertheless every box was full, especially with most noble and richly dressed ladies, 600 and more in number, according to the general opinion.[5]

The Christ Church theatre included accommodation behind the stepped rows of seats for standing spectators, on top of a 'skraene'. Entry was through a passage between and under the scaffolding, with two staircases giving access to the seats from the back. One is struck by the narrow access provision. There is a reasonably wide aisle leading to the King's chair, and giving access to the lords' seating at the front, but access to the area at the back would have meant an undignified scramble over the rows of bench-seats. However, descriptions of court behaviour at masques during the reign of James I are unanimous about its lack of dignity and rapacity, so the need to find one's place by means of a jostling scramble may not have seemed out of harmony with the occasion.

Basil's stately theatre (the entranceway at the back was to be enriched with a portico of light wooden arches, hung with coloured lamps; the square staircases giving access to the upper rear seating and standing were to be lit with lanterns hung in their central wells; and there was provision for lighting the passage under the scaffold to the lower levels of seating) presented a harmonious and integrated vision of the events that it was designed for – but Suffolk's objections show that some members of the court had no sympathy with or conception of that vision.

The source for Basil's design is known to have been Sebastiano Serlio's *L'Architettura*, which includes a plan and section for a perspective theatre (see illustration on p. 154). Serlio designed seating in the form of tiers of steps, unless benches were to be placed upon the tiers, whereas Basil's design clearly shows the benches set on to the framework. While Serlio's fore-and-aft allowance is no greater than Basil's, the step arrangement allows for a little more space, since some interlocking of the knees with the backs of those in front is possible – in Basil's theatre the legs have to be slotted in behind the benches in front. Serlio's design also shows a raked stage, which we know Inigo Jones provided from descriptions (the stage area designs do not survive) – though Jones went to Vitruvius for his scene designs.[6]

The Christ Church theatre is the earliest English theatre design extant. It shows how a court theatre was fitted into a rectangular hall at the beginning of the seventeenth century. Basil did not take the course which is nowadays adopted when such halls are used as temporary theatres – closing off one end as stage in a horizontal line, and then arranging rows of chairs parallel to the stage front. Instead, the rectangular space was adapted to provide a curved auditorium, with raked seating on scaffolds, and the dais, where the king was located forming a projecting appendage to Jones's raked Vitruvian perspective stage. The problems which the University and its designers had with the conservative courtiers was due not to a revolutionary shape for the auditorium but to the courtiers' inability to grasp the concept of perspective scenery. The perspective scene is the ultimate in exclusive art: there is only one point in the theatre from which it may be perfectly viewed and understood, and the viewer in that spot becomes the cynosure of the set. Its whole purpose is to exist for the entertainment of one person, and until that person is seated, it does not come alive. The purpose of an evening at which an important person watches a drama enacted on a perspective scene is that the court or public may witness the harmonic moment at which perfect set and perfect viewer combine. Both the King and the stage are part of the spectacle in the Basil-Jones theatre at Christ Church, and this is acknowledged in the design of the auditorium, in which the King's dais is separated from the audience and incorporated into the design where the stage would be in a thrust-stage theatre. The shape of the dais is, like that of the thrust stage of the Rose, a section of a polygon. Basil's theatre resembles a rectangular section taken through a polygonal playhouse, with the whole area, instead of just the surrounding galleries, filled with seating, and the yard incorporated into the overall design.

INIGO JONES'S THEATRE PLANS

Theatre plans exist by Inigo Jones and his pupil and heir John Webb.[7] They have in common a projecting stage with seats at the sides, and a curved seating plan in the auditorium. The automatic design for the auditorium seating seems to have been a horseshoe, either curved or polygonal. The horseshoe makes acoustic sense. The

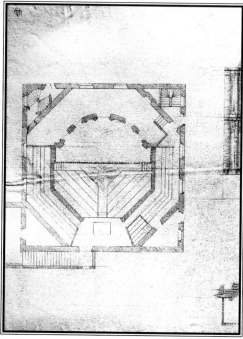

John Webb's plans and stage elevation for the 1660–2 restoration of the Cockpit-in-the-Court theatre, Whitehall, first designed by Inigo Jones in 1629–31. (The Provost and Fellows of Worcester College, Oxford)

surrounding galleries catch and augment the sound (a comparatively small hall, with high curved galleries of seating, is now the preferred shape for a concert hall), they provide good sight-lines for those seated in them, and, in an age in which a trip to the theatre was frequently an exercise in self-display, they allow a large proportion of the audience to put itself on view. Busino's description of the crush at the masque he attended in the first Banqueting House in Whitehall indicates that, while the most distinguished members of the audience were placed near the King on stools, the rest were accommodated in boxes surrounding the floor area on which the masque was enacted, the spectacular set forming a backdrop from which the various players and masquers emerged to perform their parts in the centre of the floor. A similar arrangement may be seen in pictures of masques at the French court.

The surviving building originally intended for the performance of masques is the Inigo Jones Banqueting House in Whitehall. Although this was not used for an extensive period, because of the fear that the Rubens ceiling would be damaged by smoke from the candles, the initial plan was for a building which would replace the earlier Banqueting House, used for masques, which was destroyed by fire in 1619 – although as soon as the Rubens ceilings were commissioned it was obvious that the building's use as a masquing chamber would be limited, and another masquing house had to be constructed once the ceilings were installed. What Jones designed is the idea of a masquing house, but one in which the only masque that may ultimately take place

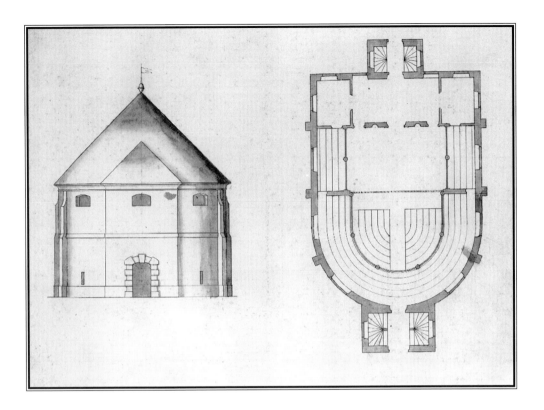

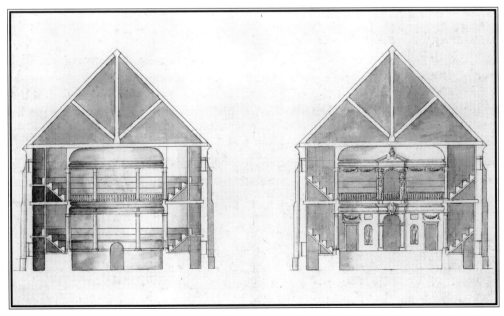

Inigo Jones's plan, elevation and sections thought to be for a projected theatre for Sir William Davenant in Fleet Street, 1639. (The Provost and Fellows of Worcester College, Oxford)

is the apotheosis of James I painted on the ceiling – a permanent painted version of what had taken place metaphorically many times in the masques presented before him in the earlier buildings on the same site. It seems possible that the puzzling cantilevered gallery which lines the interior of the Banqueting House at first floor level, but to which there is no access, is a representation of what was felt to be a necessary adjunct to a hall designed for quasi-theatrical performances – surrounding accommodation for spectators – even though the installation of the Rubens paintings meant that the hall could never be used as such. The overall impression is of a hall in which any performance which takes place may be surrounded at an·upper level by onlookers.[8]

Jones's plans for the Cockpit-in-the-Court theatre, which was adapted for private court theatrical performances, are known only from John Webb's designs for its restoration in 1660–2, after the Restoration, but there seems little doubt that the restitution adhered closely to the original designs. The shape of the building limited Jones's architectural options: the stage is backed by a curved *frons scenae* with five stage level entrances and a single upper acting area, but projects only shallowly and in a rectangular shape into the auditorium. Nevertheless, this shallow projection is flanked by some seating, and the seating in the pit is arranged in diagonal lines parallel to those two walls of the octagon comprising the interior of the building which adjoin the entrance wall. The effect of this diagonal seating is to place the audience as if looking across a projecting stage which does not exist. The angled seating may be a device to ensure that the maximum number of spectators has optimum views of the vanishing point of a perspective set. The lower level, under the gallery shown on the plan, evidently consisted of seating degrees – boxes in Webb's alteration, but possibly simple steps of seats with one royal box in Jones's original conversion. The Cockpit-in-the-Court stage is specifically classical in its design: the classical orders, the busts, the figures over the central opening all proclaim that this is a building which descends (via Renaissance Italian art) from the theatres of Greece and Rome.

Another set of plans and designs for a playhouse exists from Jones's hand, although there is some debate about the playhouse's identification, and whether it was ever built. Glynne Wickham assigned the drawings to the Salisbury Court theatre of 1629–30; John Orrell argues that it is a design for the Cockpit in Drury Lane, built by Christopher Beeston in 1616;[9] but in the most recent study of all Jones's architectural drawings, John Harris and Gordon Higgott maintain that the drawings must stylistically be assigned to the late 1630s, and that the theatre in question must therefore have been William Davenant's projected playhouse in Fleet Street.[10] This was planned in 1638–9, ran into difficulties, and was postponed by the Civil War, although Davenant was still playing with the idea of building it in 1660–1, which, Harris and Higgott argue, explains why Webb's designs for Davenant's *The Siege of Rhodes* (1658) are for a stage with the exact dimensions of the one in Jones's design. Earlier commentators, assuming the theatre to have been built within four years of the second Globe, had remarked on the projecting thrust stage, and linked it to common practice in the public playhouses, but Harris and Higgott argue that the late date means that the playhouse was designed to be dual-purpose: suitable for plays written both for the traditional open thrust stages, in which case the seats on either side of the stage would be used, and for the newer perspective scenic stages, which were to be viewed exclusively from the front.

Whether the Jones design should be dated to the teens, twenties or thirties of the seventeenth century,[11] it, like the Cockpit-in-the-Court design, accepts the basic idea of a playhouse as having a projecting stage and a curved or polygonal auditorium surrounded by galleries. The use of the curved form is more interesting if the late date is right, for the early date was based on the premise that the theatre was altered from an existing building, the Drury Lane Cockpit, and that the curved shape of the auditorium was imposed by the building's previous use.[12] If a curve or polygon was felt to be the natural shape for an auditorium even in a building where the previous use did not prescribe it, and where the shape does not produce the ideal seating arrangement for viewing the scenic stage, then it is probable that the form was felt to be the proper one for all theatres, private as well as public.

This is important because of the scant information available about the form of the private playhouses during the Elizabethan and Jacobean period, and particularly about the second Blackfriars, created by James Burbage and eventually the winter house of the King's Men, while their summer house remained the Globe. The history of the second Blackfriars suggests that James Burbage was intending as early as 1596 to transform public drama into an indoor entertainment, a move which did not ultimately take place until the Restoration.

THE FOUNDING OF THE SECOND BLACKFRIARS THEATRE

The lease held by James Burbage on the Theatre was due to expire on 13 April 1597. In the previous months, Burbage tried to negotiate a new one with the ground landlord, Giles Allen, but the negotiations could not be brought to any satisfactory conclusion, and Burbage sought alternative accommodation. He bought the frater of the former Blackfriars priory for £600 and spent several hundred more on turning it into a theatre. The Blackfriars was ideally situated from Burbage's point of view: it was central, on the north bank of the river in an upper-income residential district, and had already been the home of a theatre – the first Blackfriars playhouse, set up by Richard Farrant, Master of the Children of Windsor Chapel, and a temporary replacement for William Hunnis as Master of the Children of the Chapel Royal. Farrant was one of the entrepreneurs who moved into the entertainment industry while pretending to run educational establishments, and put on a professional basis the tradition of child acting which formed part of the Elizabethan educational system. He set up his theatre in 1576, in a different part of the former ecclesiastical complex from that later converted by Burbage, and the theatre continued to be used, under different masters, until 1584, when Farrant's landlord, Sir William More, who had thought he was leasing a schoolroom and tried indignantly for years to regain his property once he found it was a theatre, eventually obtained possession and threw the children out. Farrant's playhouse seems to have been created by knocking out partitions between rooms to form a single large rectangular hall, but little else is known about it.[13]

Burbage's portion of the Blackfriars was more suited to theatrical use than Farrant's had been, comprising the former refectory of the complex, which would have been a large hall, situated on an upper floor of the building. Unfortunately, Burbage had not sufficiently grasped the implications of Farrant's and his successors' struggle with their landlord. The children's troupes had survived at the Blackfriars because they managed to retain a façade of educational purpose – they appealed to the *cognoscenti*, and attracted an exclusive audience. They were regular performers at court, and their commercial activities subsidized their role as entertainers to the Queen, who was as notable as later conservatives for her reluctance to underwrite the arts. The boys enjoyed the protection of powerful courtiers, including the Earls of Leicester and Oxford. Once the aristocratic inhabitants of the Blackfriars grasped that there was going to be a public playhouse in their midst, they exploded with indignation. The Lord Chamberlain's Men were in a vulnerable position with regard to court patronage. Henry Carey, Lord Hunsdon – their original protector, and one of the courtiers closest to the Queen – had died early in 1596, and although his son George had taken over his father's sponsorship of the company (and would, in 1597, take over his office of Lord Chamberlain) he had neither his father's personality nor his closeness to the Queen and influence at court – added to which, he lived in the Blackfriars himself and had as little wish as his neighbours to see his own company of players encouraging anyone who had a penny to spare to enter this exclusive enclave. The inhabitants of the Blackfriars accordingly petitioned the privy Council against the theatre:

one Burbage hath lately bought certaine roomes in the . . . precinct neere adjoyning unto the dwelling houses of the right honorable the Lord Chamberlaine and the Lord of Hunsdon, which roomes the said Burbage is now altering and meaneth very shortly to convert and turne the same into a comon playhouse, which will grow to be a very great annoyance and trouble, not only to all the noblemen and gentlemen thereabout inhabiting but allso a generall inconvenience to all the inhabitants of the same precinct, both by reason of the great resort and gathering together of all manner of vagrant and lewde persons that, under cullor of resorting to playes, will come thither and worke all manner of mischeefe, and allso to the great pestring and filling up of the same precinct, yf it should please God to send any visitation of sicknesse as heretofore hath been, for that the same precinct is allready growne very populous; and besides, that the same playhouse is so neere the Church that the noyse of the drummes and trumpetts will greatly disturbe and hinder both the ministers and parishioners in tyme of devine service and sermons; – In tender consideracion wherof, as allso for that there hath not at any tyme heretofore been used any comon playhouse within the same precinct, but that now all players being banished by the Lord Mayor from playing within the Cittie by reason of the great inconveniences and ill rule that followeth them, they now thincke to plant them selves in liberties.[14]

So distinguished a group of petitioners won the day, and Burbage was forbidden to use his new theatre. In addition to the amalgamation of a belief that if a public theatre is introduced, bang will go the neighbourhood, and speciousness (since Burbage had purchased the frater from the same Sir William More who had been Farrant's landlord, the petitioners must have known that the claim that there had never been a public playhouse in the Blackfriars could be maintained only by adhering to the transparent falsehood that Farrant's enterprise had been an educational establishment), the petition contained one reasonable complaint: that the area would be clogged up by playgoers. When the by then King's Men finally got the use of their theatre in the Blackfriars, traffic jams did prove to be a problem:

> there is daylie such resort of people, and such multitudes of Coaches (whereof many are Hackney Coaches, bringinge people of all sortes) that sometymes all our streetes cannot containe them. But that they Clogg up Ludgate alsoe, in such sort, that both they endanger the one the other breake downe stalles, throwe downe mens goodes from their shopps. And the inhabitantes there cannott come to their howses, nor bringe in their necessary provisions of beere, wood, coale or haye, nor the Tradesmen or shopkeepers utter their wares, nor the passenger goe to the common water staires without danger of their lives and lymmes.[15]

Once again, the petition is at least as concerned about the pollution of the neighbourhood by the hoi polloi as about the traffic congestion: the hackney-coaches, which may contain anybody, are far more offensive than the private coaches of the rich, although they took up equal amounts of space. The true reason behind this 1619 petition was religious disapproval: the principal mover was the minister of a church adjacent to the Blackfriars, who was a Puritan and objected to the daily afternoon performances (even during Lent) interfering with access to his church.[16] The Privy Council was still promulgating traffic regulations to deal with the congestion caused by the Blackfriars theatre in 1634:

> Here hath been an Order of the Lords of the Council hung up in a Table near Paul's and the Black-Fryars, to command all that Resort to the Play-House there to send away their Coaches, and to disperse Abroad in Paul's Church-Yard, Carter Lane, the Conduit in Fleet-Street, and other Places, and not to return to fetch their Company, but they must trot afoot to find their Coaches, 'twas kept very strictly for two or three Weeks, but now I think it is disorder'd again.[17]

The realization that traffic jams, parking problems and planning controversies existed in Shakespeare's London should not blind us to the results for the Burbages of the 1596/7 petition. James Burbage died early in 1597, with his theatrical ventures and financial affairs in chaos. His company were about to lose their old home and could not use their new one, and the capital which he had sunk in the new unusable theatre had left his sons with insufficient money to build yet another playhouse. Out of this crisis developed the triumphant solution of some of the sharers in the company becoming also shareholders in the new playhouse, a factor which perhaps more than any other gave the Lord Chamberlain's/King's Men a stability lacking in other companies and ensured their survival until the closure of the theatres at the beginning of the Civil War. It also occasioned the Portia-like legal thinking which led to the removal of the Theatre from the ground on which it stood, and the consequent litigation – gratifying and informative, if sometimes misleading, to theatre historians.[18] This overall triumph must be modified by the reflection that it was shortage of money which led to the first Globe's being roofed with thatch, and its consequent brief life.

The discovery of John Brayne's involvement with the Red Lion may have provided evidence that he, rather than his partner in the Theatre, James Burbage, was the greatest innovator in theatrical architecture in the sixteenth century, but the second Blackfriars playhouse, although so little is known about it, must restore Burbage's claim to that position. The idea of moving his company from the Theatre to an indoor venue was a revolutionary and imaginative one, and involved a major financial gamble. The Theatre was a large house. Even if Orrell's conviction that it was the same size as the First and Second Globes is misplaced (the timbers of the Theatre were used at the Globe 'in an other forme',[19] and there is plenty of evidence for the reuse of timbers from framed buildings – provided the sides of the polygon were no longer, the frame from a building with twelve or fourteen sides, like the Rose, might easily be incorporated into one with over twenty sides as the second – and therefore first – Globes are believed to have had) and it was in fact only the same size as the Rose, the Theatre must have been capable of holding up to 2,000 people. The second Blackfriars cannot have accommodated anything like that number. The costs of running an indoor playhouse would have included an extra bill for the lighting, and may have imposed a different style of acting, and a different type of play, on the company (although some scepticism has greeted attempts to trace the change in style of Shakespeare's plays after the great tragedies to his company's acquisition of the Second Blackfriars as a production site).

The disadvantages of the smaller audience might be compensated for by an increase in prices. The cheapest seats in the private, or indoor, houses cost as much as the most expensive ones in the amphitheatre playhouses, but this was based on the premiss that they were educational establishments being patronized by the *cognoscenti*. In making the move to a private theatre, with a consequent increase in prices, Burbage was proposing to write off a portion of his audience. Even if he did not intend to raise prices to the levels which became conventional in the private theatres (and his prospective neighbours feared most of all the fact that he would not lose the lower economic sections of his audience),[20] he would be aiming only at those who paid for gallery space, as opposed to yard space, and he would be redefining the nature of his theatre, as a location for the *cognoscenti*. The implications of this may be assessed by the fact that when the first Globe burnt down, after the King's Men had for several years been established in James Burbage's Blackfriars theatre, they still chose to rebuild the Globe in an even more splendid form, thus retaining a summer venue for their popular audience as opposed to the richer clientele who visited their winter house. The proven success of the business management of the Lord Chamberlain's/King's Men shows that the decision to make the large capital investment needed to rebuild the Globe cannot have been based solely on emotional attachment to the open-air playhouse: by the time this decision was made, the company was finding that both its audiences were sources of financial gain, and seventeen years after James Burbage's attempt to abandon the less affluent parts of his audience, the company which he founded reversed his decision, even though they had, after a gap of ten years, at last gained possession of the indoor playhouse which he had built. (It may be that their difficulty in gaining tenure of the Blackfriars theatre made them regard their occupation of it as vulnerable to official intervention.) Studies of the repertoire of the various theatrical companies have shown that the Lord Chamberlain's/King's Men tended to appeal to a more intellectually sophisticated clientele: they performed a larger section of the dramas, besides those of Shakespeare, which have since been considered works of merit, and they were willing, as was the case with *A Game at Chess* (which insulted the Spanish ambassador and enraged the King), to take financial and political risks – perhaps confident that they had the artistic and political clout to ride an ensuing storm.

What James Burbage was proposing in his attempted move was an action of symbolic as well as practical importance. The practical considerations are obvious. For a reduction in the size of the audience, he was trading a probable increase in entrance prices. The playhouse had a location which was an improvement on those of the Theatre, the Curtain and the Southwark houses (the Rose and the Swan by this date). It was central and yet, because of the anomaly of its having been a religious house, outside the jurisdiction of the civic authorities. Audiences would no longer have to trek in appalling weather (this was the period of the Little Ice Age, with frost-fairs on the Thames) to the northern suburbs, or either brave the traffic jams on London Bridge or add to the expenses of their trip to the theatre by paying for a water-taxi in order to reach Southwark. The Blackfriars was more conveniently located than either the northern or Southwark playhouses for the Inns of Court, Whitehall and Westminster, and for the expanding westward development which was linking the City of London to Westminster and the court. It was from the courtiers and the students at the Inns of Court that Burbage must have been hoping to draw his higher-paying audience, as well as from the wealthier citizens. The reason that the Blackfriars was an upper-class residential district was its convenient location for courtiers between the nearer court centres of Whitehall, Westminster and the Tower and the further ones of Hampton Court and Greenwich – all easily reachable by river. An indoor location meant that performances would no longer be subject to the vagaries of the weather, which might reduce the size of the audience even if it did not force the actors to cancel (there is some evidence that the Lord Chamberlain's Men may have used an inn playhouse – the Cross Keys in Gracious Street – as a winter venue even before this date).[21] There would be less hazard to costumes from the effects of precipitation (John Orrell argues that the Theatre may have had no stage-cover),[22] and properties such as those listed in the Henslowe inventories, which the Lord Chamberlain's Men must have possessed, would be better protected in an indoor theatre.

THE SOCIAL IMPLICATIONS OF THE INDOOR PLAYHOUSE

In moving a commercial company into an indoor theatre, James Burbage was making claims for their place in contemporary society. That Elizabethan professional theatre companies were regarded as 'rogues and vagabonds' is a cliché; it was to protect them from the consequences of such a status that they assumed the role of servants of their aristocratic patrons. Whatever the reason for the development of the outdoor playhouses – whether they developed from the animal-baiting arenas or from the tradition of playing civic religious drama outdoors (almost invariably in summer) – the outdoor nature of the playhouses, as well as their suburban location, tended to emphasize the fact that theatre was a form of entertainment outside society. The theatre was, in both the nature of its buildings and their location, outside – other.

Indoor theatrical entertainments often took place at times in which the normal constraints of society were institutionally unloosed – at Christmas or other seasons of celebration. Festival traditions, such as the Boy Bishop or the Lord of Misrule, celebrated the stability of society by allowing a time of contrast: masters serving servants, transvestism. These were times for the reversal of social, sexual and age-based roles. At such periods, it was appropriate for drama – which embodied all these reversals as an intrinsic part of its nature – to be performed at court. Any court performance threw the protective aegis of authority over the drama. But at such performances the players performed under their quasi-fictive roles as the servants of a great magnate (in the reign of James I they became servants of the royal family, as its various members took over patronage from the courtiers).

The other cover for indoor drama – even when institutionalized at a permanent theatre, such as Farrant's first Blackfriars – was education. Although it is difficult to see much educational benefit from events such as the Inns of Court celebratory pieces, or the *Parnassus* plays from Cambridge – which are closer to a modern university revue than they are to the Plautine or Terentian comedies written for performance by schoolboys – they came at the end of a process in which the public performance of plays, either classical or specially written in English or Latin, provided both an educational experience for the children involved and a showcase for the school to display its own success. Those who visited such performances were both showing their approval of education and demonstrating their learning, for the pieces played were designed for an audience of *cognoscenti*, either because they were in a language available only to the learned or because, like the plays of John Lyly, they were written for a sophisticated coterie.

Burbage's proposed move involved a double invasion. Not only would a company of professional actors be invading a space – a purpose-built indoor playhouse – which had hitherto been the premise of amateurs (however much the amateur status was a convenient fiction – as it was with Farrant's boys), and doing so the whole year round, without the appropriateness and royal sanction conferred upon their festival visits to give indoor performances at court, but they would also be bringing with them the repertoire of the public playhouse, and therefore the public playhouse audience.

Burbage's move was overweening. He was effectively claiming that the professional companies had the same status and rights as the boys with their fictive amateur status and coterie audience. It was not until the Lord Chamberlain's Men had for six years been the King's Men that his sons were able to make the move that he had planned.[23]

The Chamberlain's Men spent two years hanging on in the Theatre, moving to the Curtain and finally, in 1599, demolishing the Theatre and building the Globe (an operation which must have taken months of planning). The second Blackfriars stood empty for three years, and then in 1600 the Burbage brothers managed to lease it to a revived company of Chapel Children, under the direction of Nathaniel Giles and Henry Evans who had been associated with the first Chapel Children and the first Blackfriars theatre. The career of this sleazy pair as managers of children's companies was marked by lawsuits and frequent changes of company name. Evans virtually kidnapped one boy into his troupe. As the boy was a gentleman's son, the result was a prosecution, after which Evans was forbidden to engage in management of a children's troupe again – an injunction which he contrived to get round. In 1608 the company, by then called the Children of Blackfriars, was finally closed down, and the King's Men entered into possession of their theatre.[24] John Orrell points out that it was still – twelve years after James Burbage had hoped – the first fully professional indoor theatre.[25] The advantage for Evans's and Giles's aristocratic neighbours was that the children's companies, adhering to the fiction of their amateurishness, performed only once a week and appealed to a select audience – to the sort of people who lived at the Blackfriars. They were not aiming to attract a large popular audience, and the inhabitants of the Blackfriars could console themselves, if they were disturbed by performances, that it was only once a week and that the audience was composed entirely of People Like Them.

THE DESIGN OF THE SECOND BLACKFRIARS THEATRE

Little is known about the design of the theatre which James Burbage had installed in the former ecclesiastical refectory. The room was on an upper floor, and measured 46 by 60 feet internally: an area of 2,760 square feet – tiny, compared with the Globe or the Rose. This was the area into which seating galleries, stage, and tiring-house had to be fitted. When the King's Men transferred their productions from the Globe to the second Blackfriars for the winter, they were moving into a house of a completely different nature. The differences cannot simply have been confined to the size and shape of the stage (which are in both cases unknown, although the stage of the Blackfriars was probably smaller than that of the Globe) but must also have related to lighting, acoustics, and the change from a large open space, however intimate the final feel of the building, to a small indoor hall. Such a move must have involved major adaptations of all the plays produced in both venues. It is not necessary to suppose that what Burbage built inside his upper hall was as close an approximation to a miniature outdoor arena as he could achieve in a rectangular hall.

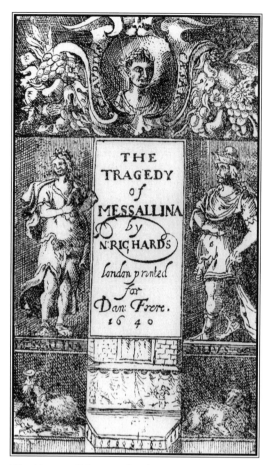

The title-page of The tragedy of Messallina the Roman *emperesse, by Nathaniel Richards (London, D. Frere, 1640), showing a tiring-house façade at lower centre. (By permission of the British Library, 162.b.15*

Conclusions may be drawn from the various illustrations of plays which are generally thought to show productions in indoor private playhouses, and from the various designs for playhouses and adaptations of halls for theatrical purposes. The two title-page vignettes for *Roxana* (see illustration on p. 91) and *Messallina*, and the illustration to Francis Kirkman's *The Wits*,[26] have common features. All show a tiring-house façade which has some relationship to that represented in the Swan sketch (see illustration on p. 72), and which supplies the features that we know from textual evidence to have been required by contemporary plays. There is an upper area above the stage. In the case of *Roxana*, where the whole stage is not in the picture, only two bays are shown, both apparently occupied by spectators. The *Messallina* vignette shows a curtained central space, set in a projecting façade either constructed from or painted to represent masonry. *The Wits'* tiring-house façade has a gallery running across the whole back stage and extending along the back wall of the performing space on either side of it. The centre space is curtained off, although the curtains are parted to show activity within – possibly that of musicians (the diagonal line may represent the throat of a cello or bass). On either side the gallery is occupied by spectators. Although the rail in front of both groups of spectators and visible in the curtained-off section seems continuous, the central section shows that it is supported on a balustrade, while in front of the spectators there are representations of martial scenes, either replacing the balustrade or on painted cloths or tapestries hung over and concealing it. The gallery also seems to be divided into boxes – or at least to have vertical posts rising from the rail of the balustrade.

If what is represented in *The Wits* is the adaptation of a private room to a temporary playhouse, the gallery is difficult to explain. It cannot be a hall screen, as the wall against which the stage is erected is blank and does not display the typical massive carving of a hall screen. Some screens (for example that in the Middle

Temple) do display a vertical division at gallery level such as is shown in *The Wits* picture, but this is unusual, and the combination with a balustrade would be extremely rare. The fittings of some of the private theatres are known to have been stripped out during the Commonwealth: it is possible that *The Wits* may represent a temporary restoration in one of the vandalized theatres. The two designs for private theatres connected with Inigo Jones show upper areas on the tiring-house façade analogous to those from the playtexts. The Cockpit-in-the-Court has an upper level decorated with niches, with one central bay – a more elaborate version of the *Messallina* façade – while that for the projected Fleet Street playhouse has raked seating on either side of a central arch which forms an upper acting level or music room, all the elements being united by a balustrade.

An illustration to The Wits: or, sport upon sport, *by Francis Kirkman (London, E. C. for F[r]ancis Kirkman, 1662), showing a tiring-house façade. (By permission of the Syndics of Cambridge University Library)*

The lower levels of the three playtext illustrations all show an element missing from the Jones-connected designs: some form of curtain covering the tiring-house façade at stage level. The *Messallina* and *Roxana* vignettes show purpose-made stage curtains, perhaps of tapestry or painted cloth – there are figures (Cupid aiming his bow at another person) visible on the *Messallina* curtain – constructed with loops which enable them to be pulled along a pole. *The Wits'* curtain seems a more ad hoc affair, suspended from a rope or wire, or pinned across the central entrance at the back of the stage. The presence of curtains is a constant feature of references to the theatre: although the Jones/Webb designs and the Swan drawing do not show them, one must assume that they were the norm. Their absence from the Swan drawing adds weight to the argument that if what is shown is an actual occasion, as opposed to the figures being placed solely to indicate the uses of the various parts of the playhouse, then it must be a rehearsal – one would not expect fabric hangings to be left exposed to the weather, and references to different coloured hangings for the various types of plays suggests that they were put up as part of the preparation of the stage for each performance.[27] The rear of the stage seems the most appropriate place for such hangings, and this is borne out by the vignettes. *Roxana* implies two entrance doors behind the rear-stage hangings; *The Wits* one; that relating to *Messallina* is unclear. The Jones/Webb designs show three entrances in the tiring-house façade for the Fleet Street project; five in the curved façade of the Cockpit-in-the-Court. Despite the evidence for only two backstage entrances in the Swan drawing, the general consensus is that the norm was three, with the central one probably combining its function with that of discovery-space. If curtains were hung across the tiring-house façade, then the central discovery-space need not have had a back access to the tiring-house, as set-ups might have been performed from one of the side entrances under cover of the back-hangings: the presence of only one entrance in *The Wits* drawing argues against its showing a purpose-built playhouse.

Both the *Messallina* and *Roxana* vignettes show trapezoidal stages, edged with a low balustrade. *Messallina* is known to have been first performed at the Salisbury Court, while the *Roxana* illustration, it has been suggested, may depict the Cockpit. It is the shape of the stages, as well as the apparent sitting position of the spectators in the *Roxana* vignette, that has been the basis for asserting that these pictures represent private indoor playhouses, but the recent revelation that the Rose stage was trapezoidal makes this assertion less certain. *The Wits* shows a rectangular stage without railing, adding to the impression that it may have been a temporary erection on trestles. Also, unlike either of the other two drawings, *The Wits* drawing shows both floor and overhead lights – a row of double candles in holders across the front of the stage and two massive chandeliers suspended above it, apparently towards the back and rather to the side. The stage shapes of the Jones/Webb designs have been discussed above: neither shows any indication of how it is to be lit. The eighteenth-century Drottningholm court theatre in Sweden has a parallel system of candle footlights. *The Wits* was printed seventy years after James Burbage embarked on his indoor theatre – after the innovations in perspective scenery and stage machines of Inigo Jones and his collaborators. It is perhaps too uncertain to take it as a model of how the second Blackfriars might have been lit. *Messallina* shows a stage trap, and also an apparently projecting tiring-house façade. *The Wits* may also show a projecting façade, but the drawing is not precise enough to be certain. In *Roxana*, insufficient of the stage is shown to know whether the façade projects or not. There is no projection on the Jones/Webb designs: the tiring-house façade for the Fleet Street project is level across the back of the stage, that of the Cockpit-in-the-Court follows a recessed curve.

Although the private playhouses illustrated in the Jones/Webb designs and the playtexts all date from some decades after the construction of the second Blackfriars, they are consistent enough for some arguments to be advanced about that playhouse on the basis of them. It seems certain that Burbage's second[28] theatre had a tiring-house façade like those of the public playhouses, if on a smaller scale. A projecting stage would have been the norm, although the excavations at the Rose combined with the *Roxana* and *Messallina* vignettes should preclude the assumption that it was necessarily rectangular.

There are two other considerations which must be examined in assessing the likeliest form for Burbage's auditorium. The first is the habit – which has become a cliché in treatments of the theatre of this date – of some members of the audience sitting on stools on the stage. The evidence for this relates almost entirely to the private playhouses: when Thomas Dekker, in his *The Gul's Hornebooke*, advises his aspiring fashionable young man about town to demand a seat on the stage at a public playhouse, he may be offering misleading advice on the lines of 'Try the famous echo in the British Museum Reading Room'. Gurr points out the disadvantages of having members of the audience (however rich and fashionable) sitting on the stage in a public playhouse — they would certainly interfere with the sight-lines of those standing in the yard, and probably of those in the lowest tier of the galleries.[29] Both *The Gul's Hornebooke* and Webster's Induction to Marston's *The Malcontent* (written for the King's Men, who took over the play, as well as the Blackfriars playhouse, from the childrens' company), which also posits an ignorant young man about town who thinks that he may sit on the stage in a public as well as in a private house, indicate that those members of the audience whose view of the stage is interfered with are likely to object vociferously. Evidence from the private playhouses suggests that those members of the audience who took up their places on the stage only interfered with the views of other members of the audience if they actually stood up.[30] This suggests that reconstructions of the Blackfriars which argue for an auditorium with galleries, and perhaps even raked seating on the lines of that provided in the Christ Church theatre, are correct: the conventional arrangement of a modern set-up in a hall, with parallel rows of seating facing the stage would not have been compatible with having members of the audience seated on stage. Nor would such an arrangement have been acoustically viable. Acoustics can be a problem in hall theatres (the rearrangement of Basil's original designs for the Christ Church theatre meant that there were problems with the audibility of the plays performed in it), and the concert halls which have the best acoustics are smallish, usually curved, and in any case with tiers of curved galleries and a good deal of surface variation in walls and ceiling. This is the arrangement which would have been present at the public playhouses — the only difference being the absence of a roof and, in some cases, size. There are no surviving complaints about problems of audibility in the public playhouses, which suggests that the acoustics must have been as good as one might expect from their shape. The natural grouping for a crowd which gathers to watch a street performer is circular, and the models for theatres, both ancient and Renaissance, posited curved auditoria. One would expect that the theatre which James Burbage inserted in the great room high in the Blackfriars would have had curved and raised seating.[31]

However the auditorium was arranged, it can only have seated about 600, or at the most 700 people, but with a minimum entry fee of sixpence, rising to a shilling later in the period, the proceeds from a full house must have been at least £15 per performance. Allowing one penny for accommodation in the yard and twopence for each gallery place, a full house at the second Globe must have brought in a minimum of £25, but that was from an audience nearly six times the size of that of the Blackfriars. If the Theatre was smaller than the first and second Globes, Burbage may have calculated that he could make more from a smaller, exclusive audience in a private theatre than he could from building another amphitheatre playhouse. A private theatre would also be less at risk from the authorities, who were less disturbed by an assembly

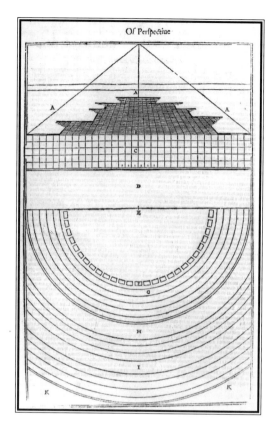

A plan and elevation for theatres from The first [− the fift] booke of Architecture − *the first English edition of Sebastiano Serlio's* L'Architettura *(book 5, Venice, 1569; translated by Robert Peake; London, Simon Stafford for Robert Peake, 1611) − one means by which the knowledge of classical architecture was disseminated. Peake had connections with the theatrical world through his work for the Office of the Revels. (By permission of the Syndics of Cambridge University Library)*

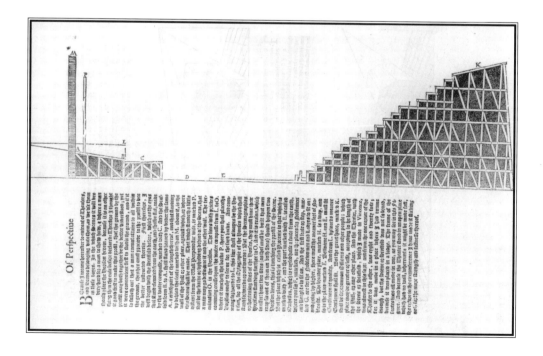

of the élite than by an assembly of the mob, especially with an audience whose demographic make-up might afford it more protection were it to be threatened with closure. Burbage's mistake was to assume that the élite audience who trekked to the northern suburbs to visit his playhouse would welcome its being moved to their own doorstep.

The rooms which were used as temporary theatres in the English Renaissance, and which might, in some cases, be converted to permanent ones, were the same as those which are now used for this purpose – school or college halls; the halls of public buildings; large rooms in inns. That the rooms were the same does not mean that their conversion to theatres was done in the same way. Modern performances in such spaces are done under the influence both of a later theatrical tradition than that of the Renaissance and of the cinema. Both these forms demand an audience which sits in more or less straight lines in front of a set presented in perspective or a flat screen. A Renaissance audience was accustomed to surround, at least partially, the entertainment which was in progress, and might have a dual focus: witnessing not only the play but also the high-status members of the audience who were present at it. The conflict between the need to see the King seeing the play and the need to see the play, has been noticed in connection with Basil's adaptation of the Christ Church theatre; in the case of Elizabeth I's visit to Cambridge, the problem was solved by raising both Queen and play on a scaffold, both forming equal foci for those who were present at the spectacle. Burbage's adaptation of the Blackfriars seems to have included an ingenious answer to the problem posed by the fact that the highest-paying members of the audience regarded themselves as part of the spectacle, and that some of the rest of those attending may have agreed with them. From the quarrel over the fact that Lord Thurles, standing on the stage, interfered with the view of the Essex family party, sitting in a box (Captain Essex attempted to move him out of the way, and Lord Thurles tried to run Captain Essex through, but missed) we may infer the existence of boxes situated beside the stage.[32] Such boxes concentrated both the actors and the fashionable in the same area, so that both could be conveniently viewed by the rest of those present. The same solution may have been found in the public playhouses by siting spectators in the gallery over the stage: it seems likely that the threepenny gallery seats were in those parts of the playhouse galleries closest to the stage. The Thurles-Essex quarrel makes it clear that the lowest tier of gallery seats in the Blackfriars abutted the stage.

We cannot know if Burbage's original plan was to accommodate spectators on stools on the stage. This seems to have arrived as a practice in the performances by children's companies, where there was some pretence that both audience and child actors were taking part in a school performance, and where the presence of some spectators among the players may have added to the informal and in-group tone of the event. By the time the King's Men eventually got the Blackfriars, it was too well-established a custom to abolish, even had they wanted to. The arrangement of the boxes at the Blackfriars was presumably analogous to those in Jones's Fleet Street project – flanking the stage, but raised slightly above it.

Theatre historians are divided between those who favour an auditorium with

The interior of Rycote Chapel, Oxfordshire, showing an early seventeenth-century pew which gives some idea of what a playhouse 'box' may have looked like. (English Heritage Photo Library)

galleries and a level pit,[33] like those of the public theatres (although the first version of the Rose had a raked yard), and those who favour a raked pit in an auditorium more on the lines of those in the Jones/Webb designs and related to the Serlian design used by Basil in the Christ Church theatre.[34] The auditorium certainly had galleries, a pit, boxes around the stage, an upper acting area and three entrances from the tiring-house façade. It was also almost certainly curved – or rather, since the interior fittings were most probably wood-framed in construction, polygonal. While no contemporary theatre survives in England, an idea of the appearance of the boxes may be gained from the form of private pews in churches of this date. The two pews at Rycote in Oxfordshire, supposedly built for a royal visit to the Norris family, are perhaps more elaborate than would have been the case with playhouse fittings (although one must not forget the universal comment on the gorgeousness of such buildings); but less elaborate family pews survive and private accommodation may have been constructed on such lines although with more decoration than in standard family pews.

DECORATION

The lavishness of theatre interiors, such as that at Drottningholm, is part of a tradition which dates back to before the Restoration. The lavishness of nineteenth-century theatre interiors is seen as part of a different tradition from the honest populism of the Elizabethan theatre, but both traditions offered make-believe in a setting which emphasized luxury and escapism – for the two hours' duration of the play all who could afford the entry fee might buy themselves a place in their own palace. The marbled classicism of the Elizabethan playhouse was as much a reflection of palace decoration of its date as the gilding and allegorical figures of the nineteenth-century theatre were of the great houses of that period.

Even temporary theatres of the Elizabethan period were decorated and conceived with great splendour. Panels which are said to have come from Nonesuch Palace, but which may be connected with the Office of the Revels – the department of the Royal household responsible for arranging the staging of entertainments, masques and plays –

survive at Loseley in Surrey. They date from the years 1543–7, and consist of grotesques and figures painted on canvas – the type of decoration which is known to have been used in the temporary halls erected as part of celebrations such as those of the Field of the Cloth of Gold.[35] Temporary theatres were of immense elaboration: John Orrell has examined the evidence for the decoration of temporary structures during the reigns of Henry VIII and Elizabeth I,[36] and the grotesques and allegorical personages at Loseley chime closely with what is known of these. Even in those cases where the interior walls of temporary structures were covered with tapestry, there would still be some painted canvas: the elaborate accommodation erected at Elvetham in 1591 by the Earl of Hertford for the entertainment of Elizabeth I was hung with arras, but the roof was covered with 'works of ivy leaves'.[37]

While temporary adaptations of public rooms for ad hoc theatrical performances were unlikely to have included more than the stage and some sort of tiring-house façade, perhaps on the lines of the booth theatres known from the Dutch tradition – any temporary building or theatrical adaptation of an existing building connected with a royal audience – and certainly any permanent theatre, would have been decorated in lavish style.

The prevailing mode in London and the surrounding area at the time of the adaptation of the Blackfriars theatre was Netherlandish classical; the prevailing mode of theatre design might have been Serlian. James Burbage had already nailed his colours to a classical mast in giving his first playhouse the name 'Theatre'; it is

One of the 'Nonesuch' panels from Loseley, Surrey, perhaps connected with the decoration of temporary entertainment structures under the care of the Office of the Revels. (Courtauld Institute/Loseley Hall)

possible that in his second he produced an exercise in the classical mode, even if it was not one which would have been recognized by an educated eighteenth-century classicist. John Orrell argues that Inigo Jones should not be seen as a great innovator in the playhouse interiors which he designed, but rather as an adaptor of a strong and already existing tradition.[38] Even if the structure was not built using classical principles, it is most likely that it would have been covered with classicizing decoration. Whatever the architectural mode which James Burbage used for his second Blackfriars theatre in 1596, it was still acceptable for his sons and their company to use it in 1609, and the Blackfriars remained a fashionable venue until the closure of the theatres at the outbreak of the Civil War, despite the opening of a number of rival private houses. The dispute between Captain Essex and Lord Thurles took place in 1632, and the clientele at the Blackfriars was then a fashionable one. In an age when playhouses might degenerate into unusability within fifteen years, like the Rose, or become so *demodé* that no fashionable person would dream of being seen there, like the Curtain, it suggests that the design of James Burbage's second playhouse was at least up-to-date, and perhaps even in advance of its time.

CHAPTER SEVEN

THE ROSE AND GLOBE EXCAVATIONS

On 10 January 1587 Philip Henslowe, Citizen and Dyer of London, and John Cholmley, Citizen and Grocer of London, entered into a partnership over a plot of ground 94 feet square between Rose Alley and Maiden Lane in Southwark, on the south bank of the Thames. Henslowe was to be responsible for a playhouse 'now in framinge and shortly to be ereckted' on the plot; Cholmley was to be free to employ a small dwelling house on the south part of the site, near Maiden Lane, as a location for selling victuals to the anticipated audience. Both men were to share the profits from the playhouse. Cholmley invested £816 in the enterprise, to be paid quarterly in instalments of £25 10s. The actual construction of the playhouse was in the hands of John Grygge, Carpenter.[1]

Cholmley's investment was a substantial one. The latter part of the sixteenth century saw a boom for the English building industry, both in the number of new buildings and in innovations in design. In the 1570s most of Longleat was built for £8,000 (with the addition of freestone, timber and fuel for brickmaking); Wollaton cost Sir Francis Willoughby £8,000 between 1580 and 1588.[2] These are two of the great 'prodigy houses'. Cholmley cannot have been putting up all the capital for the Rose (the fact that he retained the whole refreshment concession as well as half the playhouse takings suggests that his capital input may have been greater than Henslowe's), but that the cost of a playhouse was even one-tenth that of a prodigy house suggests the size of the undertaking.[3]

Little is known about John Cholmley, and he quickly fades from the records. But the Rose in which he was a partner is the best documented of all the Renaissance playhouses. Henslowe's papers record its history, the various refurbishments which it underwent, the names of many of its company and their private affairs, the writers who provided its plays, and their small fees, the comparative success or failure of those plays, the nature of the costumes and properties which were used in productions, and how much those items cost. Scholarly and popular interest has centred upon the first Globe, the playhouse with which Shakespeare is associated (although the Theatre and the Blackfriars played important parts in his career), but much of what is assumed about production methods at the Globe is posited on what we know of the Rose.

THE DISCOVERY OF THE ROSE

It was serendipitous when, in 1989, archaeologists from the Museum of London, carrying out a rescue excavation in advance of redevelopment on the parcel of land

The site of the Rose theatre from the south showing the remains and the position of the piles. (Andrew Fulgoni)

about which Cholmley and Henslowe had made their agreement over 400 years earlier, came upon the foundations of a polygonal timber-framed building which could only be the Rose. The site was known to be that of the Rose, although the theatre's exact location in the plot was not fixed, but it was thought that any traces left by the short-lived playhouses (the Rose existed for less than twenty years, and its rapid deterioration on a water-saturated site by the river was assumed to point to its having been jerry-built on insubstantial foundations) would have been destroyed by later intensive development, particularly in the nineteenth century, when most buildings were constructed with cellars. The last development of the site had been in 1957, when Southbridge House was built. No archaeological remains had been noted at that time, and it was assumed that the piles driven in to support that building would have substantially damaged any remains (in fact, they turned out to have mostly landed in the playhouse yard, where the damage they inflicted was minimal). Only the archaeological consultant Richard Hughes, who believed that it was possible that remains of the Rose had been preserved, and in 1971 reported to a potential developer of the site that 'This should be considered one of those areas where public action could make excavations and preservation a national issue', showed any prescience. His opinion remained unknown to the 1989 developer, Imry Merchant (which behaved correctly throughout the ensuing debacle).[4]

Although literary sentiment dictates that, given a choice of all the Renaissance playhouses, one would most like to come upon the well-preserved remains of the Globe, the Rose, accompanied as it is by substantial documentation, is that which has the potential to be most useful to the scholar. From the point of view of scholarship, there was only one way of dealing with this unique survival – excavation in order to obtain the maximum possible information from the site.[5] But, at this point, other interests began to intrude on the ideal world.

Despite years of education by bodies such as the Council for British Archaeology, Rescue and the York Archaeological Trust, and numerous television programmes, including that about the spectacular raising of the Mary Rose, there is little understanding, even among the well-educated public, of the processes of archaeology. An archaeological excavation is a labour-intensive and time-consuming operation, in which a piece of ground is demolished, grain by grain, often using dental picks and toothbrushes rather than the picks and shovels of popular imagination. In dealing with most urban sites, it is now considered best to uncover the whole site and deal with it as an organic unit, rather than concentrating on particular disputed areas in isolation from the rest.[6] Archaeological excavation is destructive. During excavation, a site is taken apart, sorted into its component fragments and then reassembled in laboratory and study, its nature being revealed only in the final excavation report. A properly excavated site will be unavailable to subsequent excavators except through its finds and excavation report. This is the reason for the slowness of the process of excavation on a unique site. Scholarly integrity requires precise recording of every stage of excavation for the benefit of future scholars.

Nor is it possible, having exposed it, to leave a site like the Rose while discussions continue about its optimum treatment. Timber-framed and thatched buildings are best preserved, as the Rose was, in a sealed deposit on a water-logged site, but exposure to the air causes rapid deterioration in waterlogged organic materials, which are frequently of the consistency of stewed meat. They cannot be conserved *in situ*: public display of such a site involves dismantling it, conserving the materials in laboratories and then returning them to the place where they were found. The lifting and preservation of such materials is also time-consuming and labour-intensive. In some cases, organic materials may have rotted away but their existence can be traced in the form of changes in soil texture and colour. Such materials require delicacy and care, and again provide an argument for a large-scale excavation on an open site: if they are encountered in a small test-excavation they may be damaged – or missed altogether. Archaeological, and theatre-historical interests therefore demanded that the Rose site be excavated as minutely as possible, without any pressures from deadlines. As a unique – and possibly perpetually unique – survival of one of the most important aspects of the English cultural heritage, it was a national treasure on a par with Tutankhamun's tomb.

There were, however, other considerations in the way in which the site was dealt with. These stemmed in part from a widespread failure to realize the importance of the discovery. The picture of Shakespeare's theatre – the Globe, the wooden O – was so popularly familiar that few people outside the theatrical and academic communities realized how little evidence there was for this reconstruction. Even in academia, those outside the fields of literature and history were sometimes unaware that the only visual evidence for the internal appearance of a Renaissance playhouse was one drawing. In Europe, archaeologists tend to regard post-medieval remains (unless they may be classified as 'industrial archaeology') as intrinsically uninteresting, because of the abundance of standing buildings of the period: post-1500 stratigraphy represents the boring trowel-work which must be performed in order to get at the riches below. The archaeological community as a whole, as opposed to those who were performing the excavation or who had experience of post-medieval work, was slow to realize the importance of the finds which were about to be reburied under an office block.[7] The developer was anxious to proceed with the building, as delays in its construction schedule meant losing money. It agreed to a ten-week postponement of construction work, but this was far from meeting the needs of the archaeologists. The planning permission for the new building could have been cancelled by the direct intervention of the Secretary of State for the Environment, but, since the developers had acted in good faith throughout, they would have been entitled to substantial compensation – estimated at £5–25 million.[8] The then Secretary of State, Nicholas Ridley, noted for his unsentimental attitude to the national cultural heritage, refused to schedule the Rose as an ancient monument.

THE CAMPAIGN TO SAVE THE ROSE

The credit for saving the Rose, insofar as it has been saved, must go to those people, led by members of the theatrical community, who on the night of 13–14 May 1989 physically prevented the developers from bringing on to the site the machinery with which they planned to start work. They gained time for various preservation strategies to be discussed, and ensured that some steps were taken to preserve the remains before building eventually took place. It was their action, and the attendant publicity, which probably convinced Imry Merchant that, in acquiring the plot of land developed by Henslowe and Cholmley four centuries earlier, it had acquired a major potential tourist attraction and money-spinner.

But the theatrical lobby's convictions had their own limitations. In order to gain the maximum publicity, it invoked the name of Shakespeare and made unsustainable and unproven claims about his supposed connection with the playhouse. The tentative suggestion that Shakespeare may at one time have been a member of the theatrical troupe Strange's Men, and therefore played at the Rose, was turned into fact, and contemporary actors standing on the Elizabethan ground level proclaimed that these were the very boards that the Swan of Avon had himself trodden – thus disturbing both archaeologists, who knew that if Shakespeare had trodden any boards there those boards had been located approximately at his twentieth-century successor's head level, and theatre historians and literary critics, who regarded the idea that Shakespeare acted at the Rose as at best unproven and at worst one of a number of theories about his early theatrical career, and not necessarily the most plausible one. Similarly unsustainable claims were made about the Rose as the site of the putative premiere of some of Shakespeare's early plays. Henslowe's accounts for 1594 contain records of productions of 'titus & ondronicus', marked as 'ne' on its first appearance on 23 January 1594.[9] This is agreed to be Shakespeare's *Titus Andronicus*. But while the endorsement by the performance of 23 January may indicate that this was the first performance of the play at the Rose, it is unlikely that it was the first performance ever. *Titus Andronicus* is generally agreed to be an early play, conventionally dated to the period 1584–92.[10] It was printed in 1594 with the information on the title-page that it had been 'plaide by the Right Honourable the Earle of Darbie, Earle of Pembrooke, and Earle of Sussex their servants'. 'Sussex's Men' was the name that the Rose company were acting under in 1594, and the wording on the title-page suggests that the other companies mentioned had preceded them in their productions of the play.[11] While *Titus Andronicus* was performed at the Rose, it almost certainly did not, as the thespian lobby claimed, have its first performance there. (Gurr's suggestion that Henslowe bought the play from Pembroke's Men after that company's failure in 1593 seems plausible.)[12] Problems, although less serious ones, also attach to the claim that the play 'harey the vi', which entered the repertory of the Rose (marked 'ne') performed by Strange's Men on 3 March 1591, and was played fifteen times between then and 31 January 1593, was Shakespeare's *Henry VI Part I*.[13] This is plausible, but not certain: plays did have duplicate titles at this date. The *Henry V* which appears in Henslowe's papers between 28 November 1595 and 15 July 1596 is known to be the surviving anonymous *Famous Victories of Henry VI*, rather than Shakespeare's play of that title. (One should perhaps be grateful that the fact that the Rose's repertoire in 1594 included a *Hamlet*[14] (probably by Thomas Kyd) did not become generally known.)

More serious than the spurious and inflated claims made for the Rose as the cradle of Shakespeare's thespian and literary genius (the opportunity to promote it as the theatre of Christopher Marlowe was unaccountably missed, although Marlowe's tabloid life might have proved as attractive a vehicle for attracting publicity as the magic name of Shakespeare) were the demands of the theatrical lobby for the preservation of the Rose exactly as it was in May 1989, without further disturbance of the finds by excavation, and with no appreciation of the fact that, unless the excavation was properly completed and the finds removed for conservation before being replaced *in situ*, the Rose remains would inevitably deteriorate and eventually be lost.

In the midst of these conflicting interests, the best strategy for the preservation of the Rose became lost, and this loss was compounded by an apparent failure of nerve on the part of the archaeologists responsible for digging the site when, after the government had finally agreed to pay Imry Merchant £1,000,000 for a thirty-day delay in starting building operations while the options for dealing with the site were discussed, archaeological excavation ceased. This was despite the fact that the site might deteriorate under exposure to the air,[15] that there was no guarantee that the controversy would be decided in a way that would permit further exploration of the site at a later date (the stance of the Secretary of State made it plausible that the eventual decision might involve destruction of the remains, or at least substantial damage to them), and that the thirty-day breathing-space might have been profitably used to extend the sum of human knowledge through further excavation.[16] Distinguished archaeologists experienced in dealing with structures of the period, notably Professor Martin Biddle,[17] urged strongly that excavation should proceed through the grace period, but their advice was rejected.

The eventual decision was that Imry Merchant should redesign its building to minimize intrusion on the Rose site, that the remains should be recovered, with precautions taken against deterioration and damage during construction work, and that excavation, leading to eventual public display of the site, should resume after the Imry Merchant building was finished.[18] This was done, and the Rose, briefly exposed, was returned to the obscurity in which it spent four centuries.

Before its extinction there was another unseemly scholarly squabble, this time confined to the archaeological community. The initial excavations had been undertaken by a team from the Museum of London. English Heritage, the government body which has overall responsibility for national historical monuments and antiquities, had conducted the negotiations with Imry Merchant over the future of the site. The redesigned Imry Merchant building was at one point very close to the edge of the Rose site as it had been projected from the excavations so far achieved, in the area where it seemed likely that there might be remains of the doorway to the playhouse and traces of staircase access to the galleries, areas of particular interest.[19] English Heritage asked the Museum team to do some 'keyhole excavations' in the areas threatened by the redesigned piles, but the Museum team, believing that this technique was inappropriate on a site which should be dealt with by open-area excavation, demurred. English Heritage therefore put in its own Central Excavation Unit to do the work. This proved inconclusive, but it seems unlikely that excavators unfamiliar with the site could gain anything useful from tiny exposures.[20]

By 1995 no date had been set for the resumption of the excavation: it is to be hoped that the steps taken to ensure the Rose's conservation will prove to have been effective, and that the site has not suffered disturbance from the building activity taking place around and above it. Should it prove, when uncovered, to have suffered substantial deterioration, the month's hiatus in excavation before its final fate was decided will seem even more deplorable.

THE DISCOVERY OF THE GLOBE

The discovery of the Rose made it seem possible that remains of the Globe might also survive, and the owners of its site, the Hanson Group, asked the Museum of London to undertake excavations there well in advance of planned redevelopment.[21] In October 1989 the archaeologists uncovered a small section of the gallery walls, and what is probably one of the external staircase towers of the second Globe playhouse.[22]

While these exploratory excavations were a model of good archaeological practice, making feasible a well-planned and unhurried excavation of as much of the Globe site as is not located under listed buildings and major roads, cooperation between scholarly disciplines seems, as in the case of the Rose, to have left something to be desired.

The second Globe had been the subject of a piece of brilliant scholarly reconstruction in John Orrell's *The Quest for Shakespeare's Globe*,[23] and archaeologists from the Museum of London had certainly encountered Professor Orrell during the Rose excavations earlier in 1989. In his book, Orrell worked back from Wenceslaus Hollar's *Long View of London* (see illustration on p. 60), published in 1647, but based on drawings done more than a decade earlier, and used his knowledge of seventeenth-century surveying, map-making and topographical drawing techniques to project the dimensions and the exact location of the second Globe. Since this is believed to have been built on the foundations of the first Globe, the dimensions and locations of that building were also fixed by this process. Orrell came to the conclusion that the Globe measured between 101.37 feet and 102.32 feet in diameter, and he fixed its position with some precision on the piece of ground where it was known to have stood.[24] Despite the fact that the fragment of the Globe uncovered turned up within inches of Orrell's projected location, no reference was made in the evaluation of the site to Orrell's work (the most recent book on theatre history cited was W. W. Braines: *The Site of the Globe Playhouse, Southwark*, and this not the revised edition of 1924 but the original of 1922)[25] and the computer projection for the dimensions of the Globe produced by the archaeologists differed from Orrell's by as much as one-fifth. This produced some anguished correspondence in the letters column of *The Times*,[26] and one presumes that the London archaeologists' apparent ignorance of Orrell's published work has now been silently amended.

The *Evaluation* and the related article in the *London Archaeologist* also display other evidence of a failure on the part of those responsible for the excavation to read the background material on the Globe before starting excavation. Both are illustrated with Visscher's view of the Globe from his panorama of London of 1616. This has long been discredited as having any status as an accurate representation of the playhouse, and, at the time of publication, a version of Visscher's view, with a careful exposition of why both it and the engraving upon which it was based had to be considered spurious, was on view at the British Museum in the exhibition entitled *Fake? The Art of Deception*.[27]

THE LESSONS FOR HANDLING FUTURE EXCAVATIONS

Both the Rose and the Globe excavations expose the problems faced by an increasingly fragmented scholarly community. The problem is not as simple as lack of cooperation, for at the Rose a high degree of cooperation was achieved – particularly in the campaign to ensure the preservation of the remains. It is heartening to point out that in both cases the owners of the site acted correctly and cooperatively throughout, although Imry Merchant was perhaps slow to appreciate the commercial potential of

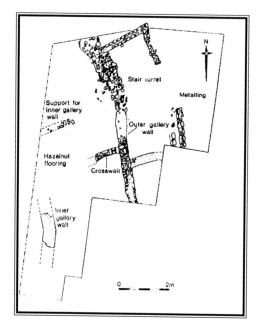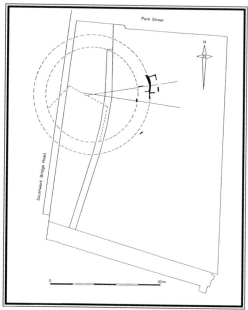

A plan of the excavated galleries of the Globe theatre and its projected outline from the test excavations (Figs 3 and 7, Antiquity 66: 315–33). (Museum of London).

what had been found in its basement. Sam Wanamaker's Globe is a few yards away, and cooperation with this enterprise, which incorporates all the commercial and hygienic features thought necessary to the modern tourist,[28] would ensure a commercial benefit to the company which it cannot have anticipated when it acquired the site. But the excavations, which should have been a joint exercise – the archaeologists profiting from the substantial researches of the historians of the theatre, and the theatre historians themselves learning from the archaeologists – suffered from both sides' ignorance of the other's discipline. The failure of the archaeologists fully to assimilate the substantial work which had been done on the buildings they were excavating is less egregious in the case of the Rose, where they had little expectation of finding anything, than in that of the Globe, where it was hoped that they might and where the experience of the Rose dig should have drawn to their attention the existence of the theatre historians' work. But the theatre historians themselves perhaps made the assumption – common among the learned – that a piece of information which they regard as commonplace is shared by everyone. The archaeological community did not realize that not only had none of the great Renaissance playhouses survived the Commonwealth, but that there was only one contemporary picture of a playhouse interior. The unconscious assumption that the familiar image of the Elizabethan playhouse (usually the Globe) was based on a great deal of available evidence was the more natural for the nearby site of the projected reconstruction of the Globe. In fact, any image we have of the playhouses, apart from rather generalized images of the exterior of the second Globe and the stage area of the Swan, are based, according to preferred definition, on rigorous scholarly inquiry into a variety of sources leading to informed deduction, or guesswork.[29]

Nor did the literary community in general appreciate the nature of good archaeological evidence. The Rose remains are substantial, incorporating bricks, stone, chalk foundation walls and timbers, as well as the general scatter of debris found on any site that has been used by human beings.[30] The outlines of both stages and of the galleries are clearly visible. But most non-archaeologists are unused to seeing sites in the course of excavation, being familiar with archaeology only from visits to excavations which have been completed, with the finds displayed and labelled in a way that makes them easier for the untrained visitor to comprehend. Archaeologists working at the site were amused by the numbers of overheard comments which indicated that visitors believed that the concrete piles of the 1950s building were part of the Rose.[31] Such ability to misunderstand and misread a site became harmful when, during the controversy over whether the site should be saved, members of the literary community who had visited the site dismissed it on the radio as having 'hardly anything left'[32] – a judgement with which no archaeologist could have agreed. Nor was there a general appreciation that the excavation was far from complete. What was exposed was only the top of the finds: further and complete excavation to the bottom of the Elizabethan foundation level will be necessary before the full value of the site can be appreciated.

Future projects of this type (and the survival of both the Rose and the Globe provides a compelling argument that preliminary archaeological surveys should be undertaken at the sites of the other playhouses of this era, to assess the chances of similar finds there) must involve a greater exchange of views and methodology on the part of scholars from the various disciplines involved, and an attempt by the archaeologists to make sure that those who visit the site understand what they see. Public incomprehension may not damage a site which is protected and where long-term excavation is assured, but it can be dangerous if public opinion is being enlisted in defence of a threatened site. A general effort on the part of those whose excavations are on public display to make sure that they explain what is going on and what each visible feature represents may help to avert the sort of damaging and ill-informed generalizations that were made in the case of the Rose.

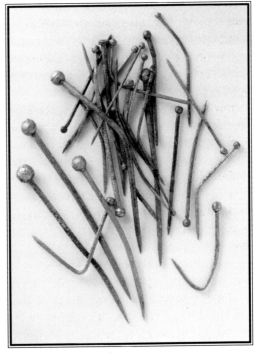

Dress pins from the Rose excavation site. (Photograph by Andy Chopping; Museum of London)

THE FINDINGS OF THE ROSE EXCAVATION

The Rose is an informative site. While there is a great deal of data about the plays mounted in the Rose, the companies who put them on and the management of the playhouse, until its discovery little was known about the building itself. It was built in 1587, worked on in 1592, and repaired, with the addition of a throne in the heavens, in 1595.[33] The last recorded performance there was in 1603, and it had been demolished by 1606.[34] The agreement between Henslowe and Cholmley proves that it was a timber-framed building (the contract refers to it as 'now in framing' – the timber frame was being prefabricated before being taken apart to be re-erected on the site).[35] Timber-frame construction meant that the building was likely to be polygonal, but the number of sides of the polygon was a guess. Nor were the dimensions of the playhouse known. Although the size of Henslowe's plot precluded the Rose reaching the projected dimension of the Globe and Swan, Orrell's work on the Globe, together with de Witt's linking of the Rose with the Swan, might have led scholars to expect that the playhouse would have a diameter of up to 90 feet.[36] In fact, it had a diameter of 72 feet. The lists of building materials purchased by Henslowe for his 1592 works at the playhouse – the nature of which was not known before the excavation – showed that the building was at least partly thatched (and that the ironmonger where Henslowe made substantial purchases of nails and other hardware was located in Southwark and called The Fryingpan).[37] The roof of the Rose may be seen poking out from among trees on Norden's panorama of London (see illustration on p. 61). The 1592 alterations had included making a 'penthowsse shed at the tyeringe hosse doore' out of 'owld tymber'.[38] The playhouse was at least partially painted and plastered, the staircases, or perhaps the fronts of the galleries, had turned balusters; and in 1592 the lord's room and 'the room ouer the tyerhowsse' had ceilings installed. The alterations in 1592 cost Henslowe over £105; those of 1595 cost £108 19s, with an additional £7 2s for the installation of a throne in the heavens above the stage.

The tantalizing entries in Henslowe's papers were to some extent elucidated by the archaeological discovery of the site. Not only was the Rose much better preserved than had been anticipated, but it provided far more information than could have been hoped. About 70 per cent of the playhouse was exposed to view.[39] Despite the fact that it functioned as a playhouse for only sixteen years, its history as a building fell into at least two periods, and Henslowe's expenditure in 1592 turned out to have been on an enlargement of the building which increased its audience capacity by about 15 per cent.

THE 1587 BUILDING

The first playhouse, of 1587, was a polygon with thirteen or fourteen sides (the part of the theatre adjacent to Southwark Bridge Road which remained unexcavated precludes a more precise decision). The fact that the polygon had many short sides rather than few long ones settles a decades-long debate: deductions made from Hollar's depiction of the Globe, rather than other engravings, were correct. What was a surprise (although perhaps it should not have been in view of the comparative irregularity of other contemporary vernacular timber-framed buildings) was the irregularity of the shape – the factor which precludes certainty about the exact number of sides. The yard was surrounded by two roughly parallel walls, about 10 feet apart, which contained the galleries.

The construction of the outer wall, so far as it has been excavated, consisted of a series of piles, formed out of large stone blocks, over which lay brick-strengthened chalk pile caps, which supported a chalk foundation wall. On the basis of contemporary building practice, the archaeologists suggest that this foundation layer would have been surmounted by a low brick wall on top of which would have lain the sleeper beams which were the load-sharing members for the superstructure. The inner wall seems to have been 'a trench-built structure of chalk and flint', but there are some

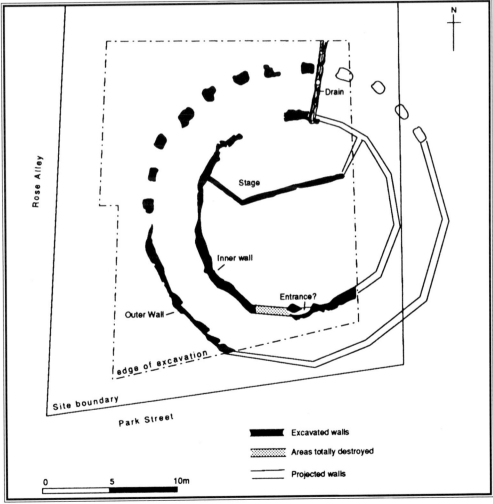

A plan of the first Rose, as revealed by the excavations. (Excavation plan drawn by Alison Hawkins; Museum of London)

places where parts of a brick superstructure remain. The stage of this first playhouse was a trapezium jutting out from the line of the inner wall, slightly west of north. (The fact that both stages of the playhouse faced south–east was a blow to most recent scholarly opinion,[40] which had been almost unanimous that the playhouses were oriented north–east, away from the afternoon sun.) It was 15 feet 6 inches deep, and a maximum of 37 feet 9 inches wide, tapering to a minimum of 27 feet 6 inches wide at front and at the rear, where it abutted the inner gallery wall. No evidence remains of whether the tiring house façade extended across it at stage level (which was probably about 5 feet above its surviving foundations) but, assuming there was no encroachment upon the playing space, this gives a maximum stage area of less than 500 square feet. The Fortune's stage area, again assuming that it was not encroached on by the tiring-house, was 1,682 ½ square feet, so that of the Rose was much smaller. Also, unlike the stage of the Fortune and that of the second Globe, on the basis of Hollar's depiction of the stage-canopy, the Rose's stage did not project to the midline of the yard. Even if the assumption made on the basis of Hollar's panorama is correct, and the line of the cover does reflect the extent of the stage beneath it, there are reasons for using the Rose stage as a basis for questioning whether the stages of all the playhouses were, like those of the Swan and the Fortune, rectangular. The Fortune is anomalous among the playhouses for its rectangular shape, whether that was caused by its insertion into an existing building, or by the exigencies of the plot of ground on which it was erected. The Boar's Head had a rectangular stage, but it was built in an inn-yard. The Fortune contract specifies the general dimensions of the playhouse and the aspects in which it is to differ from its model, the first Globe, which had just been erected by the same builder, Peter Street.[41] After describing the dimensions of the stage, and that it is to be paled in with oak boarding, the contract continues that it is to be in all other proportions like the stage of the Globe. This leaves the possibility that the stage of the Globe itself was not rectangular. The stage of the Rose is a more logical shape, and more aesthetically pleasing, than a rectangular projection, granted the multi-sided polygonal arena. The *Roxana* and *Messallina* vignettes (see illustrations on pp. 150, 91) depict stages which may be trapezoidal. John Webb's 1660–2 restoration of Inigo Jones's 1629–31 Cockpit-in-the-Court theatre has a curved tiring-house façade to the rear of the stage, echoing, as the rear line of the Rose stages seem to do, the general shape of the internal auditorium wall.[42] The Swan, which was a polygonal playhouse with a rectangular stage (if the de Witt sketch is to be trusted), was not built by a person from the entertainment world, and did not have a record of success as a playhouse. The Rose excavation makes it necessary that we re-examine the evidence and question whether the rectangular or trapezoidal stage should be taken as the Elizabethan norm.

It was the feeling – remarked by the excavators – of those employed in the modern professional theatre who stood on the stage of the Rose that both stage and auditorium were pleasantly shaped and related to each other well. It would have been a good place to act in. The shape of the Rose stage means that the accommodation in the yard for those standing was a better shape at the sides of the stage than the 6 by 27½ feet corridors into which they had to cram themselves on a full day at the Fortune. The bulk of the audience accommodation in the playhouses was, contrary to the popular impression, in the more expensive galleries, rather than in the cheaper yard,[43] so presumably the places with restricted view at the sides of the stage would be occupied only on days when the playhouse was filled to maximum capacity, but the overall sight-lines must have been better at the Rose than at the Fortune.

The stage of the first Rose shows no evidence of foundations for a stage cover, nor of any projecting façade such as that probably shown in the Swan sketch. Since the playhouse exists only at foundation level, the presence of a projecting façade supported on the stage itself cannot be ruled out, but the foundation for the front of the stage ('a solid wall of brick and timber') might not have been strong enough for any projection on to the stage to be substantial in nature. The already small size of the stage militates against there being any extensive incursion into it by a projecting façade. John Orrell has argued that a stage-cover or heavens were a comparatively late innovation in playhouse design, and that the partial cover observable in the Swan drawing represents a transitional phase between the Theatre and Curtain, where there is no evidence for any heavens, and the second Globe, where the heavens may be seen on Hollar's panorama to have been massive.[44] However, much of Orrell's argument rests on his interpretation of the view of the two northern playhouses, which is a matter of minute and unclear detail. The amount of money expended on costumes, together with the nature of the materials from which they were made (water marks are fatal to silk, and the heavy padding of much Elizabethan costume would have caused water penetration to be a problem) makes it seem unlikely that these resources would be risked by being exposed to the English climate without any cover, unless the actors covered their costumes with cloaks every time the weather was inclement. A comparatively lightweight heavens (perhaps made of wooden shingles, which were found during the excavation) mounted on pillars based on the stage would have been feasible even in the 1587 Rose, and the 1592 remodelling may have included this feature in a version substantial enough for the insertion of a flying mechanism into it a few years later. There is no convincing evidence for the presence of a stage cover in the first Rose; but nor is there any certainty that one did not exist. The stage seems to have been supported at the front on a brick and timber wall. Archaeological interpretation of this area of the early playhouse suffers from the fact that the stage area was rebuilt in 1592, and so there is not even the small amount of building debris for this stage of the building which is left from the demolition of its second phase.

Apart from the shape and orientation of the stage, the most surprising aspect of the first Rose was the fact that the yard floor was raked, with the northern half of the yard sloping down to the front of the stage. The archaeologists describe this feature as 'logical', but it must have presented many problems. The Rose was built on damp ground near the river; the presence of a timber box drain running from the rear of the stage to a ditch which formed the northern plot boundary indicates that drainage of the site was a problem. The source for the water which fed into this drain is still unknown. There are traces in the first yard of erosion round the edges of the floor, where rain dripped off the gallery roof, and against the front of the stage, which the archaeologists ascribe either to the action of water or to the effect of the standing members of the audience pressing forward to the foot of the stage. Andrew Gurr puts forward the tentative suggestion that both these features might be linked with the presence of a stage cover in the pre-1592 playhouse, pointing out that two of the plays known to have been performed in it seem to demand the use of stage posts[45] Experience of the English climate suggests that those standing at the foot of the stage would frequently find themselves standing in puddles, as the rake on the auditorium caused surface water to drain towards the stage. The wear noted may be due either to an excess amount of standing water in that area or to the effect of the feet of the groundlings on a saturated area of the yard. It is assumed that the groundlings would have pressed forward to the foot of the stage, but this is not necessarily the logical behaviour for an audience in such an arena: a forward position is advisable in order to avoid having to look over the heads of those in front, but would not necessarily give the best view of the overall action. If the stage height was, as seems to have been the norm, about 5 feet, which was about eye-level for a population whose overall average height may have been rather less than it is today, a position against the front of the stage might involve a disagreeable craning of the neck. The places closest to the stage were the cheapest in the house, and this cannot have been related solely to the fact that no seats were provided – rather, the decision not to provide seats in this area may have been related to the fact that it supplied the worst view. At the Swan theatre at Stratford-upon-Avon, a better view may be obtained from seats set back from the thrust stage, rather than immediately below it, with the optimum view coming from the lower-level of galleries – the galleries being more expensive in the Elizabethan public playhouses. The wear observed is not necessarily to be ascribed to the feet of eager playgoers, who, except on occasions when the playhouse was very crowded, may have chosen to stand further back from the stage, at the raised southern end of the yard, from which the best view might be obtained.

The entrance has not been pin-pointed, but the presence of brick footings in the south-eastern part of the internal wall, opposite the stage, suggests that it may have been located here. The English Heritage dig found the foundations of the outer wall to have been parallel to the inner at this point, and close to the boundary ditch of the property. It is known that access to the playhouse was gained by a footbridge over a ditch, and the location of the entrance in the early playhouses has generally been thought to be opposite the stage. The absence of any sign of an entrance to the playhouse in the Swan drawing has always been taken as suggesting that it was behind de Witt's vantage-point in the sketch.

The presence of three brick cross-walls in the western gallery is suggested by the excavators to be connected with entrances to the gallery from the yard, by analogy with those shown in the Swan drawing. There is, as yet, no trace of the staircases which would have been necessary to gain access to the upper galleries which are assumed to have existed. The logical place for the location of these, in the absence of any external staircase towers, would have been near to the gallery entrance. The other possible explanation for these cross-walls is that they mark the site of the 'lords' room', or private box, which is known to have existed in Elizabethan playhouses but whose location is uncertain. Lords' rooms are believed to have been located in the gallery over the stage (also in use as a music-room and to provide an upper acting area). The brick cross-walls are sited at one of the points in the galleries where an optimum view of the stage might be obtained, and one at which the occupants of the galleries would be clearly visible to other members of the audience. (The fact that the rich and aristocratic Elizabethan went to the playhouse to be seen rather than to hear the play is one of the strongest arguments put forward in defence of the theory that the lords' rooms were in the over-stage gallery, because this location would have a seriously restricted viewpoint, and be uncomfortably close to the music, besides being liable to disruption during plays with scenes set above.) Comparatively little is known about the exact divisions and arrangement of Elizabethan public playhouse seating: Thomas Platter writes about his 1599 visit, during which he saw a play at the Curtain, that

> whoever cares to stand below only pays one English penny, but if he wishes to sit he enters by another door, and pays another penny, while if he desires to sit in the most comfortable seats which are cushioned, where he not only sees everything well, but can also be seen, then he pays yet another English penny at another door.[46]

In Henslowe's account of his expenses for the 1592 building works at the Rose, the items relating to the ceilings of the room over the tirehouse and the lords' room, together with wages for a plasterer – which suggests that they were plaster, not board ceilings – are adjacent, which may indicate that the lords room was in the tiring house gallery. If two of the cross-walls in the Rose galleries do relate to an access stairway therefore, the third may relate to some division in the galleries – perhaps the point at which the twopenny gallery was separated from the more expensive seating, situated in the northern section adjacent to the stage.

THE 1592 REDEVELOPMENT

Henslowe's accounts reveal that a great deal of work was done at the Rose in 1592. The excavations have shown what this was. The playhouse was extended northward; the tiring-house area, the northward galleries and the stage were rebuilt, and the yard was resurfaced. The alterations changed the shape of the playhouse, making it into an angular horseshoe with a curved, closed end. The stage retained its basic shape, but, because there was now more yard space at its sides, it appeared to thrust out more into the auditorium. The excavators note that the alterations increased the size of the yard by just over 15 per cent, but more important from Henslowe's point of view would have been the increase in the capacity of the galleries, in the area where the more expensive seats were located. The emphasis in studies of audiences in the Elizabethan playhouse always seems to be on the groundlings, but estimates of the capacity of the yard of the enlarged Rose vary between about 800 and 1,000, while the enlarged galleries would have held about 1,650. This compares with figures for the earlier stage of the building of

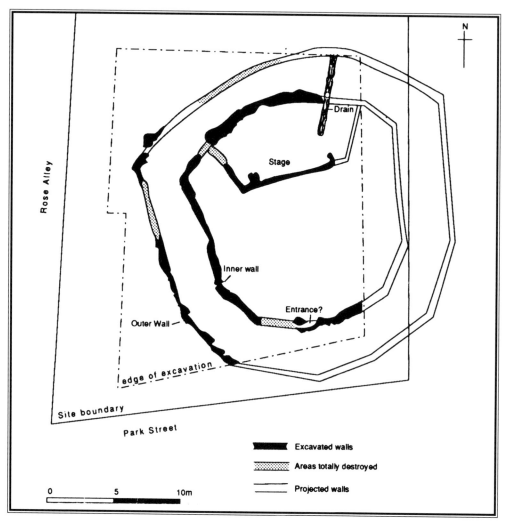

N

Rose Alley

Drain

Stage

Inner wall

Entrance?

Outer Wall —

edge of excavation

Site boundary

Park Street

Excavated walls

Areas totally destroyed

Projected walls

0   5   10m

A plan of the Rose after the alterations of 1592, as revealed by the excavations. (Excavation plan drawn by Alison Hawkins; Museum of London)

600 in the yard, and 1,400 in the galleries. The enlargement therefore increased the Rose's possible takings (using the more conservative figure for the yard capacity) by 200*d* (or 16*s* 8*d*) in the yard, but by 41*s* 8*d* in the galleries.[47] The interest of all in the Elizabethan theatre industry must have been, as a matter of economics, focused on the galleries rather than on the ground. Since Henslowe's share of the playhouse takings seems to have been half the gallery receipts, this is the area in which he would have been most interested.

The new stage was more massively constructed than the first, and there is definite evidence, in the form of pillar bases just inside its front wall, that it had a canopy. The heavier construction overall suggests the addition of a stage hut. The Norden panorama of 1600 shows the Rose, like the first Globe, with a gable jutting forward at the same level as the gallery roofs, rather than with a stage hut rising above the galleries, as is shown in the Swan drawing and, Orrell suggests, in the view of the northern playhouses[48] – an arrangement common in contemporary vernacular building. Norden shows this gable as thatched, but the presence on the floor of the second yard of wooden shingles, as well as thatch, left from the playhouse's demolition, suggests to the excavators that these were used for the stage canopy. Wooden shingles would be the logical material to use for such a purpose. They are frequently found in conjunction with thatch on penthouse areas where a lighter cover is needed (thatch is a heavy material if used in the correct density) and where it is impossible to achieve sufficient slope for the adequate drainage of thatch.[49] It is not clear if the new stage cover was guttered, as later covers, such as those of the Fortune and Hope, are known to have been. The archaeologists suggest that a thin erosion line in the new yard floor about 3 feet in front of the stage might represent rainwater run-off from the stage roof. This would have created an area in which it was unpleasant to stand on wet days. That the heavens at the redesigned Rose were of the type in which a throne (probably a mechanism for flying in supernatural characters, rather than a chair of state which could be raised or lowered) might be inserted is assumed because of the later insertion of just such a throne in 1595.

The design of the yard itself was also altered in association with the extension of the playhouse. The rake was abolished, and the level was raised to cover the traces of the former stage and internal gallery walls. The alteration of the design of the yard surface suggests that the rake did prove impracticable because of the soggy results of internal drainage. The new floor was of better quality than its predecessor. The first floor had been made of mortar, but its successor was a mixture of compacted earth, cinder and cracked hazelnut shells, which have also turned up in the floor of the excavated fragment of the Globe, and so may be presumed to have been a satisfactory flooring material. It is, according to the excavators, still 'rock-hard', and would have given better drainage than the mortar floor.[50] Standing where it did, close to the river, on a plot surrounded by ditches, and on naturally wet ground, drainage seems to have been a constant problem at the Rose, and the site may have been a factor in Henslowe's decision, when the Globe was built on a neighbouring site in 1599, to replace the Rose with a new playhouse built on the other side of the river and well away from its banks, rather than simply rivalling the Globe with a new, better, Rose.

The new stage was much the same size and shape as its predecessor, and there are once again no traces at foundation level of a projecting tiring-house façade, although the same considerations apply as for the first stage: if the tiring-house façade had been built on the stage itself, then there would be no archaeological trace of it; but a projecting tiring-house façade would further restrict the available space on a small stage. The debris scattered on the yard floor includes shoes and a spur, as well as the expected human detritus of rings and small change, all of which may date from the site's years of dereliction. Most of it confirms what is known from Henslowe's accounts of the materials from which the Rose was constructed: besides the unexpected wooden shingles, there is lath, wall plaster, thatch and a few timbers. The building was demolished, and most of its materials were taken for re-use elsewhere.

There is nothing so far to indicate the nature of the decorative scheme at the playhouse but it was probably a spectacular one. All accounts of the playhouses remark on their splendour, and they presumably looked much like those tombs, so garish to modern sensibilities accustomed to centuries of white marble, which retain their original colouring. In the 1595 Lent accounts for the work on the Rose, Henslowe includes at least nine items relating to payments to a painter, as well as payments to carpenters and for their materials.

In its early form the Rose was a compact and pleasant playhouse. Visitors to the site remarked on the comfortable feeling given by the startlingly tiny space (the site gave the impression of being even smaller than it was), and on the excellent view which must have been obtainable from the galleries. The alterations changed the shape of the yard, but cannot essentially have changed its character. Modern places of entertainment are distinctive in character, with their own strengths and disadvantages: it would be unrealistic to expect that the Elizabethan entertainment industry, with its highly competitive nature, would have produced a set of uniform buildings. As more is learned about the individual buildings, their distinctiveness from each other becomes more apparent. One of the most valuable aspects of the Rose excavation is how unlike de Witt's Swan the Rose turns out to have been. The Swan drawing does not show a building which is particularly convincing as a venue for the staging of plays. The stage fits uncomfortably into the multi-angular yard, the inadequate stage cover looks impractical and if the tiring-house façade did project as it is apparently shown doing, the sight-lines from the area where the most expensive gallery seats were perhaps placed, would have been badly restricted. Looking at the Swan, there has been an uneasy mistrust – can the glories of English drama, in which most of the playwrights seem to have so instinctive a grasp of what makes good theatre, really have been written for such impractical stages? This is perhaps one of the reasons – besides the obvious sentimental attachment to Shakespeare – why reconstructions of theatres of the age have mainly claimed to be the Globe, where all must ultimately have been based on inference and imagination, rather than the Swan, where there was some hope of reconstructing a tiring-house façade for which there was visual evidence. The Swan does not look as though it can ever have really worked. Stepping into the Rose one knew that it did – the stage was a pleasing shape when related to the yard, the view from almost everywhere must have been good, the general feeling of intimacy must have encouraged the establishment of rapport between players and audience.

What produced the greatest surprise was the size of the building. Theatre historians, notably C. Walter Hodges and John Orrell, have over the years stressed the massive size of the Renaissance playhouses: the fact that contemporary estimates of their audiences at 3,000 were not inconceivable, granted that the second Globe and the Hope at least, and therefore probably the first Globe, the Swan, and possibly even the Theatre, were 100 feet in diameter. Plays like Marlowe's *Tamburlaine*, which was put on at the Rose, seem to demand a massive home for their large-scale spectacle. Alleyn's style of acting was bravura. It was known that the Rose could not have been as large as its neighbours, but there was no expectation that it would turn out to be so small.

WHAT THE ROSE SITE MAY YET TELL US

The Rose has increased our knowledge of the Elizabethan playhouse, and the site may have more information which will be revealed as the excavation is resumed and as the finds are analysed, but there are limitations to the information it can provide, and a number of puzzles remain. That it was demolished precludes any substantial information being gained about the tiring-house: the size of the stage makes it most probable that it was contained within the backing galleries, but some invasion into the acting-space at stage level cannot yet be ruled out. No traces of its painted decorations remain, yet it was painted. Even the plaster fragments from the demolition, which were concentrated in the stage area, show, as yet, no signs of the pigmentation which might have been expected. Unless some new certain visual representation of the interior of a public playhouse is discovered, the tiring-house will remain an area for deduction and speculation.

The stage of the Rose is known, from the plays produced on it, to have possessed a trap. *Titus Andronicus* II.iii involves the concealment of Bassianus's body in a pit, into which two other characters subsequently fall. The live and dead bodies are removed from the pit and carried off-stage at the end of the scene, so it was not necessary, for this play, for the pit to have had access to the tiring-house – it had merely to be big enough to accommodate three actors. The stage-directions of Marlowe's *Dr Faustus* simply demand that Mephistophiles should enter when Faustus conjures him, but the invocation demands that Mephistophiles should 'rise',[51] and the title-page of the 1624 edition of the play shows Mephistophiles rising through the floor to the conjuring Faustus, as he would do were he to rise from a stage-trap. The edition with the woodcut is too late to provide solid evidence for theatrical practice at the Rose (that Mephistophiles's first entry was in the form of a dragon may be deduced from the entry in Henslowe's 1598 inventory of properties which lists 'j dragon in fostes'),[52] and may in any case not reflect actual stage practice; but the site of the Rose's stage-trap ought to be ascertainable from the excavations,[53] and if it is located, there must be a search for any evidence of access to it from the tiring-house, as well as from the stage above. The Globe stage-trap seems to have been accessible from the tiring-house: in *Hamlet,* the actor playing Ophelia must have made his way backstage from under the stage, after his deposition in his grave, although Hamlet and Laertes return to stage level to exit after their fight. (The action in this scene, as in Hamlet's conversation with the Gravedigger, implies a probable support for the actors at about 3 feet below stage level, rather than at ground level if the Globe's stage was about 5 feet high, as seems to have been the norm at the time – it is difficult to accept that the scene could be played satisfactorily with only the heads of those acting in the grave visible above stage level.)

The Rose shows so far no signs of flooring to raise above the damp ground the valuable costumes of any actors forced to go below the stage, nor any indication of facilities for lighting the under-stage area. Andrew Gurr argues that the Swan must have had access from under the stage into the auditorium, on the basis of the promises held forth in the trailer for *England's Joy*, which was supposed to be performed at the Swan in 1602, that devils would come out from under the stage and run among the audience.[54] But *England's Joy* was a confidence trick, and even if contemporaries were taken in by its unfulfilled and unfulfillable promises, there is no reason for twentieth-century theatre historians to treat these promises with like belief. We remain ignorant about the understage arrangements of the Elizabethan playhouse, and the Rose has so far provided little help.

As well as finding traces which add weight to speculation about the location of the Rose's entrance, the English Heritage archaeologists uncovered evidence for a building in the south-western corner of the site, which it is assumed might be the house, mentioned in the Cholmley-Henslowe agreement, that Cholmley planned to use as a base for the supply of refreshments.

The excavators state in their report that 'the plan of the theatre's outline reveals a tradition of vernacular design rather than imported Vitruvian styles'. There are problems with this statement, based on the fact that, while the plan of the Rose confirms the belief that the playhouses must have been laid out using traditional methods, and must therefore have been polygonal rather than round, we have little idea – and no evidence from the excavation – of the style of anything which stood above the foundations. Those who worked in the Elizabethan theatre, and foreigners who visited it, interpreted it in terms of the tradition of ancient Greece and Rome. It is believed that no native artist working in England before Inigo Jones fully understood the principles of Vitruvian design. This is not wholly true; there is good evidence, in a group of surviving monuments and buildings executed for men who seem to have formed the circle of Protector Somerset and the Duke of Northumberland, of a serious attempt to introduce the principles of classical art and architecture into England in the 1550s.[55] By the time the Rose was built, the visual language in which artists worked, particularly in London, contained enough classical detail for us to argue that they saw themselves working in a classical tradition, even if the eyes of modern knowledge see that they did not understand it. The shell was that of a timber-framed building – although by no means a conventional one – the first purpose-built playhouse, whose shape we do not know, may have been built only twenty years before the Rose, and only two, or at the most three, other playhouses had been built since then, so there were no real conventions for playhouse design –

The Gardiner chantry chapel in Winchester Cathedral – a three-bay classicizing façade used as a background for figures, c. 1555–60. (RCHM England)

but the language with which that shell was clothed would have been Elizabethan-classical. By the time the Rose was built, London was full of large buildings, whose subsequent destruction has allowed us to forget their existence, which were conceived and executed in a visual language which their builders thought of as classical. Much is made of the timber-framed medieval city which was destroyed in the Great Fire, but there were also spectacular modern buildings like Somerset House and Gresham's Royal Exchange which demonstrated the use of classical elements in the heart of the capital.[56] It can be no coincidence that the new form of the public playhouse (whatever its origins) was developed during the period which has been described as 'the false dawn of an English Renaissance':[57] one of innovation and experimentation in English architecture. London was full of evidences of the use of the classical idiom. To the modern eye they do not look classical, but to those who manufactured them they did. The recessed rear wall of the Rose stage invites treatment as a three-bay classicizing façade of the type so common at the time. It must surely have been in this idiom that it was executed.

The first truly classical theatre of the Renaissance was the Teatro Olimpico in Vicenza, designed by Palladio in 1580, but not completed until 1584.[58] It was visited by Inigo Jones, but cannot have influenced any of the early English playhouses. The Dutch Rhetoricians' theatres have obvious affinities with the monumental architecture erected in England, frequently by Netherlandish refugees, and so, it may be presumed, with English playhouses.[59] The spread of English acting troupes in Europe in the later years of the sixteenth and seventeenth centuries led to English playhouse construction influencing that of the countries they visited: it has been claimed that the Fortune theatre in Danzig was an exact copy of Henslowe's Fortune,[60] and that the design of the still partially-surviving Ottoneum in Kassel may have been influenced by the English troupes who used it.[61] Foreign visitors found the English playhouses strange, but not barbaric. The Dutch stages were temporary constructions, having affinities with pageant architecture, but erected by learned societies, to whom Serlio was available.[62] The influence of Serlio should not be discounted on the grounds that no English edition had been published at the time of the building of the early playhouses: it was present in the monument industry, which had Dutch roots, and any Englishman who had had a grammar-school education would have been capable of reading Serlio. Inigo Jones's claim to be the first architect to apply classical principles to the theatre in England has to remain unproven. The Rose's recessed façade would have lent itself to classical treatment, but, until the emergence of further evidence, we cannot pronounce on the matter.[63]

THE FINDINGS OF THE GLOBE EXCAVATION

The excavators who went on to the Globe site in the same year as the discovery of the Rose were fired by a hope which had not been possible for their predecessors, and they were rewarded. In a location predicted by John Orrell from his study of Hollar's panorama, they uncovered part of the gallery and the north-eastern stair turret. The excavation reports are hampered by the excavators being evidently ignorant of the existence of Orrell's work, but they believe that they have discovered traces of both the Globes – the first built in 1599 and burnt down in 1613; the second erected immediately afterwards and demolished in 1644. Because of the speed of its construction, it has always been believed that the second Globe was built on the foundations of the first, but the excavations show problems with this, and further exploration may shed more light on the topic. The fire may have damaged the foundations of the first playhouse as well as its timber-framed superstructure, so that differences in construction materials and techniques may be accounted for by the need for patching before rebuilding. The foundations of the inner and outer gallery walls of the Globe were apparently of different construction. It remains to be proved by further excavation whether the excavators have indeed found the outer gallery walls of both the first and the second Globes – the second using the chalk and timber foundations of the first, but reinforced with brick – but the inner gallery wall of only the second playhouse, which one would have expected to follow its predecessor like the outer gallery wall. The most interesting find was the stair-turret, which may, on current archaeological evidence, be connected with the second, but not the first, Globe. The existence of stair-turrets on playhouses has been a matter of dispute. The second Globe certainly had them, the Rose, on archaeological evidence, did not. The view of the northern playhouses has been interpreted as showing the Theatre with stair-turrets.[64] Neither of Norden's versions of the playhouses – cartographer's conventions though they may be – incorporates stair-turrets. As Andrew Gurr explains, stair-turrets were an innovation which added efficiency to the process of admitting the audience to the playhouse.[65] They reduced the number of gatherers necessary, and increased the audience accommodation. Access to the galleries no longer had to be obtained by pushing through a yard already containing the cheaper members of the audience – a benefit which may have appealed to a society with a liking for enforcing visible difference between the classes. The staircase turrets represent not only an innovation in crowd-control, but also a stage in the process of marking social divisions in the audience.

There is still a puzzle connected with the evidence that the Swan seems to have had both stair-turrets and access from yard into the lower gallery. These features are not necessarily incompatible. If the Swan was as large as the Globe, with similar capacity, then it would have accommodated 600 people in the yard, 1,000 in each of the first and second galleries, and 750 in the top gallery.[66] To send those wishing to enter the higher galleries up the stairs, but those wishing to enter the lower gallery through the yard, might have been an efficient way of processing the audience and would have allowed standers to change their minds and buy themselves a seat in the galleries without having to fight their way back through a crowded yard to the stair-towers. Orrell argues that in the Fortune at least, the most prestigious gallery was the middle one, so that this system would not involve the mingling of high and low status members of the audience.[67]

The portion of the Globe uncovered, small though it was, forced a modification in Orrell's Hollar-based reconstruction. While there is no universal agreement on the matter, it now seems likely that the polygonal Globe had twenty, rather than twenty-four, bays. R. A. Foakes, stressing the importance of the rod (16 feet 6 inches) as a basic unit of measurement, argues for a playhouse either of eighteen bays of 1 rod each, giving a diameter of 95 feet and a circumference of 298 feet, or of twenty bays of 1 rod each, giving a diameter of 105 feet and a circumference of 329 feet 8 inches. John Orrell prefers bays 11 feet 6 inches wide at the yard front, 15 feet 6 inches wide at the rear, and 12 feet 6 inches deep, giving a diameter of 99 feet. Andrew Gurr prefers a depth of just over 10 feet for the galleries. Foakes argues that the discoveries at the Rose strengthen the case for the Globe's stage being tapered, but Orrell and Gurr stay with the rectangular model.[68]

Perhaps the most important aspect of the discovery of this corner of the Globe is its implication for the remainder of the site. The Globe was, like the Rose, demolished, so that substantial illumination of the vexed tiring-house area is no more likely from this site than it proved to be at the Rose. But the Rose excavation has raised substantial doubts about what, on the evidence of the Fortune contract and the Swan drawing, has always been taken as one of the truisms of Elizabethan theatre history – the rectangular thrust stage jutting into the playhouse yard. On the evidence of the Rose, the Globe's stage was not necessarily this shape, and it would harmonize much better with the great stage cover of the second Globe visible on Hollar's panorama if what it covered was a trapezoidal stage, rather than a rectangular thrust. The other area of possible enlightenment is the line of the foundations of the tiring-house façade. Absence of evidence at foundation level of a projecting façade would not necessarily prove its absence, as it could have been erected on the stage itself, but its presence might certainly be proved by the presence of foundations for it. And if the Globe stage proved to be, like that of the Rose, rather smaller than might have been expected from studies based on documentary evidence (the great stage projecting half-way down the yard of the Fortune contract is possibly one of the aspects in which the Fortune is to differ from the recently completed first Globe), then, as at the Rose, the further restriction of the available acting area by a projecting façade would seem to be unlikely. The depth of the deposit above the portion of the Globe uncovered has raised hopes that a substantial portion of the stage area may lie undamaged and preserved under the cellars of Anchor Terrace – a listed building. If a way can be found to excavate the area without damaging Anchor Terrace, then there may be hopes that excavation can provide valuable information from this part of the Globe site.

One further question is raised by the discovery that the Globe does indeed survive archaeologically. In the eighteenth century, Mrs Thrale, the friend of Doctor Johnson, lived with her husband at the brewery on the site. She claimed that she saw the ruins of the Globe. For years her claims have been dismissed as fanciful, with only Dr Frances Yates – often dismissed as fanciful herself – supporting her.[69] Mrs Thrale's account must now be re-examined to see if what she was describing was indeed the Globe and if so, what exactly she saw. It may be that generations of male theatre historians owe one intelligent and well-educated eighteenth-century lady a profound apology.

Sam Wanamaker's Globe under construction. (The Shakespeare Globe Trust)

SAM WANAMAKER'S 'GLOBE'

Sam Wanamaker's Globe playhouse has now been completed close to the site of its namesake. Designed with the advice of leading theatre historians, the building stands 30 feet high, and is a twenty-sided polygon with an external diameter of 100 feet. It has a thatched roof, and three galleries look down on to the stage in its open yard. The initial design was modified to take account of the conclusions drawn from the Rose and Globe excavations, the number of sides being reduced from twenty-four to twenty, although the shape of the stage remains rectangular.

The 'Globe' will give audiences the chance to see Shakespeare's plays performed close to the site of the premieres of some of them in a building which goes some way to recreating Renaissance theatre conditions. There is no reason to suppose that a visit will be anything other than interesting, entertaining and moving. But to claim that this 'Globe' is any more authentic than Olivier's 'Globe' in *Henry V* is to mislead. The frame is based on a combination of Hollar's view of the second Globe, and Norden's view of the first, so that the hut is a thatched single-gable, as in Norden, but has a lantern, as in Hollar. The tiring-house façade and stage combine the de Witt sketch of the Swan with elements of the Jones/Webb theatres. The style of the interior seems to incline to the opinion, currently fashionable, and most strongly propounded by John Orrell, that there was a pre-Jones classicism in English theatre design. This produces a more restrained effect than would have been produced by following the views of Richard Hosley, and modelling the façade on an elaborate hall screen. The decorative scheme appears to be more restrained in its use of colour than it would have been had contemporary funeral monuments been taken as a model. The lantern does not seem to rely on surviving lanterns close in date to the first and second Globes, such as that on Hunsdon's tomb in Westminster Abbey (1596), or the monument to Sir Anthony Mildmay (d. 1617) at Apethorpe, Northamptonshire. Olivier's 'Globe' incorporated the most up-to-date conclusions of mid-twentieth-century scholarship; Wanamaker's 'Globe' incorporates the most up-to-date conclusions of late twentieth-century scholarship; neither is free from the taste of the era which produced it. We do not know what the interior of Shakespeare's Globe was like – Wanamaker's 'Globe' is based just as much on guess-work as any other attempt at reconstruction. It is worrying that almost none of the findings of the Rose excavation has modified the design, and that the publicity material still relies on versions of the Visscher view. To visit the 'Globe' will be fascinating, but it will not be authentic.

CONCLUSION

In this book I have used the evidence of literary history, theatre history, surviving architectural designs and costumes, together with dramatic groupings suggested by contemporary funerary monuments – and, of course, Shakespeare's plays themselves – to suggest some bases for reconstruction of the physical context within which those plays were performed. While primary documentation of Shakespearean playhouses and staging was, until the discovery of the foundations of the Rose and Globe, almost non-existent, and is even now sparse, such secondary and circumstantial evidence can be surprisingly informative. By viewing the Elizabethan and early Jacobean theatre within the broad context of contemporary culture I have, I hope, been able to indicate areas which may be useful in extending the range of material on which playhouse reconstructions may be based, while indicating the paucity and therefore the value of the material available, and the

The tomb of Sir Anthony Mildmay, d. 1617, at Apethorpe, Northamptonshire, showing the lantern, which may resemble the lantern of the second Globe. (Norman Hammond)

need to treat any extension of it with enormous care. The study of Shakespeare's theatre must, however, be an interdisciplinary effort, involving archaeologists, iconographers, literary critics and theatre historians, if we are to escape parochial interpretations and incomplete understanding: the unfortunate events at the Rose must never be repeated.

NOTES

References to Shakespeare's plays are to William Shakespeare: *The Complete Works*, ed. Peter Alexander (London, Collins, 1951).

CHAPTER 1 (pp. 1–16)

1   The first child of the marriage, who evidently died as an infant, probably during 1559 or 1560, when the Stratford registers are incomplete. She was certainly dead by 1569 when the second Joan Shakespeare was born. See S. Schoenbaum: *William Shakespeare: A Compact Documentary Life*, rev. edn (Oxford, Oxford University Press, 1987), pp. 23ff; in this chapter I am heavily indebted to this and to Schoenbaum's *William Shakespeare: A Documentary Life* (Oxford, Oxford University Press, 1975).

2   Lawrence Stone: *The Crisis of the Aristocracy 1558–1641*, corrected edn (Oxford, Oxford University Press, 1979), pp. 599–600.

3   William Harrison: *A Description of England*, ed. Lothrop Withington, with Introduction by F. J. Furnivall (London, Walter Scott, n.d.), p. 118.

4   Notably E. A. J. Honigmann, who also accepts Shakespeare's involvement with Catholicism: *Shakespeare: The 'Lost Years'*, (Manchester, Manchester University Press, 1985). F. W. Brownlow: 'John Shakespeare's Recusancy: New Light on an Old Document', *Shakespeare Quarterly* XL, 1989, pp. 186–90, argues forcefully that the Shakespeares were Catholics.

5   See Lawrence Stone: *The Family, Sex and Marriage in England 1500–1800* (London, Harper & Row, 1977), pp. 46ff.

6   Leeds Barroll: *Politics, Plague, and Shakespeare's Theater: The Stuart Years* (Ithaca, Cornell University Press, 1991), pp. 208ff, suggests that Shakespeare's output was more intermittent, and conditional upon the playhouses being open, but his views have not met with universal acceptance.

7   Robert Greene: *Groats-worth of witte, bought with a million of Repentance* (London, 1592), sig. A3v. Reproduced in Schoenbaum, *Shakespeare: A Documentary Life*, p. 115.

8   Not a carpenter – his training was in the small-scale use of wood, rather than in large-scale construction. Stephen Harrison, who made the pageant arches for the entry of King James I into London in 1604, was a joiner.

9   Some scholars have suggested that Shakespeare joined them on this occasion. See, for instance, Robert E. Burkhart: 'Finding Shakespeare's "Lost Years"', *Shakespeare Quarterly*, XXIX, 1978, pp. 77–9.

10 For a description of the entertainment at Kenilworth, see Muriel Bradbrook: *Drama as Offering: the princely pleasures at Kenelworth* (Houston, Rice Institute, pamphlet XLVI, 1960) and Jean Wilson: *Entertainments for Elizabeth I* (Woodbridge, D. S. Brewer and Rowman & Littlefield, 1980), pp. 119ff. There is also a description in Walter Scott's *Kenilworth* (1821). Some biographers have dismissed the idea that William Shakespeare could have been taken to see this, on the grounds that the distance between Stratford and Kenilworth is too great, but Shakespeare's father had made trips to London, the family was certainly prosperous enough at that date to be able to afford horses (even if not, it is only a three-hour walk), and the circle in which the Shakespeares moved in Stratford seem to have maintained social and societal links which suggest that twelve miles would be regarded as well within the local area – several of them became members of the religious guild at Knowle, some fifteen miles distant. See Mark Eccles: *Shakespeare in Warwickshire* (Madison, University of Wisconsin Press, 1961), pp. 4, 13, 14, 16, 45.

11 Recent discussions include Peter Thomson: *Shakespeare's Professional Career* (Cambridge, Cambridge University Press, 1992), pp. 23–104, and Andrew Gurr: 'Three Reluctant Patrons and Early Shakespeare', *Shakespeare Quarterly*, XLIV, 1993, pp. 159–74.

12 The closeness of the relationship between Elizabeth and her Carey cousins may be gauged from the autobiography of Robert Carey, Hunsdon's youngest son. Robert Carey: *Memoirs of Robert Carey*, ed. F. H. Mares (Oxford, Oxford University Press, 1972).

13 Philip Henslowe: *Henslowe's Diary*, ed. R. A. Foakes & R. T. Rickert (Cambridge, Cambridge University Press, 1961), pp. 123, 124.

14 See A. L. Rowse: *Shakespeare's Southampton, Patron of Virginia* (London, Macmillan, 1965).

15 Essex was the grandson of Mary Boleyn's daughter Catherine Carey, sister of Lord Hunsdon, whose great-nephew he was. He was Elizabeth's first cousin twice removed, and may, if Catherine Carey was the daughter of Henry VIII, and therefore Elizabeth's half-sister, have been the Queen's great-nephew.

16 J. B. Leishman, ed.: *The Three Parnassus Plays 1598–1601* (London, Ivor Nicolson & Watson, 1949).

17 See Herbert Berry: *Shakespeare's Playhouses* (New York, AMS Press, 1987), pp. 19–46.

18 The authenticity of the commonly accepted signatures of Shakespeare on legal documents has recently been questioned and it is argued that clerks were accustomed to sign legal documents on their clients' behalf: a signature on a document may be no guarantee that the apparent signer was actually present at the transaction. (Jane Cox: 'Shakespeare's will and signatures', in *Shakespeare in the Public Records*, ed. David Thomas (London, HMSO, 1985), pp. 24–35.

19 The date of Shakespeare's retirement is usually put earlier, but this is on the grounds of a change of mood seen in the later plays, and a diminution in his speed of output, rather than any objective evidence. In March 1613 Shakespeare was engaged with Richard Burbage (a talented artist) in executing a tournament shield for the Earl of Rutland, a commission not easily performed if one of those engaged on it was over 100 miles from London. The Blackfriars gatehouse purchase is more easily explained as being for his own use rather than simply a speculative investment. The trauma of the burning of the Globe seems a more likely occasion for his withdrawal from the world of the London theatre, and this coincides with his ceasing to write, though his rate of production had slowed in the previous six or seven years. He was still visiting London at the end of 1614. Recent scholarship is tending to put his retirement later. See Barroll: *Politics, Plague, and Shakespeare's Theater*, pp. 208–9; Thomson: *Shakespeare's Professional Career*, pp. 186–7.

20 For a revisionist view of the importance of the king's patronage, together with a discussion of the status conferred by the rank of Groom of the Chamber, see Barroll: *Politics, Plague, and Shakespeare's Theater*, pp. 23–69.

21 Cox, in 'Shakespeare's will and signatures', argues that the signatures may not in any case be by Shakespeare himself.

CHAPTER 2 (pp. 17–39)

1 E. K. Chambers: *The Elizabethan Stage* (4 vols, Oxford, Oxford University Press, 1923), vol. 1, p. 123, vol. 4, pp. 61f. On a visit to Coventry in 1567, several of the pageants from the Coventry mystery cycle were erected to greet Elizabeth. See Chambers, vol. 4, p. 83.

2 The great Holkham Bible Picture Book, British Museum MS Add. 47682, has been used as evidence for the staging of medieval biblical dramas. See Gail McMurray Gibson: 'Long Melford Church, Suffolk: Some Suggestions for the Study of Visual Artifacts and Medieval Drama', *Research Opportunities in Renaissance Drama*, XXI, 1978, pp. 103–16, and Pamela Sheingorn: 'On Using Medieval Art in the Study of Medieval Drama: An Introduction to Methodology', *Research Opportunities in Renaissance Drama*, XXII, 1979, pp. 101–10.

3 For an idea of the amount of drama lost, see R. M. Wilson: *The Lost Literature of Medieval England*, rev. edn (London, Methuen, 1972).

4 For the medieval drama, see Glynne Wickham: *Early English Stages 1300–1660* (3 vols, London, Routledge & Kegan Paul, 1959–1981) and E. K. Chambers: *The Medieval Stage* (2 vols, Oxford, Oxford University Press, 1903).

5 Corpus Christi College, Cambridge, Manuscript B.5.

6 Wickham, *Early English Stages*, vol. I, pp. 179ff.

7 See Karl Young: *The Drama of the Medieval Church* (2 vols, Oxford, Oxford University Press, 1933) and Richard Axton: *European Drama of the Early Middle Ages* (London, Hutchinson, 1974).

8 See Roy C. Strong: *The Cult of Elizabeth: Elizabethan Portraiture and Pageantry* (London, Thames and Hudson, 1977), pp. 17ff.

9 See J. Wilson, *Entertainments*, pp. 5ff.

10 See Wickham, *Early English Stages*, vol. I, pp. 51ff.

11 Based on the fabliau *Dame Siriz and the Weeping Bitch*; see Celia Sisam (ed.): *The Oxford Book of Medieval English Verse* (Oxford, Oxford University Press, 1970), p. 50.

12 Wickham, *Early English Stages*, vol. I, pp. 191ff.

13 Chambers, *Elizabethan Stage*, vol. 2, p. 365. Chambers also provides evidence of displays of tumbling and fencing by troupes of players (vol. 4, pp. 79, 97).

14 Painting was one of the subjects which was recommended for a gentleman's education.

15 Chambers, *Elizabethan Stage*, vol. 2, pp. 295–350, passim.

16 For the Derby family patronage, see Thomson, *Shakespeare's Professional Career*, pp. 23–51. The descendants and

connections of this family were later to commission *Arcades* and *Comus* from John Milton. They had close family connections with the Tudors: the first Earl was the stepfather of King Henry VII.

17 Chambers, *Elizabethan Stage*, vol. 4, pp. 75ff.

18 *Ibid.*, vol. I, pp. 106ff.

19 Andrew Marvell, *An Horatian Ode upon Cromwell's Return from Ireland*, ll. 53–8, in *The Complete Poems*, ed. Elizabeth Story Donno (Harmondsworth, Penguin Books, 1972), pp. 55ff. On the theatricality of this occasion, see Wickham, *Early English Stages*, vol. 2, part I, plate XXXII, and the note to it, p. 387.

20 He was married to More's younger sister, Elizabeth. His son William, also a printer, married Winifred Clement, the daughter of More's foster daughter Margaret Gigs.

21 F. P. Wilson: *The English Drama 1485–1585*, ed. G. K. Hunter (Oxford, Oxford University Press, 1969), p. 23.

22 Wickham, *Early English Stages,* vol. 2, part 1, pp. 166–7.

23 Chambers, *Elizabethan Stage*, vol. 2, p. 306.

24 Janet S. Loengard: 'An Elizabethan lawsuit: John Brayne, his carpenter, and the building of the Red Lion Theatre', *Shakespeare Quarterly*, XXXIV, 1983, pp. 298–310.

25 *Ibid.*, p. 299n.

26 For example, Chambers, *Elizabethan Stage*, vol. 2, p. 379.

27 Modern house names may have symbolic significance, referring to the names of previous owners (Dilley's Cottage), location (Drift Cottage), distinguishing features of the house or its garden (The Gables; Yew Tree Farm), or some fact relating to the owner (Dunroamin; Billswin), but they are rarely visual as well as verbal symbols.

28 John Orrell and Andrew Gurr: 'What the Rose can tell us', *Antiquity*, 63 (1989), pp. 421–9 (a revised version of 'What the Rose can tell us', *Times Literary Supplement*, 9–15 June 1989, pp. 636, 649). When dealing with Elizabethan measurements, one should bear in mind the warning of S. P. Cerasano: 'To say that the Fortune was 80 feet square on the outside, with a courtyard of 55 feet within, tells us that those distances were measured according to Street's "London rod" but will not tell us the exact inner dimensions of the playhouse'. S. P. Cerasano: 'Shakespeare's Elusive Globe: Review Article', *Medieval & Renaissance Drama in England*, III, 1986, pp. 265–75, pp. 269–70.

29 The dimensions of the height of the tower in proportion to the stage area are analogous to those suggested by Wickham for his conjectural reconstruction of the pageant-wagon stage (*Early English Stages*, vol. 1, p. 173).

30 See Herbert Berry: 'The First Public Playhouses, Especially the Red Lion', *Shakespeare Quarterly*, XL, 1989, pp. 133–48.

31 Wickham, *Early English Stages*, vol. 2, part 1, pp. 186ff. There is some incontrovertible evidence that plays were, on occasion, put on in inn-yards. See, for instance, Donald F. Rowan, 'The Players and Playing Places of Norwich', in John H. Astington, ed., *The Development of Shakespeare's Theater* (New York, AMS Press, 1992), pp. 77–94.

32 A great deal of work is being done in local records on the locations of dramatic performances in the provinces, which may mean that this statement will need modification. See, for instance, Rosalind Conklin Hays: 'Dorset Church Houses and the Drama', *Research Opportunities in Renaissance Drama*, XXXI, 1992, pp. 13–24.

33 Wickham, *Early English Stages*, vol. 2, part 1, pp. 187–96.

34 Tennis courts were, of course, converted to theatres after the Restoration. See Wickham, *Early English Stages*, vol. 2, part 2, pp. 93–4.

35 John Orrell: *The Human Stage: English theatre design 1567–1640* (Cambridge, Cambridge University Press, 1988), pp. 7ff, Herbert Berry: *The Boar's Head Playhouse* (Washington, Folger Books, 1986).

36 Wickham, *Early English Stages,* vol. 2, part 2, pp. 101ff.

37 David Wiles: *Shakespeare's Clown: Actor and Text in the Elizabethan Playhouse* (Cambridge, Cambridge University Press, 1987), pp. 11ff deals with Tarlton at length.

38 Henslowe, *Diary*, pp. 304–6.

39 Schoenbaum, *Shakespeare: A Compact Life*, p. 206.

40 Wickham, *Early English Stages*, vol. 2, part 1, p. 188.

41 For the liking of the period for self-confident children, see Jean Wilson: 'The Noble Imp', *The Antiquaries Journal*, vol. LXX, part 2, 1992, pp. 360–79.

42 See Michael Shapiro: *Children of the Revels: The Boy Companies of Shakespeare's Time and their Plays* (New York, Columbia University Press, 1977), pp. 1ff.

43 Schools putting on plays were not confined to the capital. It is possible that William Shakespeare's first experience of drama was taking part in a school play.

44 Chambers, *Elizabethan Stage*, vol. 4, pp. 81, 83. For other academic plays, see *ibid.*, pp. 373–9, and Leishman, *Parnassus Plays*.

45 See Chambers, *Elizabethan Stage*, vol. 4, p. 111.

46 Wickham, *Early English Stages*, vol. 2, part 1, page 186.

47 *Ibid.*, part 2, pp. 63ff.

48 R. A. Foakes: *Illustrations of the English Stage 1580–1642* (London, Scolar Press, 1985), pp. 52–5; van Buchell was a man of considerable artistic sensibility, and is the first person known to have mentioned Rembrandt. (Seymour Slive: *Frans Hals* (London, Royal Academy of Arts, 1989), p.142).

49 Wickham, *Early English Stages*, vol. 2, part 2, pp. 68ff.

50 The Fortune was claimed to have survived in the form of an inn in the early nineteenth century, although C. Walter Hodges disputes this. (*The Globe Restored*, 2nd edn (Oxford, Oxford University Press, 1968), pp. 111–12).

51 Schoenbaum, *Shakespeare: A Compact Life*, pp. 167ff.

52 For the way in which the costumes and properties for the miracle cycles were distributed around their home cities, see Wickham, *Early English Stages*, vol. 1, pp. 291ff.

53 This is most clearly seen in the frequently-remarked change in the nature of the clown's roles when Armin succeeded Kempe in the Lord Chamberlain's Men.

54 Henslowe, *Diary*, pp. 16–47 passim, 170.

55 *Ibid.*, pp. 36–7.

56 For Kempe, see Wiles, *Shakespeare's Clown*, pp. 24ff.

57 Quoted in Andrew Gurr: *Playgoing in Shakespeare's London* (Cambridge, Cambridge University Press, 1987), pp. 96–7. For other testimonies to Burbage's greatness, see *ibid.*, p. 233.

58 *Ibid.*, p. 69.

59 Schoenbaum, *Shakespeare: A Compact Life*, pp. 205–6.

60 Gurr, *Playgoing*, p. 265, n. 34.

61 In, for instance, the appearance of John Skelton as the leading figure in comic anecdotes in jestbooks, for example Anon.: *Tales and quicke answeres, very mery, and pleasant to rede*, printed by Thomas Berthelet (?1535), and *Merie Tales . . . made by Master Skelton Poet Laureate*, printed by Thomas Colwell (1567). Both reprinted in P. M. Zall (ed.): *A Hundred Merry Tales and other Jestbooks of the Fifteenth and Sixteenth Centuries* (Lincoln, Nebraska, University of Nebraska Press, 1963).

62 See the instances given by Gurr, *Playgoing*, pp. 191–251 passim.

63 *Ibid.*, p. 191. Barroll, *Politics*, pp. 70–116, argues that the measures taken to stop the spread of the plague were reasonable and effective.

64 Andrew Gurr: *The Shakespearean Stage, 1574–1642*, 3rd edn (Cambridge, Cambridge University Press, 1992), pp. 8–9.

65 Wickham, *Early English Stages*, vol. 2, part 2, p. 58.

66 Gurr, *Playgoing*, pp. 191–251, passim.

67 Wickham, *Early English Stages*, vol. I, pp. 179ff.

68 *Ibid.*, pp. 184f.

69 The association in the general mind of the theatre with prostitution may be seen in the incident on Shrove Tuesday 1617, when a group of apprentices, out on their traditional Shrove Tuesday treat of wrecking a few brothels, turned their attention to the new Cockpit playhouse which had just opened in Drury Lane and wrecked that. (Gurr, *Shakespearean Stage*, p. 14.)

70 Schoenbaum, *Shakespeare: A Compact Life*, p. 321, gives figures which suggest that 35 per cent of the yeoman class, and 44 per cent of the tradesman and craftsman class, from which most players seem to have been drawn, were able to sign their names. He points out that reading and writing do not invariably go together, although reading invariably precedes writing. Overall, 70 per cent of Englishmen seem to have been unable to sign their own name.

71 Schoenbaum, *Shakespeare: A Compact Life*, pp. 217–19.

72 *Ibid.*, pp. 252–3.

73 *Ibid.*, p. 219.

74 John Donne: *Sermons*, ed. G. R. Potter and E. M. Simpson (10 vols, Berkeley, University of California Press, 1953–62); Hugh Latimer: *Sermons*, ed. H. C. Beeching (London, Dent, 1906).

75 G. R. Owst: *Literature and Pulpit in Medieval England*, rev. edn (Oxford, Oxford University Press, 1961).

76 See Gurr, *Playgoing*, p. 237.

CHAPTER 3 (pp. 40–58)

1 The most entertaining account of Essex's execution is in Lytton Strachey: *Elizabeth and Essex* (London, Chatto & Windus, 1928), pp. 260–3.

2 For Ralegh, see Stephen Greenblatt: *Sir Walter Ralegh: The Renaissance Man and his Roles* (New Haven, Yale University Press, 1973). I am greatly indebted to Greenblatt in my exploration in this chapter of the way in which the Elizabethans saw life as a performance.

3   For colour symbolism at this date, see George Ferguson: *Signs & Symbols in Christian Art* (Oxford, Oxford University Press, 1961 (paperback edn)), pp. 151–3. It is interesting that Mary Queen of Scots, who certainly believed that her death was a martyrdom, had chosen to perform it in the same symbolic colours as Essex. See Antonia Fraser: *Mary, Queen of Scots* (London, Weidenfeld & Nicolson, 1969), pp. 536ff.

4   See the chapter on Essex in Strong, *Cult of Elizabeth*, pp. 56–83.

5   For the martyrdoms of Cranmer and Latimer see John Foxe: *Actes and Monuments (The Book of Martyrs)* (London, John Day, 1563), pp. 1376f, 1503f.

6   See Denis Meadows: *Elizabethan Quintet* (London, Longmans, Green & Co., 1956), pp. 238–63.

7   For Sidney as Protestant knight, see J. Wilson, *Entertainments*, pp. 1–63 passim, and Alan Young: *Tudor and Jacobean Tournaments* (London, Sheridan House, 1987), passim.

8   Carey, *Memoirs*, pp. 30–1.

9   Queen Elizabeth's parsimony in rewarding her courtiers is remarked in Stone, *Crisis of the Aristocracy*, pp. 65ff.

10 The previous female rulers had been Matilda in the early Middle Ages, and Elizabeth's immediate predecessor, her elder sister Mary Tudor, both of whose reigns must be reckoned fairly disastrous episodes in English history. Margaret Beaufort, mother of Henry VII, never raised her claim to the throne, although his claim to the throne derived from her and she was a highly intelligent, well-educated and capable woman. See Michael K. Jones and Malcolm G. Underwood, *The King's Mother: Lady Margaret Beaufort, Countess of Richmond and Derby* (Cambridge, Cambridge University Press, 1992).

11 For the cults surrounding Elizabeth I, see E. C. Wilson: *England's Eliza* (Cambridge, Mass., Harvard University Press, 1939), F. A. Yates: *Astraea: The Imperial Theme in the Sixteenth Century* (London, Routledge & Kegan Paul, 1975), Strong, *Cult of Elizabeth I*, J. Wilson, *Entertainments*, A. Young, *Tudor and Jacobean Tournaments* and Philippa Berry, *Of Chastity and Power: Elizabethan Literature and the Unmarried Queen* (London, Routledge, 1989), pp. 61–110.

12 See Strong, *Cult of Elizabeth*, and Janet Arnold: *Queen Elizabeth's Wardrobe Unlock'd* (London, Maney, 1988).

13 Arnold, *Elizabeth's Wardrobe,* fig. 129 and plates III and IVB.

14 *Ibid.,* fig. 217.

15 *Ibid.,* figs 26, 128.

16 *Ibid.,* figs 20, 79, 140, 448.

17 *Ibid.,* p. 369.

18 *Ibid.,* p. 370.

19 *Ibid.,* fig. 71.

20 *Ibid.,* fig. 140.

21 Roy C. Strong: *The English Icon: Elizabethan and Jacobean Portraiture* (London, Routledge & Kegan Paul, 1969), pp. 143f.

22 Arnold, *Elizabeth's Wardrobe*, pp. 84ff.

23 A. Young, *Tudor and Jacobean Tournaments*, p. 151.

24 *Ibid.,* p. 139.

25 Portrait of Sir James Scudamore by an unknown artist, c. 1595–1600, (*Ibid.*, p. 142).

26 Portrait miniature of the Earl of Essex by Nicholas Hilliard, c. 1593–95 (*Ibid.*, p. 171).

27 Portrait miniature by Isaac Oliver of Edward Herbert, 1st Baron Herbert of Cherbury, c. 1610–14 (Roy C. Strong and V. J. Murrel: *Artists of the Tudor Court: The Portrait Miniature Rediscovered 1520–1600* (London, Victoria and Albert Museum, 1983), plate xxiii).

28 *As You Like It*, IV.i.10ff. Timothy Bright's *A treatise of melancholie, containing the causes thereof* (London, T. Vautrollier, 1586) and Robert Burton's *The Anatomy of Melancholy* (Oxford, J. Lichfield, 1621) are dedicated to the subject.

29 By Isaac Oliver, 1590–5 (Strong and Murrell, *Artists of the Tudor Court*, cat. 268).

30 By Nicholas Hilliard, 1590–5 (*Ibid.*, cat. 266).

31 By Isaac Oliver, c. 1595–1600 (*Ibid.*, cat. 161).

32 Strong, *English Icon*, pp. 28ff, and figs 22, 23 and 24.

33 *Ibid.,* fig. 284, and pp. 28ff. It has been suggested that the picture may be connected to the Ditchley Entertainment of 1592 (Christopher Lloyd: *The Queen's Pictures: Royal Collectors through the Centuries* (London, National Gallery Publications, 1991), cat. 10).

34 In Greek mythology, Tereus, King of Thrace, married Procne, daughter of the King of Athens, who bore him a son, Itys; but Tereus then fell in love with her sister Philomena, cut out Procne's tongue, concealed her and claimed she was dead in order to marry Philomena. Philomena learned of Tereus's crime and encouraged Procne to seek revenge. Procne served Itys to Tereus in a stew, and, as Tereus sought revenge on the sisters, all three were transformed by the gods into birds: Procne became a swallow, Philomena a nightingale and Tereus a hoopoe. See Robert Graves: *The Greek Myths*, rev. edn (2 vols, Harmondsworth, Penguin, 1960), vol. I, no. 46 passim.

35 F. P. Wilson: *English Drama*, p. 154.

36 For the widespread practice of drama in schools at this period, see *ibid.*, pp. 151ff.

37 *Ibid.*

38 Gurr, *Shakespearean Stage*, p. 97.

39 John Harris and Gordon Higgott: *Inigo Jones: Complete Architectural Drawings* (London, Royal Academy of Arts, 1990), p. 90. John Orrell emphasizes the closeness of the relationship between Arundel and Alleyn during the last years of the latter's life in 'The Architecture of the Fortune Playhouse', *Shakespeare Survey*, XLVII, 1994, pp. 15–43.

40 Stone, *Crisis of the Aristocracy*, pp. 672ff.

41 Edmund Spenser: *The Faerie Queene: Letter to Raleigh*, in *Poetical Works*, ed. J. C. Smith and E. de Selincourt (Oxford, Oxford University Press, 1912), p. 407.

42 F. P. Wilson, *English Drama*, p. 103.

43 *Ibid.*, pp. 108ff.

44 For a description of the gates, see Royal Commission on Historical Monuments England: *City of Cambridge* (3 vols, London, HMSO, 1959), vol. I, pp. 72ff. See Orrell, *Human Stage*, pp. 56–7.

45 For a description and interpretation of the welcome for King James, see David M. Bergeron: *English Civic Pageantry 1558–1642* (London, Edward Arnold, 1971), pp. 71ff. and Marie Axton: *The Queen's Two Bodies: Drama and the Elizabethan Succession* (London, Royal Historical Society, 1977), pp. 131ff.

46 See the description of this procession in Neville Williams: *Elizabeth, Queen of England* (London, Weidenfeld & Nicolson, 1967), pp. 56ff., and Robert Withington: *English Pageantry: An Historical Outline* (2 vols, New York, Benjamin Blom, 1918, repr. 1963), vol. 2, pp. 199ff. For interpretations of this show, see Bergeron, *English Civic Pageantry*, pp. 11ff. and Wickham, *Early English Stages*, vol. I, p. 72.

47 Withington, *English Pageantry*, pp. 199–200.

48 *Ibid.*, p. 200.

49 *Ibid.*, p. 201.

50 *Ibid.*

51 *Ibid.*, p. 202.

52 Anon.: *The Royall Passage of her Majesty from the Tower of London, to her Palice of White-hall, with all the Speaches and Deuices, both of the Pageants and otherwise, together with her Majesties Seuerall Answers and most pleasing Speaches to them all* (London, S. S[tafford], n.d. [?1559]), and *The passage of our most drad soueraigne lady Quene Elyzabeth through the citie of London to Westminster the day before her coronacion* (London, Richard Tottil, 1558/9).

53 These pageants are described in Withington, *English Pageantry*, pp. 222ff.

54 Spenser, *Poetical Works*, pp. vii–viii.

55 Tho[mas]. Dekker: *The Magnificent Entertainment: giuen to King Iames, Queen Anne his wife, and Henry Frederick the Prince, vpon the day of his Maiesties Tryumphant Passage (from the Tower) through his Honourable Citie (and Chamber) of London, being the 15. of March, 1603. As well by the English as by the Strangers: With the speeches and Songes deliuered in the seuerall Pageants* (London, Thomas Man, 1604); Jon[son], B[en], *His Part of King James his Royall and Magnificent Entertainment through his Honorable Cittie of London, Thurseday the 15. of March, 1603, so much as was presented in the first and last of their Tryumphall Arch's* (London, Edward Blount, 1604). There are several other descriptions of the event – see Withington, *English Pageantry*, pp. 222–3.

56 Quoted Withington, *English Pageantry*, p. 226.

57 *Winter's Tale*, IV. Prologue. 20.

58 John Buxton, *Elizabethan Taste* (London, Macmillan, 1963), pp. 59–60. Orrell, *Human Stage*, pp. 49–60, discusses emblematic buildings of the period.

59 Nikolaus Pevsner and Bridget Cherry: *The Buildings of England: Wiltshire* (Harmondsworth, Penguin Books, 1975), pp. 303ff.

60 Quoted Buxton, *Elizabethan Taste*, p. 137. Buxton takes this to mean that the order was for portraits of Sir Thomas and Lady Fermor in the modern sense of representations of them as they were during life, but I do not think that the passage will bear this interpretation.

61 See Williams, *Elizabeth*, pp. 276ff.

CHAPTER 4 (pp. 59–103)

1 Which should possibly not be classed with the amphitheatres at all, but with the converted inns.

2 See Christine Eccles: *The Rose Theatre* (London, Nick Hern Books, 1990), p. 124. The classic exposition of the way that contemporary fashion influenced conjectural reconstructions of Elizabethan playhouses is C. Walter Hodges: 'The Lantern of Taste', *Shakespeare Survey* XII, 1959, pp. 8–14.

3   See Mark Jones (ed.): *Fake? The Art of Deception* (London, British Museum Publications, 1990), p. 156.

4   Reproduced in Schoenbaum, *Shakespeare: A Compact Life*, p. 133, and Orrell, *Human Stage*, pp. 26–7. The whole panorama which shows the northern playhouses is discussed by James P. Lusardi: 'The Pictured Playhouse: Reading the Utrecht Engraving of Shakespeare's London', *Shakespeare Quarterly*, XLIV, 1993, pp. 202–27.

5   Henslowe, *Diary*, p. 281.

6   Quoted in Schoenbaum, *Shakespeare: A Compact Life*, pp. 138–9.

7   Quoted in Gurr, *Playgoing*, pp. 213–14. The original German is quoted by Chambers, *Elizabethan Stage*, vol. 2, pp. 364–5n.

8   Chambers, *Elizabethan Stage*, vol. 4, pp. 199–200.

9   Quoted Gurr, *Shakespearean Stage*, p. 7. Gurr dates this to post-1576, on the assumption that the first playhouse built was the Theatre, but it was first dated by Furnivall to 1572, and the discovery of the documents relating to the Red Lion make this date possible. See Harrison, *Elizabethan England*, p. 268. See also Chambers, *Elizabethan Stage*, vol. 4, p. 269.

10 See Jean Wilson: *Romance Themes in The Faerie Queene* (Ph.D. dissertation, Cambridge University, 1973).

11 Strong, *Elizabethan Image*, pp. 13ff.

12 Wickham, *Early English Stages*, passim.

13 Harrison, *Elizabethan England*, pp. 215–16.

14 See Buxton, *Elizabethan Taste*, pp. 151ff and plate 13 and Nikolaus Pevsner: *The Buildings of England:Herefordshire* (Harmondsworth, Penguin Books, 1963), pp. 78ff. Pevsner thinks that the monuments are by different hands; he does not consider the possibility that even if by different hands they may be the products of the same workshop.

15 Harrison, *Elizabethan England*, pp. 3–4.

16 Quoted Schoenbaum, *Shakespeare: A Compact Life*, p. 190.

17 Sir Philip Sidney: *A Defence of Poetry* in *Miscellaneous Prose*, ed. Katherine Duncan-Jones and Jan Van Dorsten (Oxford, Oxford University Press, 1973), pp. 74, 114.

18 Hodges: *The Globe Restored*, passim.

19 See the illustrations to Orrell, *Human Stage*, passim.

20 Schoenbaum, *Shakespeare: A Compact Life*, p. 136.

21 John Orrell: *The Quest for Shakespeare's Globe* (Cambridge, Cambridge University Press, 1983), pp. 117–20. The practice of the reuse of timbers for buildings of entirely different form is much commoner in vernacular architecture than Professor Orrell allows.

22 Chambers, *Elizabethan Stage*, vol. 2, p. 358. Kiechel also notes that double prices were charged for a new play, and that the ban on playing on Friday and Saturday was not observed.

23 See S. Schoenbaum: *Shakespeare: A Documentary Life*, p. 105. The Theatre is surveyed in Herbert Berry (ed.), *The First Public Playhouse: The Theatre in Shoreditch 1576–1598* (Montreal, McGill-Queen's University Press, 1979).

24 Gurr, *Shakespearean Stage*, p. 132.

25 Henslowe, *Diary*, p. 281.

26 Gurr, *Shakespearean Stage*, p. 136.

27 Gurr (*ibid.*, pp. 131ff) argues that the figures are placed to indicate the uses of various areas, rather than to represent an actual scene, but is undecided whether the stage gallery represents privileged seating, space for musicians, an upper acting area, or all three.

28 The Norden view has the usual problem about the shape of the Theatre in his panorama and in his plan; the sketch by Webb for a scene from *Britannia Triumphans* (Stephen Orgel and Roy Strong: *Inigo Jones: The Theatre of the Stuart Court*, 2 vols (London, Sotheby Parke Bernet and University of California Press, 1973), vol. 2, pp. 670–1) shows an apparently circular building, but presumably, in so distant a view, the same conventions apply as to the Hollar view of the second Globe (see Orrell, *Quest for Shakespeare's Globe*, pp. 158ff).

29 For Peter Street, see Mary Edmond: 'Peter Street 1553–1609: Builder of Playhouses', *Shakespeare Survey*, XLV, 1993, pp. 101–14.

30 The Globe was said to have been built with the same timbers as the Theatre, but 'in an other forme' (Gurr, *Shakespearean Stage*, p. 120). It may well be that de Witt is an accurate reporter, and that the Swan, and subsequently the first and second Globes, were much bigger than the Theatre. Certainly the Rose, which also belongs, with the Theatre and the Curtain, to what Gurr calls the 'first generation' of playhouses, was much smaller than the projected size of the second Globe, the magnitude of which seems to have been confirmed by recent excavations on the site.

31 Henslowe, *Diary*, pp. 306ff. Contractions expanded, 'u' and 'v' normalized, and some punctuation added.

32 John Orrell, 'Architecture of the Fortune Playhouse', passim.

33 Malcolm Rogers: *Montacute House Somerset* (London, The National Trust, 1991), p. 15.

34 Orrell, *Quest for Shakespeare's Globe*, passim.

35   Hodges, *Globe Restored*, p. 111.

36   It has been suggested that the substantial heavens for the second Globe (visible in Hollar's engraving) might also have been carried on the playhouse's frame, without the need for supporting pillars on the stage – see C. Walter Hodges: *Shakespeare's Second Globe; the missing monument* (London, Oxford University Press, 1973), pp. 52ff.

37   Gurr, *Shakespearean Stage*, pp. 153–4, quotes the contract.

38   *Bartholomew Fair*, Induction, ll. 46ff., in Ben Jonson: *Three Comedies*, ed. Michael Jameson (Harmondsworth, Penguin Books, 1966), pp. 321ff.

39   Hodges, *Shakespeare's Second Globe*, pp. 70f.

40   Orrell, *Quest for Shakespeare's Globe*, passim.

41   Gurr, *Shakespearean Stage*, pp. 146ff.

42   *Ibid*. 2nd edn (Cambridge, Cambridge University Press, 1980), pp. 131–2. In his later writings, Gurr prefers the term 'alcove' to 'discovery-space' (*Shakespearean Stage*, pp. 149ff., Andrew Gurr: 'The Bare Island', *Shakespeare Survey*, XLVII, 1994, pp. 29–34), and argues that the alternatives he proposed in 1980 were both correct; there was a relatively unobtrusive curtained 'alcove' as a permanent feature of the stage, but this might be supplemented with a special property, which could incorporate a curtained 'booth', where the play's action demanded it.

43   Richard Hosley: 'The Second Blackfriars Playhouse', in J. Leeds Barroll, Alexander Leggatt, Richard Hosley and Alvin Kernan: *The Revels History of Drama in English: Volume III: 1576–1613* (London, Methuen, 1975), pp. 197ff.

44   Chambers, *Elizabethan Stage*, vol. 1, pp. 227f, expresses doubts about the assumption that the screen was the natural place for the stage to be situated, and gives examples of its being located at the upper, or dais, end. Nor was the hall the invariable location for the performance of a play; *ibid*, p. 216, gives examples of dramatic performances taking place in great chambers, and other rooms, which, although large enough to incorporate a stage, would not have a screen. Alan H. Nelson: 'Hall Screens and Elizabethan Playhouses: Counter-Evidence from Cambridge', in Astington, *Development of Shakespeare's Theater*, pp. 57–76, provides a series of examples where plays were staged, as at Christ Church, at the upper end of the hall, with the screen providing accommodation for the audience. Basil's use of the word 'skraene' for the rear section of his scaffold may be further evidence that the screen was associated with the audience, not the show.

45   Buxton: *Elizabethan Taste*, p. 165.

46   *Hamlet*, II.ii.76–86. For discussions of the use of emblems in the theatre and stage design, see Wickham, *Early English Stages*, vol. 2, part 1, pp. 206ff, and Orrell, *Human Stage*, pp. 49ff.

47   This has parallels in contemporary life: after Sir Walter Raleigh's execution, his widow kept his head in a bag with her until she died. Cyril Tourneur: *The Revenger's Tragedy*, in Gamini Salgado (ed.): *Three Jacobean Tragedies* (Harmondsworth, Penguin Books, 1965), pp. 41–136, I.i.1–40. Roland Mushat Frye deals with the affinities between drama and painting at this date in 'Ladies, Gentlemen, and Skulls: *Hamlet* and the Iconographic Tradition' (*Shakespeare Quarterly*, XXX 1979), pp. 15–28 and 'Ways of Seeing in Shakespearean Drama and Elizabethan Painting', *ibid*. XXXI (1980), pp. 323–42. See also Lucy Gent, *Picture and Poetry 1560–1620: Relations between literature and the visual arts in the English Renaissance* (Leamington Spa, James Hall, 1981).

48   Vere died in 1609, but the tomb is based on that of Count Englebert II of Nassau-Dillenburg (d. 1504; tomb about 1530) at Breda, which Vere had presumably seen during his service in the Netherlands. See *Westminster Abbey: official Guide*, rev. edn (London, Westminster Abbey, 1988), p. 51.

49   H. G. Wayment: *The Windows of King's College Chapel Cambridge* (London, British Academy, 1972), pp. 9ff.

50   Monument to Sir Rowland Cotton and Lady Cotton (d. 1606) at Norton-in-Hales, Shropshire; see Harris and Higgott, *Inigo Jones Drawings*, pp. 42–4. Jones is also credited with the monument to the dramatist George Chapman (d. 1634) in St-Giles-in-the-Fields, London; see Nikolaus Pevsner: *The Buildings of England: London: Volume I: The Cities of London and Westminster* (Harmondsworth, Penguin Books, 1957), p. 263.

51   See Wickham, *Early English Stages*, vol. 2, part 1, pp. 47, 243–4.

52   *Westminster Abbey*, p. 60–1.

53   For aristocratic funerals, see Stone, *Crisis of the Aristocracy*, pp. 572ff.

54   The *Roxana* vignette must be treated with caution as evidence for the appearance of a permanent playhouse: it is an academic play, produced at Cambridge University, and the vignette may represent a temporary stage erected in a hall, rather than a playhouse proper. John H. Astington has argued that both the *Roxana* and the *Messallina* vignettes are of dubious value as they may be dependent on previously published material, rather than representing contemporary dramatic practice. John H. Astington: 'The Origins of the *Roxana* and *Messallina* Illustrations', *Shakespeare Survey*, XLIII, 1991, pp. 149–69.

55   Glynne Wickham uses a late seventeenth-century monument of a different type, in which the figure of the deceased is revealed under a tent-like canopy, to suggest one form of discovery – that of Hermione's statue in *The*

Winter's Tale (V.iii.). But he subordinates his argument to his conviction that Renaissance staging was descended from the medieval tradition of 'houses', and posits the discovery-tent as an isolated element erected on the forestage, without exploring the possibilities raised by earlier monuments in which discoveries are enacted against a flat façade. *Shakespeare's Dramatic Heritage: collected studies in Mediaeval, Tudor and Shakespearean Drama* (London, Routledge & Kegan Paul, 1969), pp. 249ff. George R. Kernodle: *From Art to Theatre* (Chicago, Chicago University Press, 1944), uses European tombs as analogies for *tableaux vivants* and other examples of street theatre, but gives no English examples, and, while he touches on the affinities between the tiring-house façade and funerary architecture, does not develop this (pp. 53–58, 143, etc.).

56 Hodges, *Globe Restored*, pp. 54–5. Gurr, *Shakespearean Stage*, p. 149, believes that Cleopatra's monument was a 'special property'.

57 See Stone, *Crisis of the Aristocracy*, pp. 549 ff. Timothy Mowl: *Elizabethan & Jacobean Style* (London, Phaidon Press Limited, 1993), emphasizes the coherence of style at this period in all the visual arts.

58 Similar chests are preserved at Arundel and Hardwick. The architectural decoration is apparently taken from Vredeman de Vries' *Variae Architecturae Formae* (Antwerp, c. 1560). See Gervase Jackson-Stops (ed.): *The Treasure Houses of Britain* (New Haven, Yale University Press, 1985), pp. 86–7 and Sotheby's: *English Silver Treasures from the Kremlin* (London, Sothebys, 1991), p. 23.

59 A similar classical three-bay façade, in this case used for the display of figures, may be seen in the chantry of Bishop Gardiner (d. 1555) in Winchester Cathedral (see illustration on p. 178); see Nikolaus Pevsner and David Lloyd, *The Buildings of England: Hampshire and the Isle of Wight* (Harmondsworth, Penguin Books, 1967), p. 679.

60 The Elizabethans and Jacobeans consistently referred to these as 'pyramids', and sometimes represented the Egyptian pyramids in the form of obelisks. See Margery Corbett and Ronald Lightbown: *The Comley Frontispiece* (London, Routledge and Kegan Paul, 1979) pp. 145–52.

61 Ben Jonson, *An Expostulacion with Inigo Jones*, ll. 29–58, in Ben Jonson, *Poems*, ed. George Burke Johnston (London, Routledge & Kegan Paul, 1954), pp. 302ff.

62 Orrell, *Human Stage*, pp. 97ff. Orrell later modified his ideas on plasterwork. See also C. Eccles, *Rose Theatre*, p. 138.

63 See Nikolaus Pevsner: *The Buildings of England: Buckinghamshire* (Harmondsworth, Penguin Books, 1960), p. 296.

64 Originally in the parlour. See Rogers, *Montacute*, pp. 64–5.

65 See Chapter 6.

CHAPTER 5 (pp. 104–132)

1 Arnold: *Elizabeth's Wardrobe*, passim, gives examples of the astonishing sums paid for the rich materials necessary for the Queen's wear.

2 See, for instance, the accounts for autumn 1597, printed in Henslowe, *Diary*, pp. 72ff.

3 Gurr, *Shakespearean Stage*, p. 69.

4 *Ibid.*, p. 194.

5 Chambers, *Elizabethan Stage*, vol. 4, pp. 184–259, passim.

6 See Arnold, *Elizabeth's Wardrobe*, pp. 158–9.

7 Henslowe, *Diary*, pp. 316ff.

8 Chambers, *Elizabethan Stage*, vol. I, pp. 157f, notes the variety of masquing costumes held by the Office of the Revels in the early years of the reign of Elizabeth. They included Venetian commoners, Moors and Italian women, and were supposed to be instantly recognizable. Chambers also notes the way in which costumes were transformed and made over for later masques – a process which must also have taken place in the playhouses.

9 Arnold, *Elizabeth's Wardrobe*, pp. 52ff.

10 There is a growing body of work on the history of theatrical production, for example John Ripley's *Julius Caesar on Stage in England and America* (Cambridge, Cambridge University Press, 1980).

11 Henslowe, *Diary*, pp. 47–8.

12 The illustration is discussed in Gurr, *Shakespearean Stage*, p. 198, and Schoenbaum, *Shakespeare: A Documentary Life*, pp. 122–3. A. M. Nagler doubts the authenticity of the sketch as a record of contemporary theatrical practice: *Shakespeare's Stage*, rev. edn (New Haven and London, Yale University Press, 1981), p. 88.

13 Contemporary records for court masques suggest that this may either be make-up, as worn by the Daughters of the Niger in *The Masque of Blackness* (Stephen Orgel and Roy Strong, *Inigo Jones*, vol. I, pp. 89–90), or a velvet skin-cover, as used in earlier court entertainments (Chambers, *Elizabethan Stage*, vol. I, p. 156).

14 Orgel and Strong, *Inigo Jones*, passim.

15 For instance in the drawing of *Solomon and the Queen of Sheba*, reproduced in *Holbein and the Court of Henry VIII* (London, The Queen's Gallery, Buckingham Palace, 1978), colour plate x.

16 The pictures have such close relationships in many details besides the costumes of the supernatural attendants that one should consider the possibility that they are, if not from the same hand, at least from the same workshop. The suggestion made by Horace Walpole that the monogrammatist HE was Lucas de Heere has been dismissed on the grounds that the *Three Goddesses* picture is superior to anything else known to be by him, but the close relationship of the paintings demands that it be taken seriously.

17 Arnold, *Elizabeth's Wardrobe*, pp. 317, 318, etc.

18 Philoclea is described as wearing such a costume in Philip Sidney's *Arcadia*: 'she . . . lay . . . upon the top of her bed, having her beauties eclipsed with nothing but a fair smock wrought all in flames of ash-colour silk and gold, lying so upon her right side that the left thigh down to the foot yielded his delightful proportion to the full view. . . '. (Philip Sidney: *The Countess of Pembroke's Arcadia*, ed. Maurice Evans (Harmondsworth, Penguin Books, 1977), p. 683.)

19 Reproduced Strong, *English Icon*, p. 224.

20 Sidney, *Arcadia*, pp. 130–1.

21 This picture has been extensively discussed, notably in Yates, *Astraea*, pp. 215ff; Roy Strong: *Portraits of Queen Elizabeth I* (Oxford, Oxford University Press, 1963), pp. 84ff; Arnold, *Elizabeth's Wardrobe*, pp. 81f.

22 There is a description of late-Elizabethan masque costumes for the wedding of Anne Russell and Lord Herbert in 1600: each lady had 'a skirt of cloth of silver, a rich waistcoat wrought with silks and gold and silver, a mantle of carnation taffeta cast under the arm and their hair loose about their shoulders curiously knotted and interlaced', which follows exactly this pattern. (A. L. Rowse: *Times, Persons, Places* (London, Macmillan, 1965), p. 213.) The early designs of Inigo Jones seem to exactly follow late Elizabethan court practice, and it is worth noting that, although Jones's early history is obscure, he was born in 1573.

23 For Lady Elizabeth Pope as a personification of America, see Ellen Chirelstein: 'Lady Elizabeth Pope: the heraldic body', in Lucy Gent and Nigel Llewellyn (eds): *Renaissance Bodies: The Human Figure in English Culture c. 1540–1660* (London, Reaktion Books, 1990), pp. 11–35.

24 For this picture, see Roy C. Strong: *The Elizabethan Image: Painting in England 1540–1620* (London, Tate Gallery, 1969), p. 70, and above, Chapter 3, footnote 33.

25 For the Ditchley Entertainment, see J. Wilson: *Entertainments*, pp. 96ff. As part of the general disenchantment, one of the personages freed is an old knight who has been 'a stranger lady's thrall', deserting the true object of his devotion. The costume of the lady in the Hampton Court picture and her realization that she has been deserted makes it seem possible that she might be this stranger lady. The fact that she is apparently depicted in a grove, and an enchanted grove was the site of Elizabeth's interpretation of the pictures, adds weight to the idea that this is one of the Ditchley paintings.

26 It might conceivably be an imported Middle-Eastern garment, but the embroidery on it looks typical of work found on contemporary English clothes, rather than on eastern textiles, and the cut of the sleeves also looks like coeval English fashion. However, the possibility that she is wearing a caftan – possibly one adapted to English taste – cannot be ruled out. It may also be that the garment is an English attempt to reproduce a caftan, just as Thomas Lee's shirt (see below) is a fancy-dress version of Irish costume. The garment might also conceivably be based on the figure of a Persian Captain from Cesare Vecellio's *Habiti Antichi Et Moderni* (1598), the source of Elizabeth's head-dress in the *Rainbow Portrait*.

27 This picture, by Marcus Gheeraedts the Younger, in the Tate Gallery, is connected with the same tradition as produced the *Ditchley Portrait* and possibly the Hampton Court picture. Thomas Lee was a nephew of the Queen's champion Sir Henry Lee. It would be tempting to suggest that the portrait of Thomas Lee is also connected to the Ditchley entertainment, but it lacks the sonnet inscription of the other two pictures, and Lee's service in Ireland is enough to explain his costume. Connected as he was to Sir Henry Lee, it was natural that Lee should be painted by Gheeraedts, and the choice of fancy-dress costume may also have been dictated by the tastes of his relative.

28 Strong, *Elizabethan Image*, p. 71.

29 Orgel and Strong, *Inigo Jones*, vol. 2, p. 767.

30 Knowledge of Roman dress was not dependent on an acquaintance with the antiquities of Rome: the archaeological remains of places like Verulamium and the area round Hadrian's wall were familiar enough in the early seventeenth century to be included by Speed in his atlas.

31 See Martin Holmes: 'An Unrecorded Portrait of Edward Alleyn', *Theatre Notes*, 5, 1950, pp. 11–13; and Gurr, *Shakespearean Stage*, p. 35. John H. Astington: 'The "Unrecorded Portrait" of Edward Alleyn', *Shakespeare Quarterly*, XLIV, 1993, pp. 73–86, questions the validity of Holmes's arguments.

32 Orgel & Strong, *Inigo Jones*, vol. 2, pp. 598, 623, 819.

33 See, for instance, the costume by Inigo Jones for Zenobia in *The Masque of Queens* (*Ibid.*, vol. I, p. 148).

34 Wickham, *Early English Stages*, vol. 2, part 1, pp. 47, 239, 243–6, 337, 338.

35 Harris and Higgott: *Inigo Jones Drawings*, p. 42, and Nikolaus Pevsner: *The Buildings of England: Shropshire* (Harmondsworth, Penguin Books, 1958), p. 220.

36 Nikolaus Pevsner, rev. Bridget Cherry: *The Buildings of England: Hertfordshire* (Harmondsworth, Penguin Books, 1977), p. 163; Orrell, *Human Stage*, pp. 119ff.

37 Harris and Higgott, *Inigo Jones Drawings*, p. 90.

38 Wickham, *Early English Stages*, vol. 2, part 1, p. 90; Orrell, *Architecture of the Fortune*, p. 18. For Arundel as an art-collector, see David Howarth: *Patronage and Collecting in the Seventeenth Century: Thomas Howard, Earl of Arundel* (Oxford, Ashmolean Museum, 1985).

39 Orgel and Strong, *Inigo Jones*, vol. I, p. 180; Schoenbaum, *Shakespeare: A Compact Life*, p. 272.

40 Orgel and Strong, *Inigo Jones*, vol. I, p. 38, vol. 2, p. 569; Edmond, *Peter Street*, p. 110.

41 Roy C. Strong: *Festival Designs by Inigo Jones: An Exhibition of Drawings for Scenery and Costumes for the Court Masques of James I and Charles I* (London, Victoria and Albert Museum, 1969); John Harris, Stephen Orgel and Roy Strong: *The King's Arcadia: Inigo Jones and the Stuart Court* (London, The Banqueting House, Whitehall, 1973); John Harris and Gordon Higgott: *Inigo Jones: Complete Architectural Drawings* (London, The Royal Academy of Arts, 1990).

42 For the history of the monument, see Schoenbaum, *Shakespeare: A Compact Life*, pp. 306ff. Although the Shakespeare monument is not an outstanding advertisement for its standards, the Johnson workshop was patronized by more members of the nobility than the Earls of Rutland (for one of whom, as Schoenbaum points out, Shakespeare and Burbage worked on tournament impresas). It seems likely that the major monument to the 3rd Earl of Bath (d. 1623) at Tawstock, Devon, was also from this atelier, which was situated in Southwark, near the Globe.

43 The exceptions are monuments where they are shown as dead in their shrouds, such as that of John Donne in St Paul's Cathedral; as skeletons or cadavers, such as that of the 1st Earl of Salisbury at Hatfield; and extremely rare instances where they are shown in classicizing draperies, such as the monument to John and Thomas Lyttelton (d. 1635) by Nicholas Stone in the chapel of Magdalene College, Oxford.

44 Michael Neill describes the monument as 'a kind of perpetual pageant or hearse' ('"Exeunt with a Dead March": Funeral Pageantry on the Shakespearean Stage', in David M. Bergeron (ed.): *Pageantry in the Shakespearean Theater* (Athens, GA, The University of Georgia Press, 1985), pp. 153–93, p. 181). The Harlton monument is shown in colour as the frontispiece of *RCHM West Cambridgeshire* (London, HMSO, 1968).

45 Nikolaus Pevsner, rev. Enid Radcliffe: *The Buildings of England: Essex* (Harmondsworth, Penguin Books, 1965), p. 437; Nikolaus Pevsner and Priscilla Metcalf: *The Cathedrals of England: Southern England* (Harmondsworth, Penguin Books, 1985), p. 153.

46 Jennifer Sherwood and Nikolaus Pevsner: *The Buildings of England: Oxfordshire* (Harmondsworth, Penguin Books, 1974), p. 506; Pevsner: *Buckinghamshire*, p. 174.

47 David Verey: *The Buildings of England: Gloucestershire: Volume 2: The Vale and the Forest of Dean*, corrected edn (Harmondsworth, Penguin Books, 1980), p. 308.

48 Pevsner, *Hertfordshire*, p. 211.

49 For these entertainments, see J. Wilson, *Entertainments*, pp. 43ff.

50 Gurr, *Shakespearean Stage*, pp. 193ff.

51 Gurr's treatment in *Shakespearean Stage* occupies only eight pages, two of which are devoted to full-page illustrations, in a book 231 pages long.

52 Oxford, Oxford University Press, 1936. Ann Pasternak Slater: *Shakespeare the Director* (Sussex, The Harvester Press, 1982), devotes one chapter to costume, dealing mainly with its symbolism (pp. 136–70), while John T. Williams: *Costumes and Settings for Shakespeare's Plays* (London, B. T. Batsford, 1982) suggests a plausible Renaissance mise-en-scene for *Julius Caesar* (pp. 73ff).

53 *Cymbeline*, V.iv.29ff; *The Winter's Tale*, V.iii.passim.

54 Quoted Orgel and Strong, *Inigo Jones*, vol.1, pp. 11–12.

55 *Ibid.*, p. 90.

56 See Bradbrook: *Drama as Offering*; J. Wilson, *Entertainments*, pp. 96ff.

57 For a biographical sketch of Jones, see Harris and Higgott, *Inigo Jones Drawings*, pp. 13ff.

58 Orgel and Strong, *Inigo Jones*, vol. I, p. 96.

59 See the account quoted in *ibid.*, pp. 205–6.

60 For example, in the play *Two Shakespearean Actors*, by Richard Nelson (London, Faber, 1990), staged by the RSC at Stratford in 1990 and in London in 1991, which explores two different nineteenth-century acting styles.

CHAPTER 6 (pp. 133–158)

1 In King's College Chapel, Cambridge, for example, the usual place for performances is in the antechapel (where the play was put on for Elizabeth I in 1564), with the stage erected in front of the screen, through the central doorway of which entrances and exits are made, and with the chapel itself providing back-stage facilities. Cf. Chambers, *Elizabethan Stage*, vol. I, pp. 226f. Hosley, 'The second Blackfriars playhouse', argues for the screen as the natural backdrop.

2 For a discussion of the involvement of the Queen in the entertainments put on for her, so that she herself became part of the performance, see J. Wilson, *Entertainments*, pp. 6f.

3 This division is particularly clear in King's College Chapel, Cambridge. The antechapel is for members of the public, the chapel for members of the college, and the massive screen which separates them precludes the public from even seeing what goes on inside the chapel, although they may hear the services. The screen marks off initiates – members of the college (and even the choirboys are in a sense members of the college since they attend its private school) – from the general ignoramuses who may go to the chapel to listen, but have no hope of understanding.

4 Sieur de Maisse, quoted in N. Williams: *Elizabeth*, p. 228.

5 Orazio Busino in *Calendar of State Papers, Venetian, 1617–19*, pp. 111–14; quoted in Gurr, *Shakespearean Stage*, p. 203.

6 For the Christ Church theatre, see John Orrell: *The Theatres of Inigo Jones and John Webb* (Cambridge, Cambridge University Press, 1985), pp. 24ff, and Orrell, *Human Stage*, pp. 119ff.

7 For the Jones/Webb theatres, see Orrell, *Theatres of Jones and Webb*, passim.

8 Harris and Higgott, *Inigo Jones Drawings*, pp. 108–9, suggest that the gallery may have originally been intended to have access by means of an external stair, and that its present state reflects the change of use of the building.

9 Wickham, *Early English Stages*, vol. 2, part 2, pp. 78–9; Orrell, *Human Stage*, pp. 173ff.

10 Harris and Higgott, *Inigo Jones Drawings*, pp. 266ff. This contains an elegant summary of the various arguments which have been put forward, since the first publication of the design in 1969, for the identification of this building.

11 All the interpretations rely on essentially subjective stylistic evidence – John Harris has changed his mind about the dating, having initially accepted the 1617 attribution – although the latest is by two scholars with sufficient standing for their pronouncements to be magisterial.

12 Orrell, *Theatres of Jones and Webb*, pp. 39ff.

13 For the children's theatre at this period, see Shapiro, *Children of the Revels*, passim. On the first Blackfriars theatre, see *ibid.*, pp. 14–18.

14 Chambers, *Elizabethan Stage*, vol. 4, pp. 319–20.

15 Gurr, *Playgoing*, p. 35.

16 *Ibid.*, p. 33–4.

17 *Ibid.*, p. 35, quoting a letter by George Garrard.

18 It was in the course of a case connected with the confusion about James Burbage's estate that Cuthbert Burbage made the statement that his father was the first builder of playhouses in London which led to the belief that the Theatre was the first purpose-built playhouse, only recently modified by the discoveries about the Red Lion.

19 Gurr, *Shakespearean Stage*, p. 120.

20 Later in the period, at least, there was a clear distinction made between playhouses catering to upper-income and to more popular audiences. In 1613 the Venetian ambassador went to the Curtain, which by then was 'an infamous place, where no good citizen or gentleman would show his face'. He compounded this *faux pas* by standing in the yard, rather than paying for a gallery seat. He was greeted with mockery and catcalls by the audience, who resented his presence not only because he was a foreigner but because he was a gentleman slumming. See Gurr: *Playgoing*, p. 71.

21 Schoenbaum, *Shakespeare: A Compact Life*, p. 182.

22 Orrell, *Human Stage*, p. 66.

23 Chambers, *Elizabethan Stage*, vol. I, pp. 308ff, charts the claims to the status of gentleman which were made by actors over this period. The actors' consistent defence of their own existence was their need to keep in practice for the occasions when they were called upon to play before the Queen. See Carol Chillington Rutter: *Documents of the Rose Playhouse* (Manchester, Manchester University Press, 1984), pp. 9f.

24 For the history of the second Blackfriars under the children's companies, see Shapiro, *Children of the Revels*, pp. 24ff.

25 Orrell, *Human Stage*, p. 186.

26 This differs from the other two in that it is believed to represent a performance during the Commonwealth, while

playing was officially banned, and so may represent a temporary playhouse erected in the hall of a private house. For a caution against placing too much reliance on these vignettes, see Astington, '*Roxana* and *Messallina* Illustrations', passim.

27 One must be careful about taking apparent references to theatrical practice in contemporary plays too literally; there has been a great deal of argument about where the hangings put on the stage area for individual performances were actually located. Gurr (*Shakespearean Stage*, p. 136) believes that the vague curved shapes visible under the stage on the Swan drawing represent not trestles, supporting the stage, but hangings round it – but a balance must be struck between an appreciation of the Elizabethan consciousness, 400 years before Brecht, of the theatricality of the stage world, and a desire to identify every possible allusion to parts of the playhouse as references to a specific theatrical location. If Orrell is right, and stage covers were not introduced until the construction of the Swan, then the opening line of Shakespeare's *Henry VI, Part I*, 'Hung be the heavens with black, yield day to night!', which is often taken as a reference to the stage cover and the practice of changing the colour of the fabric hangings of the playhouse to whatever was most appropriate for the play being presented, was written for a playhouse without heavens.

28 Or possibly third, if he was involved in the Red Lion project with his brother-in-law.

29 For a discussion of the custom of sitting on the stage, see Gurr, *Playgoing*, pp. 28ff.

30 See Gurr's account of a fight at the Blackfriars in 1632, *ibid.*, pp. 27f.

31 See Orrell, *The Human Stage*, pp. 186ff. Orrell argues that Burbage had constructed a Serlian theatre, but a designer whose model of a playhouse was the existing amphitheatres would in any case be likely to produce an indoor playhouse in which a projecting stage was surrounded on three sides by curved or angled galleries.

32 Gurr, *Playgoing*, pp. 27ff. Frances Yates's suggestion (*Theatre of the World*, London, Routledge & Kegan Paul, 1969, pp. 136ff) that the stage area of the Globe is represented in Robert Fludd's *Utriusque Cosmi Historia* (Oppenheim, John Theodore de Bry, 1617–19) has been met with some scepticism (see, for example, Hodges, *Globe Restored*, pp. 118f), but it would be plausible as a representation of the stage area of the Blackfriars, with private boxes lining the stage sides at a height which would permit those in them to see over the heads of anyone sitting on the stage on a stool.

33 Led by Richard Hosley, 'The second Blackfriars playhouse'.

34 Orrell, *Human Stage*, pp. 186ff. Orrell assumes that the Jones design is for the Cockpit in Drury Lane, not for Davenant's much later Fleet Street project, which remained unrealized, unlike the Drury Lane Cockpit.

35 Ian Nairn and Nikolaus Pevsner, rev. Bridget Cherry: *The Buildings of England: Surrey* (Harmondsworth, Penguin Books, 1971), pp. 353ff. Loseley was built by Sir William More, the landlord of the first Blackfriars theatre, and vendor of the Blackfriars frater to James Burbage, between 1561 and 1569. Nairn, Pevsner and Cherry point out the connections between More and Sir Thomas Cawarden, Master of the Revels and Keeper of the Tents, as well as Keeper of Nonesuch, who died in 1559. More was his executor, and may have acquired the pieces for his projected building then. Courtly rapaciousness with royal property was common – the circumstances in which the famous state bed at Knole arrived there do not bear close examination. Sir William More was the grandfather of Ann More, the wife of the poet John Donne.

36 Orrell, *Human Stage*, pp. 30ff.

37 J. Wilson, *Entertainments*, p. 100.

38 Orrell, *Theatres of Jones and Webb*, passim. Orrell has also argued that the Fortune was a Serlian structure ('Architecture of the Fortune'), but his argument is much stronger for the application of classicizing decoration (the satyrs specified in the Fortune contract) than for the use of Serlian principles in building.

CHAPTER 7 (pp. 159–183)

1 The contract is reproduced in Henslowe, *Diary*, pp. 304f.

2 For general expenditure, see Stone, *Crisis of the Aristocracy*, pp. 549ff; on Wollaton, see Mark Girouard: *Robert Smythson & The Elizabethan Country House* (London, Yale University Press), 1983, pp. 77ff.

3 Builders of playhouses had to find all the materials, which might come in part from the estate of a great house.

4 *Yesterday's World*, September/October 1989, pp. 12–13. For another view of Imry's involvement, see C. Eccles: *The Rose Theatre*, passim. This book is excellent and fascinating on the negotiations to save the site.

5 This position was summarized by John Orrell and Andrew Gurr: 'What the Rose can tell us'.

6 That Orrell and Gurr did not understand this is shown by their concluding remarks in the article cited above.

7 The general slowness to realize the unique importance of the finds (the remains of the Globe were discovered only after those of the Rose, and, more importantly, after the discovery of the Rose remains had made it seem more likely that traces of the Globe might have survived) is tacitly acknowledged in John Ashurst, Nick Balaam and

Kate Foley: 'The Rose theatre: overcoming the technical preservation problems', *English Heritage Conservation Bulletin*, 9 (October 1989), pp. 9–10, where they write, 'before the full importance of the discoveries was realized, the developers had already agreed to rebury the remains in a way which would secure their preservation.. . .' The literary and theatre-historical communities had, of course, realized the importance of the remains from the outset.

8   *Yesterday's World*, p. 13.

9   Henslowe, *Diary*, pp. 21–2.

10 William Shakespeare: *The Complete Works*, ed. Peter Alexander (London, Collins, 1951), p. xv.

11 See Schoenbaum, *Shakespeare: A Compact Life*, pp. 161ff. The title-page of the 1594 quarto of *Titus Andronicus* is reproduced in Schoenbaum, *Shakespeare: A Documentary Life*, p. 124.

12 Gurr, *Shakespearean Stage*, p. 41.

13 Henslowe, *Diary*, pp. 16–20; Schoenbaum, *Shakespeare: A Compact Life*, p. 165.

14 Henslowe, *Diary*, p. 21.

15 The extent of the deterioration is described in Ashurst, Balaam and Foley, 'Rose theatre', pp. 9–10.

16 Brian Fagan: 'The Rose affair', *Archaeology*, March/April 1990, pp. 12ff, provides a succinct account of the various options discussed during the debate over the future of the site, although he too uncritically accepts its Shakespearean associations.

17 Letter to *The Independent*, 30 May 1989.

18 *English Heritage Press Release*, 2 June 1989.

19 These are pinpointed as areas needing exploration in Orrell and Gurr, 'What the Rose can tell us', pp. 421–9.

20 The disapproval among the general archaeological community at English Heritage's action can be sensed in the last paragraph of Patrick Ottaway: 'The Campaign to save the Rose', *Rescue News*, 48 (1989), pp. 2–3.

21 Steven Brindle and Roger Thomas: 'The Globe Theatre', *English Heritage Conservation Bulletin*, 1990, pp. 8–9.

22 Simon McCudden: *Report on Evaluation at Anchor Terrace Car Park, Park Street S.E.1* (London, Museum of London, 1990); Simon McCudden with Peter Hinton: 'The Discovery of the Globe Theatre', *London Archaeologist*, vol. 6, no. 6, (spring 1990), pp. 143–4.

23 Cambridge, Cambridge University Press, 1983.

24 Orrell, *Quest for Shakespeare's Globe*, pp. 102–3, and fig. 30, *ibid*.

25 McCudden, *Report on Anchor Terrace*, p. 7. Braines (called 'Baines' by McCudden) was published by the London County Council.

26 Letters from Professors Andrew Gurr and John Orrell, 20 June, and Mr Harvey Sheldon, 26 June, 1990.

27 Jones, *Fake?*, pp. 156–7.

28 Andrew Gurr and John Orrell: *Rebuilding Shakespeare's Globe* (London, Weidenfeld & Nicolson, 1989), passim.

29 While Orrell's reconstruction of the second Globe – which does not include its interior – is admirable, his arguments that the first Globe and the Theatre must have been of the same dimensions are only probably and possibly correct, and the Swan drawing has led to almost as many reconstructions of its interior as there are theatre historians. For salutary reminders of the impossibility of any accurate 'reconstruction' of a Renaissance playhouse on the existing evidence, see Nagler, *Shakespeare's Stage*, (where he writes, 'I do not aspire to reconstruct the stage of the Globe playhouse. The undertaking strikes me as hopeless.' (p.18)) and Cerasano, 'Shakespeare's Elusive Globe'.

30 Julian M. C. Bowsher & Simon Blatherwick: 'The Rose Theatre', *Minerva*, February 1990, pp. 14–17. This report includes the unjustified assertion that *Titus Andronicus* was first produced at the Rose.

31 Personal communication.

32 Programme hosted by Ludovic Kennedy, BBC Radio 4, 17 July 1989, 9.05 a.m.

33 Henslowe, *Diary*, pp. 304–6, 9–13, 6–7.

34 Bowsher and Blatherwick, 'Rose theatre', p. 15.

35 For timber-framing construction techniques, see Orrell, *Human Stage*, passim.

36 Orrell calculated the diameter of the Hope, which is shown with the second Globe on Hollar's *Long View of London*, at between 98.99 feet and 100.99 feet (*Quest for Shakespeare's Globe*, p. 102). The Hope was to be the same size as the Swan (*ibid.*, pp. 103–4). De Witt says that the Swan was the largest of the playhouses, which presents some problems to Orrell's argument that the Theatre had the same dimensions as the Globe, but de Witt does not remark that the Rose was substantially smaller than the Swan, as the archaeological evidence suggests may be the case.

37 Henslowe, *Diary*, pp. 9–13.

38 *Ibid.*, p. 13.

39 The following summary is, unless otherwise indicated, based on Bowsher and Blatherwick, 'Rose theatre', pp. 14–15, the report by the Museum of London excavation team responsible for the Rose's discovery and most of its excavation.

40 John Orrell worked out the orientation of the second Globe (apparently correctly) in *Quest for Shakespeare's Globe*, pp. 139ff, and extends this, picking up a suggestion made by Leslie Hotson (*Shakespeare's Wooden O*, London, Rupert Hart Davies, 1959, pp. 263–6) and others that most, if not all, Elizabethan playhouses were oriented north of east. This assumption continues in Orrell's *Human Stage*, p. 92. A problem arises in that Orrell argues that Norden's panorama (which shows the first Globe) appears to agree with Hollar's in its depiction of the orientation of the Globe, suggesting that the stages of both Globes faced the same direction, but it also shows the Rose and the Globe as oriented in the same direction, which proves, for the Rose, to have been inaccurate. Norden also shows the Rose with fewer sides than it has turned out to have possessed. Norden is therefore no longer a sound basis for a pronouncement on the orientation of the first Globe, and the exact position of its stage must await further excavation, if that is possible. Norden and Hollar are not in such clear agreement as Orrell argues over the orientation of the stages, and the excavators prefer to read Norden's panorama as showing the Rose stage precisely where it has turned out to be.

41 The Fortune contract is reprinted in Henslowe, *Diary*, pp. 306–10; see also Chapter 4.

42 Harris and Higgott, *Inigo Jones Drawings*, p. 269.

43 Orrell, *Quest for Shakespeare's Globe*, p. 137, calculates that at peak capacity the second Globe was capable of accommodating 600 people in the yard and 2,750 in the galleries.

44 Orrell *Human Stage*, pp. 61ff. He reads the projection above the gallery roof-line on the view of the Theatre as the roof of a tower, like that of the Red Lion, rather than evidence of a stage-cover.

45 Gurr, *Shakespearean Stage*, p. 130.

46 Quoted Gurr, *Shakespearean Stage*, p. 214.

47 Figures based on Bowsher and Blatherwick, 'Rose theatre', p. 17, where the estimate of a yard capacity of 1,000 is given, and Orrell and Gurr, 'What the Rose can tell us', who give more conservative figures.

48 Orrell, *Human Stage*, pp. 61ff.

49 Orrell, *ibid.*, pp. 88ff, notes the slope needed for adequate drainage of thatch, and discusses tile as a roofing medium, but does not explore the possibilities of wood shingles.

50 Gurr (*Shakespearean Stage*, p. 131) suggests that this material is a result of the mixture of ash and clinker, scattered to provide a dry surface in the yard, with hazelnut shells discarded by the audience. Only further excavation can determine which theory is correct.

51 Christopher Marlowe: *Doctor Faustus*, I.iii.15ff., in *Complete Plays*, ed. J. B. Steane (Harmondsworth, Penguin Books, 1969).

52 Henslowe, *Diary*, p. 320.

53 Professor Martin Biddle believes that it may have been visible during the excavation. Personal communication.

54 Gurr, *Shakespearean Stage*, p. 136.

55 See the entry for the tomb of Sir Robert Dormer (d. 1552) at Wing, in Pevsner, *Buckinghamshire*, p. 296. See also Stone, *Crisis of the Aristocracy*, pp. 711f. The Duke of Northumberland was the father of the Earl of Leicester, who owned Italian Renaissance paintings. He and his brother, the Earl of Warwick, were patrons of theatrical companies. James Burbage at one time led Leicester's Men.

56 For a discussion of the use of the classical style see Girouard, *Robert Smythson*, pp. 28ff.

57 *Ibid.*, p. 30.

58 Kernodle, *From Art to Theatre*, pp. 167ff.

59 For the Dutch stage, see *ibid.*, pp. 111ff and 152ff.

60 Mira Bar-Hillel, 'Good Fortune for Dansk', *History Today*, 41 (February 1991), pp. 3–4.

61 Graham C. Adams: 'The Ottoneum: A Neglected Seventeenth-Century Theatre', *Shakespeare Studies*, XV, 1982, pp. 243–68, and 'The Interior Design of the Ottoneum, Kassel', *ibid.*, XX, 1988, pp. 1–14.

62 Kernodle, *From Art to Theatre*, p. 119.

63 For some account of the debate among theatre historians about the implications of the Rose excavation, see C. Eccles, *Rose Theatre*, pp. 85ff, and Franklin J. Hildy, ed.: *New Issues in the Reconstruction of Shakespeare's Theatre* (New York, Peter Lang, 1990).

64 Orrell, *Human Stage*, pp. 65ff.

65 Andrew Gurr: 'A First Doorway into the Globe', *Shakespeare Quarterly*, 41, 1990, pp. 97–100.

66 Orrell, *Quest for Shakespeare's Globe*, p. 137.

67 Orrell, 'Architecture of the Fortune Playhouse', pp. 21–2.

68 R. A. Foakes: 'The Discovery of the Rose Theatre: Some Implications', *Shakespeare Survey*, XLIII, 1991, pp. 141–8; Orrell, 'Architecture of the Fortune Playhouse', p. 19; Gurr, *Shakespearean Stage*, p. 143. Blatherwick and Gurr, 'Shakespeare's Factory', show a slightly tapered stage.

69 Yates, *Theatre of the World*, pp. 130f. Christine Eccles accepts Mrs Thrale's authority (*The Rose*, pp. 97, 109, 112).

BIBLIOGRAPHY

Alabaster, William, *Roxana tragaedia* (London, A. Crook, 1632).

Arnold, Janet, *Queen Elizabeth's Wardrobe Unlock'd* (London, Maney, 1988).

Ashurst, John, Balaam, Nick and Foley, Kate, 'The Rose theatre: overcoming the technical preservation problems', *English Heritage Conservation Bulletin*, 9 (October 1989).

Astington, John H., 'The Origins of the *Roxana* and *Messallina* Illustrations', *Shakespeare Survey*, XLIII (1991), pp. 149–69.

Astington, John H., 'The "Unrecorded Portrait" of Edward Alleyn', *Shakespeare Quarterly*, XLIV (1993), pp. 73–86.

Axton, Marie, *The Queen's Two Bodies: Drama and the Elizabethan Succession* (London, Royal Historical Society; distributed by Swift Printers, 1977).

Axton, Richard, *European Drama of the Early Middle Ages* (London, Hutchinson University Library, 1974).

Bar-Hillel, Mira, 'Good Fortune for Gdansk', *History Today*, 41 (February, 1991), pp. 3–4.

Barroll, Leeds, *Politics, Plague, and Shakespeare's Theater: The Stuart Years* (Ithaca, Cornell University Press, 1991).

Barton, Anne, *Ben Jonson, Dramatist* (Cambridge, Cambridge University Press, 1984).

Bergeron, David M., *English Civic Pageantry 1558–1642* (London, Edward Arnold, 1971).

Berry, Herbert, (ed.), *The First Public Playhouse: The Theatre in Shoreditch 1576–1598* (Montreal, McGill-Queen's University Press, 1979).

Berry, Herbert, *The Boar's Head Playhouse* (Washington, Folger Books, 1986).

Berry, Herbert, *Shakespeare's Playhouses* (New York, AMS Press, 1987).

Berry, Herbert, 'The First Public Playhouses, Especially the Red Lion', *Shakespeare Quarterly*, XL (1989), pp. 133–48.

Berry, Philippa, *Of Chastity and Power: Elizabethan Literature and the Unmarried Queen* (London, Routledge, 1989).

Biddle, Martin, Letter to the *Independent*, 30 May, 1989.

Blatherwick, Simon and Gurr, Andrew, with commentary by John Orrell: 'Shakespeare's factory: archaeological evaluations on the site of the Globe Theatre at 1/15 Anchor Terrace, Southwark Bridge Road, Southwark, *Antiquity* LXVI, no. 251 (June 1992), pp. 315–33.

Bowsher, Julian M. C. and Blatherwick, Simon, 'The Rose theatre', *Minerva*, February 1990, pp. 14–17.

Bradbrook, Muriel, *Drama as Offering: the princely pleasures at Kenelworth* (Houston, Rice Institute, pamphlet XLVI, 1960).

Braines, W. W., *The Site of the Globe playhouse, Southwark*, rev. edn (London, London County Council, 1929).

Bright, Timothy, *A treatise of melancholie, containing the causes thereof* (London, T. Vautrollier, 1586).

Brindle, Steven and Thomas, Roger, 'The Globe Theatre', *English Heritage Conservation Bulletin*, 1990.

Brownlow, F. W., 'John Shakespeare's Recusancy: New Light on an Old Document', *Shakespeare Quarterly*, XL (1989), pp. 186–90.

Burkhart, Robert E., 'Finding Shakespeare's "Lost Years"', *Shakespeare Quarterly*, XXIX (1978), pp. 77–9.

Burton, Robert, *The Anatomy of Melancholy* (Oxford, J. Lichfield, 1621).

Buxton, John, *Elizabethan Taste* (London, Macmillan, 1963).

Carey, Robert, *The Memoirs of Robert Carey*, ed. F. H. Mares (Oxford, Oxford University Press, 1972).

Cerasano, S. P., 'Shakespeare's Elusive Globe: Review Article', *Medieval & Renaissance Drama in England*, III (1986), pp. 265–75.

Chambers, E. K., *The Medieval Stage* (2 vols, Oxford, Oxford University Press, 1903).

Chambers, E. K., *The Elizabethan Stage* (4 vols, Oxford, Oxford University Press, 1923).

Chirelstein, Ellen, 'Lady Elizabeth Pope: the heraldic body', in Gent, Lucy and Llewellyn, Nigel, eds, *Renaissance Bodies: The Human Figure in English Culture c. 1540–1660* (London, Reaktion Books, 1990), pp. 11–35.

Corbett, Margery, and Lightbown, Ronald: *The Comley Frontispiece: The Emblematic Title-Page in England 1550–1660*, (London, Routledge & Kegan Paul, 1979).

Cox, Jane, 'Shakespeare's will and signatures', in Thomas, David, ed., *Shakespeare in the Public Records* (London, HMSO, 1985).

Dekker, Thomas, *The Magnificent Entertainment: giuen to King Iames, Queen Anne his wife, and Henry Frederick the Prince, vpon the day of his Maiesties Tryumphant Passage (from the Tower) through his Honourable Citie (and Chamber) of London, being the 15. of March. 1603 . . . .* (London, Thomas Man, 1604).

Donne, John, *Sermons*, ed. G. R. Potter and E. M. Simpson (10 vols, Berkeley, University of California Press, 1953–62).

Eccles, Christine, *The Rose Theatre* (London, Nick Hern Books, 1990).

Eccles, Mark, *Shakespeare in Warwickshire* (Madison, University of Wisconsin Press, 1961).

Edmond, Mary, 'Peter Street 1553–1609: Builder of Playhouses', *Shakespeare Survey*, XLV (1993), pp. 101–14.

English Heritage Press Release, 2 June, 1989.

Fagan, Brian, 'The Rose Affair', *Archaeology*, March/April 1990.

Ferguson, George, *Signs & Symbols in Christian Art* (Oxford, Oxford University Press, 1961 (paperback edn)).

Fludd, Robert, *Utriusque Cosmi Historia* (Oppenheim, John Theodore de Bry, 1617–19).

Foakes, R. A., *Illustrations of the English Stage 1580–1642* (London, Scolar Press, 1985).

Foxe, John, *Actes and Monuments . . . (The Book of Martyrs)* (London, John Day, 1563).

Fraser, Antonia, *Mary, Queen of Scots* (London, Weidenfeld & Nicolson, 1969).

Frye, Roland Mushat, 'Ladies, Gentlemen, and Skulls: *Hamlet* and the Iconographic Tradition', *Shakespeare Quarterly*, XXX (1979), pp. 15–28.

Frye, Roland Mushat, 'Ways of Seeing in Shakespearean Drama and Elizabethan Painting', *Shakespeare Quarterly*, XXXI (1980), pp. 323–42.

Gent, Lucy, *Picture and Poetry 1560–1620: Relations between literature and the visual arts in the English Renaissance* (Leamington Spa, James Hall, 1981).

Gibson, Gail McMurray, 'Long Melford Church, Suffolk: Some Suggestions for the Study of Visual Artifacts and Medieval Drama', *Research Opportunities in Renaissance Drama*, XXI (1978), pp. 103–16.

Girouard, Mark, *Robert Smythson & The Elizabethan Country House* (London, Yale University Press, 1983).

Graves, Robert, *The Greek Myths*, rev. edn (2 vols, Harmondsworth, Penguin Books, 1960).

Greenblatt, Stephen, *Sir Walter Ralegh: the Renaissance Man and his Roles* (New Haven, Yale University Press, 1973).

Greene, Robert, *Groats-worth of Witte, bought with a Million of Repentance* (London, 1592).

Gurr, Andrew, *The Shakespearean Stage, 1574–1642*, 2nd edn (Cambridge, Cambridge University Press, 1980).

Gurr, Andrew, *Playgoing in Shakespeare's London* (Cambridge, Cambridge University Press, 1987).

Gurr, Andrew and Orrell, John, *Rebuilding Shakespeare's Globe* (London, Weidenfeld & Nicolson, 1989).

Gurr, Andrew, 'A First Doorway into the Globe', *Shakespeare Quarterly*, XLI (1990), pp. 97–100.

Gurr, Andrew, *The Shakespearean Stage, 1574–1642*, 3rd edn (Cambridge, Cambridge University Press,1992).

Gurr, Andrew, 'Three Reluctant Patrons and Early Shakespeare', *Shakespeare Quarterly*, XLIV (1993), pp. 159–74.

Gurr, Andrew, 'The Bare Island', *Shakespeare Survey*, XLVII (1994), pp. 29–34.

Harris, John and Higgott, Gordon, *Inigo Jones: Complete Architectural Drawings* (London, Royal Academy of Arts, 1989).

Harris, John, Orgel, Stephen, and Strong, Roy C., *The King's Arcadia: Inigo Jones and the Stuart Court* (London, The Banqueting House, Whitehall, 1973).

Harrison, Stephen, *The arch's of triumph erected in honor of James, the first at his entrance & passage through London* (London, J. Windet, 1604).

Harrison, William, *Elizabethan England: From 'A Description of England', by William Harrison (In 'Holinshed's Chronicles')*, ed. by Lothrop Withington with Introduction by F. J. Furnivall (London, Walter Scott, n.d.).

Hays, Rosalind Conklin, 'Dorset Church Houses and the Drama', *Research Opportunities in Renaissance Drama*, XXXI (1992), pp. 13–24.

Henslowe, Philip, *Henslowe's Diary*, ed. R. A. Foakes and R. T. Rickert (Cambridge, Cambridge University Press, 1961).

Hildy, Franklin J., ed., *New Issues in the Reconstruction of Shakespeare's Theatre* (New York, Peter Lang, 1990).

Hodges, C. Walter, 'The Lantern of Taste', *Shakespeare Survey*, XII (1959), pp. 8–14.

Hodges, C. Walter, *The Globe Restor'd*, 2nd edn (Oxford, Oxford University Press, 1968).

Hodges, C. Walter, *Shakespeare's Second Globe: the missing monument* (Oxford, Oxford University Press, 1973).

Holinshed, Raphael, *Chronicles of England, Scotlande, and Irelande* (London, L. Harrison, 1577).

Holmes, Martin, 'An Unrecorded Portrait of Edward Alleyn', *Theatre Notes*, 5 (1950), pp. 11–13.

Honigmann, E. A. J., *Shakespeare: The 'Lost Years'* (Manchester, Manchester University Press, 1985).

Hosley, Richard, 'The second Blackfriars playhouse', in Barroll, J. Leeds, Leggatt, Alexander, Hosley, Richard and Kernan, Alvin, *The Revels History of Drama in English*, Volume IIII 1576–1613 (London, Methuen, 1975).

Hotson, Leslie, *Shakespeare's Wooden O* (London, Rupert Hart Davis, 1959).

Howarth, David, *Patronage and Collecting in the Seventeenth Century: Thomas Howard, Earl of Arundel* (Oxford, Ashmolean Museum, 1985).

Jackson-Stops, Gervase, ed., *The Treasure Houses of Britain* (New Haven, Yale University Press, 1985).

Jones, Mark, ed., *Fake? The Art of Deception* (London, British Museum Publications, 1990).

Jones, Michael K., and Underwood, Malcolm G., *The King's Mother: Lady Margaret Beaufort, Countess of Richmond and Derby* (Cambridge, Cambridge University Press, 1992).

Jonson, Ben, *His part of King James his royall and magnificent entertainement through his Honorable Cittie of London, Thurseday the 15. of March. 1603, so much as was presented in the first and last of their triumphall arch's* (London, Edward Blount, 1604).

Jonson, Ben, *Workes* (London, William Stansby, 1616).

Jonson, Ben, *Poems*, ed. George Burke Johnston (London, Routledge & Kegan Paul, 1954).

Jonson, Ben, *Three Comedies*, ed. Michael Jameson (Harmondsworth, Penguin Books, 1966).

Kernodle, George R., *From Art to Theatre* (Chicago, University of Chicago Press, 1944).

Kirkman, Francis, *The Wits; or, sport upon sport* (London, F[r]ancis Kirkman, 1662).

Knolles, Richard, *The Generall Historie of the Turkes* (London, Adam Islip, 1597).

Kyd, Thomas, *The Spanish Tragedy* (rev. edn, London, Augustine Mathewes, 1633: first published 1592).

Latimer, Hugh, *Sermons*, ed. H. C. Beeching (London, Dent, 1906).

Leishman, J. B., ed., *The Three Parnassus Plays 1598–1601* (London, Ivor Nicholson & Watson, 1949).

Linthicum, M. C., *Costume in the Drama of Shakespeare and his Contemporaries* (Oxford, Oxford University Press, 1936).

Loengard, Janet S., 'An Elizabethan Lawsuit: John Brayne, his carpenter, and the building of the Red Lion theatre', *Shakespeare Quarterly*, XXXIV (1983), pp. 298–310.

Lusardi, James P., 'The Pictured Playhouse: Reading the Utrecht Engraving of Shakespeare's London', *Shakespeare Quarterly*, XLIV (1993), pp. 202–27.

McCudden, Simon, *Report on Evaluation at Anchor Terrace Car Park Park Street S.E.1* (London, Museum of London, 1990).

McCudden, Simon with Hinton, Peter, 'The Discovery of the Globe Theatre', *London Archaeologist*, vol. 6, no. 6 (Spring 1990).

Marlowe, Christopher, *Complete Plays*, ed. J. B. Steane (Harmondsworth, Penguin Books, 1969).

Marvell, Andrew, *The Complete Poems*, ed. Elizabeth Story Donno (Harmondsworth, Penguin Books, 1972).

Meadows, Denis, *Elizabethan Quintet* (London, Longmans, Green & Co., 1956).

Mowl, Timothy, *Elizabethan & Jacobean Style* (London, Phaidon Press Limited, 1993).

Nagler, A. M., *Shakespeare's Stage*, rev. edn (New Haven and London, Yale University Press, 1981).

Nairn, Ian and Pevsner, Nikolaus, rev. Bridget Cherry, *The Buildings of England: Surrey* (Harmondsworth, Penguin Books, 1971).

Neill, Michael, '"Exeunt with a Dead March": Funeral Pageantry on the Shakespearean Stage', in Bergeron, David M., ed., *Pageantry in the Shakespearean Theater* (Athens, The University of Georgia Press, 1985).

Nelson, Alan H., 'Hall Screens and Elizabethan Playhouses: Counter-Evidence from Cambridge', in Astington, John H., ed., *The Development of Shakespeare's Theater* (New York, AMS Press, 1992).

Nelson, Richard, *Two Shakespearean Actors* (London, Faber, 1990).

Orgel, Stephen and Strong, Roy: *Inigo Jones: The Theatre of the Stuart Court*, 2 vols, (London, Sotheby Parke Bernet and University of California Press, 1973).

Orrell, John, *The Quest for Shakespeare's Globe* (Cambridge, Cambridge University Press, 1983).

Orrell, John, *The Theatres of Inigo Jones and John Webb* (Cambridge, Cambridge University Press, 1985).

Orrell, John, *The Human Stage: English theatre design 1567–1640* (Cambridge, Cambridge University Press, 1988).

Orrell, John, and Gurr, Andrew, 'What the Rose can tell us', *Antiquity*, 63 (1989), pp. 421–9 (rev. version of 'What the Rose can tell us', *Times Literary Supplement*, 9–15 June 1989, pp. 636, 649).

Orrell, John, 'The Architecture of the Fortune Playhouse', *Shakespeare Survey*, XLVII (1994) pp. 15–43.

Ottaway, Patrick, 'The Campaign to Save the Rose', *Rescue News*, no. 48 (1989).

Owst, G. R., *Literature and Pulpit in Medieval England* (Oxford, Oxford University Press, 1961).

The passage of our most drad soueraine lady Quene Elyzabeth through the citie of London to Westminster the day before her coronacion (London, Richard Tottil, 1558).

Pevsner, Nikolaus, *The Buildings of England: Buckinghamshire* (Harmondsworth, Penguin Books, 1960).

Pevsner, Nikolaus, *The Buildings of England: Essex*, rev. Enid Radcliffe, (Harmondsworth, Penguin Books, 1965).

Pevsner, Nikolaus, *The Buildings of England: Herefordshire* (Harmondsworth, Penguin Books, 1963).

Pevsner, Nikolaus, rev. Cherry, Bridget, *The Buildings of England: Hertfordshire*, (Harmondsworth, Penguin Books, 1977).

Pevsner, Nikolaus, *The Buildings of England: London: Volume I: The Cities of London and Westminster* (Harmondsworth, Penguin Books, 1957).

Pevsner, Nikolaus, *The Buildings of England: Shropshire* (Harmondsworth, Penguin Books, 1958).

Pevsner, Nikolaus, and Cherry, Bridget, *The Buildings of England: Wiltshire* (Harmondsworth, Penguin Books, 1975).

Pevsner, Nikolaus, and Lloyd, David: *The Buildings of England: Hampshire and the Isle of Wight* (Harmondsworth, Penguin Books, 1967).

Pevsner, Nikolaus, and Metcalf, Priscilla, *The Cathedrals of England: Southern England* (Harmondsworth, Penguin Books, 1985).

Queen's Gallery, Buckingham Palace, *Holbein and the Court of Henry VIII* (London, 1978).

Richards, Nathaniel, *The tragedy of Messallina the Roman emperesse* (London, D. Frere, 1640).

Ripley, John, *Julius Caesar on stage in England and America* (Cambridge, Cambridge University Press, 1980).

Rogers, Malcolm, *Montacute House Somerset* (London, The National Trust, 1991).

Rowan, Donald F., 'The players and Playing Places of Norwich', in Astington, John H., ed., *The Development of Shakespeare's Theater* (New York, AMS Press, 1992).

Rowse, A. L., *Shakespeare's Southampton, patron of Virginia* (London, Macmillan, 1965).

Rowse, A. L., *Times, Persons, Places* (London, Macmillan, 1965).

Royal Commission on Historical Monuments England, *City of Cambridge* (3 vols, London, HMSO, 1959).

The Royall Passage of her Majesty from the Tower of London, to her Palice of White-hall, with all the Speaches and Deuices, both of the Pageants and otherwise, together with her Majesties Severall Answers and most pleasing Speaches to them all (London, S. S[tafford]., ?1559).

Rutter, Carol Chillington, *Documents of the Rose Playhouse* (Manchester, Manchester University Press, 1984).

Schoenbaum, S., *William Shakespeare: A Documentary Life* (Oxford, Oxford University Press in association with the Scolar Press, 1975).

Schoenbaum, S., *William Shakespeare: A Compact Documentary Life*, rev. edn (Oxford, Oxford University Press, 1987).

Serlio, Sebastiano, *The first [– the fift] booke of Architecture* (trans. Robert Peake; London, Simon Stafford for Robert Peake, 1611).

Shakespeare, William, *The Complete Works*, ed. Peter Alexander (London, Collins, 1951).

Shapiro, Michael, *Children of the Revels: The Boy Companies of Shakespeare's Time and their Plays* (New York, Columbia University Press, 1977).

Sheingorn, Pamela, 'On Using Medieval Art in the Study of Medieval Drama: An Introduction to Methodology', *Research Opportunities in Renaissance Drama*, XXII (1979), pp. 101–10.

Sherwood, Jennifer and Pevsner, Nikolaus, *The Buildings of England: Oxfordshire* (Harmondsworth, Penguin Books, 1974).

Sidney, Philip, *The Countess of Pembroke's Arcadia* (London, W. Ponsonbie, 1598).

Sidney, Philip, *A Defence of Poetry* in *Miscellaneous Prose*, ed. Katherine Duncan-Jones and Jan Van Dorsten (Oxford, Oxford University Press, 1973).

Sidney, Philip, *The Countess of Pembroke's Arcadia*, ed. Maurice Evans (Harmondsworth, Penguin Books, 1977).

Sisam, Celia (ed.), *The Oxford Book of Medieval English Verse* (Oxford, Oxford University Press, 1970).

Skelton, John, *Merie Tales . . . made by Master Skelton Poet Laureate* (London, Thomas Colwell, 1567).

Slater, Ann Pasternak, *Shakespeare the Director* (Sussex, The Harvester Press, 1982).

Slive, Seymour, *Frans Hals* (London, Royal Academy of Arts, 1989).

Sotheby's, *English Silver Treasures from the Kremlin* (London, Sotheby's, 1991).

Speed, John, *The Theatre of the Empire of Great Britaine* (London, John Sudbury and George Humble, 1611 and 1616).

Spenser, Edmund, *Poetical Works*, ed. J. C. Smith and E. de Selincourt (Oxford, Oxford University Press, 1912).

Stone, Lawrence, *The Crisis of the Aristocracy 1558–1641*, corrected edn, (Oxford, Oxford University Press, 1979).

Stone, Lawrence, *The Family, Sex and Marriage in England 1500–1800* (London, Harper & Row, 1977).

Strachey, Lytton, *Elizabeth and Essex* (London, Chatto & Windus, 1928).

Strong, Roy C., *Portraits of Queen Elizabeth I* (Oxford, Oxford University Press, 1963).

Strong, Roy C., *Festival Designs by Inigo Jones: An Exhibition of Drawings for Scenery and Costumes for the Court Masques of James I and Charles I* (London, Victoria & Albert Museum, 1969).

Strong, Roy C., *The Elizabethan Image: Painting in England 1540–1620* (London, Tate Gallery, 1969).

Strong, Roy C., *The English Icon: Elizabethan & Jacobean Portraiture* (London, Paul Mellon Foundation and Routledge & Kegan Paul, 1969).

Strong, Roy C., *The Cult of Elizabeth: Elizabethan Portraiture and Pageantry* (London, Thames & Hudson, 1977).

Strong, Roy C. and Murrel, V. J., *Artists of the Tudor Court: The Portrait Miniature Rediscovered 1520–1600* (London, Victoria & Albert Museum, 1983).

Tales, and quicke answeres, very mery, and pleasant to rede (London, Thomas Berthelet, ?1532).

Thomson, Peter, *Shakespeare's Professional Career* (Cambridge, Cambridge University Press, 1992).

Tourneur, Cyril, *The Revenger's Tragedy*, in Salgado, Gamini, ed., *Three Jacobean Tragedies* (Harmondsworth, Penguin Books, 1965).

Verey, David, *The Buildings of England: Gloucestershire 2: The Vale and the Forest of Dean*, corrected edn, (Harmondsworth, Penguin Books, 1980).

Wayment, Hilary, *The Windows of King's College Chapel, Cambridge* (London, British Academy, 1972).

Westminster Abbey: Official Guide, rev. edn (London, 1988).

Wickham, Glynne, *Early English Stages 1300–1660* (3 vols, London, Routledge & Kegan Paul, 1959–1981).

Wickham, Glynne, *Shakespeare's Dramatic Heritage: collected studies in mediaeval, Tudor and Shakespearean Drama* (London, Routledge & Kegan Paul, 1969).

Wiles, David, *Shakespeare's Clown: Actor and text in the Elizabethan Playhouse* (Cambridge, Cambridge University Press, 1987).

Williams, John T., *Costumes and Settings for Shakespeare's Plays* (London, B. T. Batsford, 1982).

Williams, Neville, *Elizabeth, Queen of England* (London, Weidenfeld & Nicolson, 1967).

Wilson, E. C., *England's Eliza* (Cambridge, Mass, Harvard University Press, 1939).

Wilson, F. P., *The English Drama 1485–1585*, ed. G. K. Hunter (Oxford, Oxford University Press, 1969).

Wilson, Jean, *Romance Themes in The Faerie Queene*, Ph.D. dissertation, Cambridge University, 1973.

Wilson, Jean, *Entertainments for Elizabeth I* (Woodbridge, D. S. Brewer and Rowman & Littlefield, 1980).

Wilson, Jean, 'The Noble Imp', *The Antiquaries Journal*, vol. LXX, part 2 (1992), pp. 360–79.

Wilson, R. M., *The Lost Literature of Medieval England*, rev. edn (London, Methuen, 1972).

Withington, Robert, *English Pageantry: An Historical Outline* (2 vols, New York, Benjamin Blom, 1918, repr. 1963).

Yates, F.A., *Theatre of the World* (London, Routledge & Kegan Paul, 1969).

Yates, F.A., *Astraea: The Imperial Theme in the Sixteenth Century* (London, Routledge & Kegan Paul, 1975).

Yesterday's World, September/October 1989.

Young, Alan, *Tudor and Jacobean Tournaments* (London, Sheridan House, 1987).

Young, Karl, *The Drama of the Medieval Church* (2 vols, Oxford, Oxford University Press, 1933).

Zall, P. M., ed., *A Hundred Merry Tales and other Jestbooks of the Fifteenth and Sixteenth Centuries* (Lincoln, Nebraska, University of Nebraska Press, 1963).

INDEX